WILL CARLING
THE AUTHORISED BIOGRAPHY

To National Home Loans
for providing such crippling inspiration

WILL CARLING
The Authorised Biography

David Norrie

HEADLINE

First published in 1993
by HEADLINE BOOK PUBLISHING

10 9 8 7 6 5 4 3

British Library Cataloguing in Publication Data

Norrie, David
    Will Carling: Authorised Biography
    I. Title
    796.333092

    ISBN 0–7472–0902–2

Typeset by Keyboard Services, Luton

Printed and bound in Great Britain by
Mackays of Chatham PLC, Chatham, Kent

HEADLINE BOOK PUBLISHING
A division of Hodder Headline PLC
Headline House
79 Great Titchfield Street
London W1P 7FN

Contents

Contents

Acknowledgements

My grateful thanks go to all those who gave so generously of their time in the preparation of this book, so do my apologies to any absent from the following list. Bill and Pam Carling (not least for providing me with wine and the Carling family albums), Marcus Carling, Geoff Cooke, Roger Uttley, Rob Andrew, Jeff Probyn, Colin Herridge, Will Fawcett, John Morris, Brooke Dawse, Stephen Jones, Chris Jones, Tony Roche, Terry Cooper, Julia Smith, Jon Holmes, and Alan Brooke, Ian Marshall and all at Headline. And, of course, to Will himself for being so frank, forthright and patient.

DAVID NORRIE

Bibliography

Captain's Diary, 1989–91, Will Carling (Chatto & Windus); *Carling's England*, Barry Newcombe (HarperCollins); *England's Grand Slam 1991*, Rob Andrew and Dean Richards (Stanley Paul); *Flying Wing*, Rory Underwood with David Hands (Stanley Paul); *The Tower & the Glory*, Wade Dooley with Gerry Greenberg (Mainstream); *The Phoenix Book of International Rugby Records*, John Griffiths (Dent); *English Rugby: A Celebration*, ed. Ted Barrett (Mainstream); *Rothmans Rugby Union Yearbooks* (Queen Anne Press/Headline); *The Rugby Union Who's Who*, ed. Alex Spink (Collins Willow); various issues of *Rugby World* magazine, national daily and Sunday newspapers.

Foreword by Will Carling

I was rather surprised when David Norrie first asked me 'Isn't it time you did a book, Will?' After all, I'm only 27 and, hopefully, have far from finished my England rugby career. Then I realised that I had been through a lot in my five years as England captain.

It has been a period of phenomenal change – not only for me, but for the national side and the rugby world at large. I am not sure that those on the outside, and even the majority involved inside, have realised just how dramatic and traumatic the changes have been. The part I have played in this rugby 'revolution' has been often misconstrued.

I've enjoyed working with David, not least because it has given me the chance to set the record straight on many controversial matters. I've given my side of events and David has used these to give his overall view of the modern rugby world. He is allowed to be more outspoken than me, but this book represents a true and realistic picture of my life and career so far.

Introduction

Will Carling is the most famous rugby face in the land, a British sporting star from the top drawer, alongside Gary Lineker, Nigel Mansell, Nick Faldo and Graham Gooch. Carling's successful captaincy, his dashing style in the centre and his dark-haired good looks have made him an inspiration and hero to thousands, every mother's dream. Quite simply, Will Carling is the symbol of England's greatest ever rugby success.

This is not only the story of a great rugby player, but of a great rugby team. It is a team that includes manager Geoff Cooke and coaches Roger Uttley and Dick Best. In many ways, the side should be known as Cooke's England. His influence has been the dominant one over the past six years. The England players available are no better than those of yesteryear. But they have been a team. And a team that has not been disbanded at the first setback. Three players exemplify the change: Mickey Skinner, Paul Ackford and Mike Teague had all been on the fringes of international rugby before Cooke took over. Nobody today doubts their ability to compete with the best in the world, but none of this trio would have contributed half as much under the old system. That is the sort of talent England have wasted over the decades. Remarkably, England's achievements in recent times have never really silenced the critics. They have shifted their ground to suit their argument. Initially, Carling's England lacked tactical awareness and positive leadership. When England's safety-first, single-minded, forward-orientated approach, which was

1

attacked as they steam-rollered their way to the 1991 Grand Slam, was abandoned in the World Cup final, the team found it had got it wrong again. The underlying message was that this team could, and should, be providing more than they were delivering. Victory was not enough, although it would have sufficed in that World Cup final. Carling and his team have found it a struggle coping with the constant sniping.

England's success has been difficult to live with. England have not only been the team to beat, but the team to beat with a big stick at every opportunity. Such sadistic pleasure is rampant in the sports world. The England soccer and cricket teams have taken their fair share of abuse in recent years. Yet, while there are obvious signs that England's soccer and cricket teams are falling behind the rest of the world, the rugby side is among the very best. No visiting Five Nations country has won at Twickenham since 1988; that fact alone explains the special affection the home supporters have for Carling's England. It delivers. And delivers in style. To the Twickenham faithful, rugby is Carling, Rory Underwood, Jerry Guscott, Brian Moore, Wade Dooley and Peter Winterbottom. They are the inspiration to the thousands of youngsters who are taking up the game.

The Rugby Football Union see it differently. While the RFU have been happy to build a brand new Twickenham on the backs of England's recent sell-out achievements, the same authorities have identified Carling's team as the greatest threat to the future of Rugby Union. Rugby's increased commercialism and Twickenham's reluctance to live in the real world mean the current team's epic struggles have not been restricted to the field of play. Off the park, Carling's England has been less successful. Every time the players adopt what looks like a winning position in their negotiations, the RFU change the rules. The feeble leadership of the International Board, the game's governing body, has caused chaos and inconsistency in the rugby world. In Australia and New Zealand, where the players rule, rugby is already in the 21st century. In the home countries, where the committee man is still king, rugby is hanging on to the 19th century for dear life.

The authorities not only mistrust the players, the majority resent them. A few minutes' conversation in any club's committee-room is normally sufficient to realise that most rugby officials know as much about the modern game and its players as they do about Einstein's Theory of Relativity. They seem to treat rugby players as a necessary nuisance, a means to an end. The favourite phrase of dismissal to any player's request that might upset their cosy world is 'the game is bigger than any of the players'. But, as John Arlott said of cricket, 'The game is the players!' Unfortunately, rugby officials have never seen it that way. The game is theirs, because that's all they have got. You do not need to be bright, successful, visionary, astute or to know the game to go places in the world of rugby administration. It's the world of committees, of negative thoughts, of no change and, most of all, of perks. Mixing with players will only confuse the issues. Stay anonymous. And if anyone ever dares to question your motives, remember the game. 'This great amateur game of ours' must be defended at all costs. Those who challenge such a worthy cause can be accused of trying to destroy the very fabric of rugby. That is how even those on the RFU committee who try to move the game slowly forward are treated by the hard-liners. If you are not for us, you must be against us. Accusation by insinuation of association usually does the trick. It is McCarthyism at its most effective and most evil.

Carling has suffered, as do all sporting stars in the modern age. The sacrifices, in terms of time and effort, are part of today's world if you want to compete. And Carling does. He is better informed about his opposing centre than an England scrum-half was about his own fly-half a generation ago. He is dedicated to the job of being an international centre and an international captain. Work and life outside rugby naturally suffer. That is a price Carling is prepared to pay. That is the acceptable side of a success story.

The rest of the suffering reflects a national hang-up with success, a sport that is not being allowed to grow up and a system that allows the mediocre and long-serving to survive without any accountability. Carling is accused of being aloof and arrogant, of not caring about the grass-roots of rugby, of trying to turn rugby professional and, finally, of reaching the top on the back of a successful team. He has never denied that the efforts of others have played a significant part in his career, that he was in the right place at the right time. He realises that his reign as captain would not have lasted half as long in any other era of English rugby. Individual records do not interest him. Yet committee men and others, many unidentified, continue to sully Carling and his reputation with innuendo and allegation. When former players, especially those who have struggled with similar pressures, join in those attacks, Carling feels let down. He has learnt not to expect understanding from rugby administrators and

3

journalists, but has always hoped that those who play and have played the game would appreciate the problems. However, a few do not; some are jealous of his success, others have little comprehension of how the demands on the current players and, above all, the England captain have increased.

The press, too, have grown resentful of his achievements. 'Everyone loves a winner' is often not a true maxim in this country. Faldo, Mansell and Carling have all suffered. Faldo developed a technique that made him the best golf player in the world, yet, since then, he has been constantly ridiculed for being 'boring' and putting his golf above everything else. Any opportunity to knock Faldo is gratefully received.

Carling, like Faldo, is a true competitor ... and a winner. The problem with bidding to be the best in an amateur world was perfectly illustrated by Colin Welland in his script for *Chariots of Fire*. Harold Abrahams is carpeted by two Masters of College at Cambridge University for employing a professional coach, Sam Mussabini.

'Here in Cambridge we have always been proud of our athletic prowess. We have always believed that games are indispensable in helping complete the education of an Englishman. It creates character, fosters courage, honesty, and leadership, but, most of all, an unassailable spirit of loyalty, comradeship and mutual responsibility. In your enthusiasm for success, you seem to have lost sight of some of those ideals. You've employed a personal coach. He's a professional.'

'He's the best. What else would he be?' answered Abrahams.

'There our paths diverge. The way of the amateur is the only way to provide satisfactory results.'

'I am an amateur.'

'Being trained by a professional, adopting a professional attitude in the headlong pursuit of personal glory.'

'I am a Cambridge man, first and last. I am an Englishman, first and last. What I have achieved and intend to achieve is for my family, my university and my country. And I bitterly resent you suggesting otherwise.'

'Your aim is to win at all costs.'

'At all costs, no. But I do aim to win within the rules. Perhaps you would rather I play the gentleman and lost.'

'To playing the tradesman, yes. Your approach has been rather too plebian. You are the élite and expect to behave as such.'

'You yearn for victory just as I do. But achieved with the apparent effortlessness of Gods. Yours are the archaic values of the prep-school playgrounds. You deceive no one but yourselves. I believe in the pursuit of excellence and I'll carry the future with me,' concluded Abrahams.

Great cinema. The confrontation never took place, of course, but the conflict is real. It is as true now as it was then. Will Carling could easily step into Abrahams' role, with RFU secretary Dudley Wood taking the place of the Master of Caius. Carling will take the future with him if England want to remain a force in the rugby world. There are those on the RFU committee who believe that becoming a second-rate, or even third-rate, rugby nation would be a small price to pay for retaining the old ways and old values. But, fortunately, this great amateur sport of theirs needs ever greater injections of money. The supporters do not come to Twickenham to sit in a great stadium; they come to watch a great team. Without that team, the RFU have nothing to sell. The players, at least, know the value of a seat in Twickenham. During the last decade, England's Huw Davies was rather surprised to find himself squashed on the replacements' bench. Looking along, he saw seven sitting where six should have been. It was not difficult to spot the intruder; he was wearing a coat and an England scarf. But Davies was told not to complain. A West Country forward, also on the bench, had sold his ticket for some beer money.

Carling has made mistakes. People would have been far more suspicious of him if he had done everything perfectly over the past five seasons. He should have made more effort with the rugby correspondents of the national press. For the past few years, England's captain has had an exclusive contract with a newspaper, which has allowed him a convenient get-out from other demands. Previous incumbents, in much easier times, were more accessible. Carling did make himself more available to the press during the 1993 Lions tour and both sides were surprised that the experience was not as painful as they had feared. Carling's own *Captain's Diary 1989–91*, which he dictated into a machine was rushed out without due care and attention. It was littered with elementary mistakes and contained one of the best literals ever to escape the notice of a careful sub-editor. 'To stop Bullyoff and Galway from charging round the field, we just can't give penalties away again to Lynah.' 'Lynah' was obviously Mike Lynagh, but 'Bullyoff and Galway'? Step forward Willie Ofahengaue! It didn't stop the book from selling well.

Carling has had to cope with much more than rugby fame. He is a national celebrity. England's captain appeared on the front cover of the *Rothmans Rugby Union Yearbook* for three years in a row. He became the biggest name in rugby when Grogg, the Welsh manufacturer of sporting statues, announced that Carling had outsold even Gareth Edwards. Carling is recognised wherever he goes, as much for his TV and magazine appearances as his Twickenham ones. He is the first rugby player to have his off-the-field life investigated. Carling survives the pressure that that creates by cutting himself off from all except a close-knit circle. That has always been his way. Even at school and university, where rugby traditions were high, he was a rugby player apart. That continued when Carling was handed the England captaincy at 22. It has been a fairly lonely life since then, and a fairly turbulent one, despite England's unparalleled success on the field. The wonder is that William David Charles Carling is still around, and still smiling.

Chapter 1

He Would Say That, Wouldn't He!

I didn't need to captain the British Lions from an ego point of view. I'm not belittling the Lions. The 1993 tour was a unique experience. But, at that stage in my career, it was nice not to be given that responsibility. Maybe I was being selfish. I had long-terms plans. I'm looking to take England to the World Cup in 1995.

WILL CARLING

Will Carling's 1993 appeared to be in ruins. England's rugby captain could not help wondering why. This was supposed to be his year ... the Year of Carling. A third successive England Grand Slam would naturally lead to his appointment as British Lions captain. And the strength of English rugby seemed likely to bring victory for the Lions in New Zealand for only the second time. Yet, two weeks before the end of the tour, almost half-way through his year, Carling was contemplating retirement. The demise of the dark-haired, golden boy of English rugby was complete. He had just been left out of a rugby side for the first time in his 27 years. There had been no hat-trick of Grand Slams as England lost to the two weakest sides in the Five Nations championship. Scotsman Gavin Hastings, not Carling, had been asked to lead the Lions, and the final humiliation came when the tourists recorded an historic victory in the second Test at Wellington to level the series. All-action Carling, his services not required on the pitch, was reduced to sitting in the ITV box with commentator John Taylor.

Carling's worst fears had become a reality. Too often the Carling success story has been confused and distorted by the England captaincy. Many believe that Darling Carling has ridden to the top on the back of England's power pack. How good was the England centre without the captaincy as protection and camouflage? The rugby world was about to find out. Carling was left with nothing to play for but pride in the final fortnight of the tour. For once, he was on his own with no outside responsibilities. The easy option was to throw in the towel, settle in with the rest of the Lions' midweek side and pretend it was just a bad experience. The press, especially, watched and waited for his reaction to adversity. The character, courage and class of Carling, whose existence some doubted, was never more necessary. And it was never more evident than when the northern hemisphere's most famous player, now a dirt-tracker, played his heart out in the final two midweek matches. Carling knew it would not win him back a Test place, yet the final victory was his. Carling flew back to London with his reputation restored, if not enhanced. Now nobody doubts that England's captain can stand on his own two feet, 1993 could yet be the year of Will Carling.

CARLING

I had let myself down. I had injury problems, but they were just excuses. I wasn't concentrating on my rugby. I was missing Julia desperately. There was no edge to my play; I wasn't making things happen. I wondered if I'd been around too long. The England World Cup side was breaking up. Did I really want to stay and help re-model a new team? And, if I gave up the England captaincy, that would be it: no England, no Quins, no rugby of any sort. Getting dropped focused my mind. Did I want to carry on? I asked Geoff [Cooke] if we could have a chat. He'd been thinking along the same lines as me. 'Don't you want to do the job [the England captaincy] anymore?' he asked me. I told Geoff that the answer was yes. It still is. I was pleased with the way I came through the toughest period of my rugby life, because I had to fight. And that's never really happened to me before. My silver-spoon image had taken quite a battering in 1993. But I don't mind, I've learnt a lot and that will help me in the years ahead. The year certainly hasn't gone according to plan, but what does in this life? There are no complaints from me.

The Carling-Cooke international partnership had begun in late 1988, when the England manager offered the young centre the captaincy of the national side. Carling never had any doubts that he could handle the job. Four and a half years, two Grand Slams and a World Cup final down the road, Cooke asked Carling if he wanted another job, that of leading the 1993 British Lions to New Zealand. This time the most successful England captain in rugby history did have doubts.

Carling was 27 and at the peak of his rugby powers, but was forced to concede defeat. He replied that he did not want the job. Saying 'no' was a blow to his pride, an enormous blow. But any other answer would have been dishonest. Had the Lions selectors been in desperate straits, with no alternative captain, Carling would have reconsidered. There was no need. The feeling on all sides was that both Carling and the Lions would be better served if England's skipper took a back seat for once.

England's poor 1993 Five Nations championship showing offered only part-explanation for Carling's reluctance to accept the honour that would have capped a hitherto astonishing playing career. Even if England had completed a hat-trick of Grand Slams that spring, Carling would still have been happy to see Scotland's Gavin Hastings take the Lions to New Zealand. For Carling had been living with the Lions captaincy for a whole year before Hastings was named. Until the final weeks of the championship, England's captain was viewed as the automatic choice. But David Sole, then Scotland's captain, had already given Carling a warning during the 1992 championship. Sole, who would have been a front-runner for the job himself, had told Carling that he would be retiring at the end of the summer. That left Carling in the box seat, especially when England wrapped up a second successive Grand Slam two months later. 'Sole warned me that it would be very hard for a so-called pretty-boy Englishman to captain the Lions, with all the different nationalities. He didn't say it would be impossible, but I would have my work cut out.'

Carling had finished that 1991–92 season with a monumental performance in the Pilkington Cup final for Harlequins against Bath. Nobody was surprised when he was subsequently named *Rugby World* Player of the Year. Nothing, it appeared, could stop Carling from leading the Lions. 'I had that summer off. I loved the break from rugby. It was very important. Rugby has dominated my life since I was 6. I needed time away. I still enjoy it as much as I've always done, but it was nice to get off the treadmill for once. I've never been one for reflection, though. You have to keep improving. If you look back on achievements, there's the danger of satisfaction creeping in.'

Carling's summer was spent building up his management training business and fulfilling the various engagements that go with the role of England rugby captain, such as racing turbo-charged motor cars for charity. There was a brief split with his long-time girlfriend, Victoria, but they went on holiday together to France with friends in August. Carling started the new season refreshed, looking forward to leading England and the British Lions.

England's championship season was to go horribly wrong. Only two matches were lost, but previously high standards had provoked high expectations. The narrow defeat in Cardiff was seen as the turning point, but Carling was already struggling by that stage. He was unable to provide the perfection that he felt was demanded. The media dissection of his every move confirmed his fears that he was falling short. His previous crisis period as captain had come after defeat at Murrayfield in the 1990 Grand Slam decider. Carling had had every right to feel a victim during that spell, but this time he was more culpable, with much of the pressure coming from within.

The strain was evident early in the season when he clashed with former Wales captain Eddie Butler after the game between Australia and the Barbarians in November. Butler had suggested on BBC TV's 'Rugby Special' programme that the only breaks Carling was currently making were in the commercial world. It was a cheap shot; Carling probably should have ignored it. The cold, aloof, arrogant Carling of popular portrayal would have done. But, in a rare emotional outburst, Carling gave vent to his feelings at the post-match dinner. That was regretted straight away – not for the words, but for allowing the mask to slip.

'Will has always tried to keep his emotions and thoughts in check,' insists Colin Herridge, the Harlequins club official who helps the England team deal with the media. 'He doesn't get out of control. But when the adrenalin flows and he lets his hair down after a match, he'll tell you what he thinks. As he showed with Butler, there is a lot pent up there. Will felt that a former top-class player should have shown a better understanding of his situation, not make fun out of it. Butler has been through the mill himself.'

As England's championship, which had started with high hopes, ended in failure, so Carling had his poorest campaign as a leader and player. Geoff Cooke, England's team manager and the Lions tour manager, had considered trifling with tradition and naming Carling as captain ahead of the touring party. But that was before the championship.

CARLING

I was never obsessed by the Lions captaincy. I never sought it. So much can happen: injuries, loss of form. Shin splints had cost me my place on the 1989 Lions tour to Australia, denying me a chance of playing with players from other countries and working with coach Ian McGeechan. I took nothing for granted, although I desperately wanted to go on the tour. My main interest during that season was England. I'm sure the Lions did have a distracting influence, especially once the third Grand Slam was lost in Cardiff. Our minds wandered off the job in hand.

That defeat in Wales was the crunch. It dawned on me that the England captaincy was tiring me out a lot more than it used to. My own performance disappointed me there. I felt I needed to concentrate on my own game. 'Carling didn't want the Lions captaincy' – well, he's bound to say that. Had we won another Grand Slam, I might have felt fresher. I may have been given the Lions job, I may have accepted, and I might have done a good job. But it worked out this way, and I was happy with it.

The pressures were intense, even before Cardiff. I had been in the job since 1988, so I knew what the score was. But success brings its own pressures, and I had also created a few of my own. I set very high standards. I think I've done well, but there is still a great desire to do even better. That increases the pressure on myself. In the summer with the Lions I was relieved to take a back seat and watch another management team at work.

I've always felt the England job was a big enough challenge. I've had my fair share of captaincy. And my fair share of success. I didn't need to captain the British Lions from an ego point of view. I'm not belittling the Lions. The 1993 tour was a unique experience. But, at that stage in my career, it was nice not to be given that responsibility. Maybe I was being selfish. I had long-term plans. I'm looking to take England to the World Cup in

11

1995. The next two years will be tough enough. The summer out of the hot seat was as good as a rest.

The media were crucifying me, again. We've never really got on. I realised in the 1993 championship that I was getting even more uncomfortable with the press. I seemed to have no control over who I am. I don't think even the average international understands what it's like being England captain these days. When posed pictures of me with my new girlfriend Julia hit the front pages in March, Winters [Peter Winterbottom] said, 'Why did you do that, Will?' I told him that they would not let her alone until they got the picture they wanted. I'd been around long enough to know they meant that. You learn that you're not going to win. I didn't want Julia to have all that hassle. I was just astonished that it was considered front page news.

Carling's final split with Victoria and new relationship with Julia Smith, a former girlfriend of pop star Jeff Beck, was played out much too publicly for Carling's liking. Victoria went into print about the problems of going out with Will Carling, while photographers camped outside the office of the PR company where Julia worked. Carling gave in, and the pair were photographed together. England's captain was seen smiling, but he was gritting his teeth. This was not his style. But he felt he had been left with little option. The Lions captaincy would have offered him no respite from this life under the probing spotlight. Carling had had enough.

Cooke had noticed the strain. The Lions team manager had no worries about Carling's capacity to prepare the England rugby side. But the Lions sometimes require a more extrovert and easy-going animal. And this was one of those times.

COOKE
I always thought there were others who could do the job. There were candidates known to us all the way through. For the Lions job, we perceived that a different approach is necessary. One point of view was that Will needed a break from the whole business of being captain. The job and the make-up of the party then pushed us towards Gavin [Hastings]. The fact that the management was mainly English was all part of the process. If the Lions captain, who's an integral part of the set-up, had been Will, then three out of the four people in charge would have been

12

English. There weren't any votes during the selection discussions, not even on the captaincy. It was all done by consensus.

Will sets high standards. He puts pressure on himself. It's about finding a balance. Sometimes you get it wrong, and that causes problems. I believe the break from captaincy, so he could just play as a world-class player, has been of benefit. That doesn't mean I'm worried about him as England captain; I am very happy with him. The only doubt over his future as captain would be a loss of form. That's always been the only proviso, as far as I'm concerned.

Cooke and Carling had made their decisions well before the final international weekend in Dublin in March. That Saturday night should have been one of doom and gloom. England were no longer the best team in Europe, for the first time in three years. And Carling had lost the job he had wanted just a year earlier. But England's captain was in relieved mood, talking openly to the press about the summer. Diplomatically, he admitted that he did not expect to be named Lions captain. Carling was pleased that, for a period, however temporary, he could return to the back benches.

CARLING
There was no feeling of being slighted when the Lions squad was announced. I had already made my feelings clear to Geoff, and I don't think he was surprised with what I said. Nor did it go against what the Lions selectors were thinking. The Lions were looking for an emphasis away from the English bias. Two of the three-man management team were from England. And the English players were obviously going to provide the majority of the squad. To be Lions captain is a great honour. No one would ever turn it down. But, after five years of leading England, I was looking forward to the responsibility being with someone else. So I spoke to Cookie and said I was tired.

Gavin knew how I felt. We had discussed it when we worked together for ITV at the World Sevens. I didn't head out to New Zealand thinking, 'It should have been me.' Immediately the squad was announced, the pressure lifted. Rob [Andrew] said to me, 'You've been captain for five years now. You've never been able to enjoy the company of the lads without being their captain.' I knew then that I had made the right decision.

13

Chapter 2

Why the Hell Did He Pick Me?

One day when all my rugby is behind me, I'm going to sit down with Geoff Cooke. And, after the right amount of alcoholic influence, I'm going to try and get a straight answer to the most puzzling question of all – 'Why the hell did you pick me?'

WILL CARLING

Will Carling faced an agonising 48 hours after Geoff Cooke offered him the England captaincy in autumn 1988. Carling had no hesitation in accepting the job on that Thursday night. But the new leader was sworn to secrecy. His identity would not be announced to the England squad until two evenings later – 30 October – and the world at large would not hear the news until the morning after that.

Carling was stunned by Cooke's decision. He knew that the players and public would be, too. The public weren't his concern, but the players now were. How would they react? Especially veteran warriors such as Wade Dooley, Paul Rendall and Dean Richards, faced with this young upstart? The good-looking Harlequin centre with a university education was still wet behind the ears. The youngest England captain for over half a century was an international novice. Why, then, had Cooke given Carling something denied every other England rugby captain in modern times – job security?

Merely naming Carling as England captain was enough to shock the rugby world. Nobody saw it coming. But it was Cooke's admission that Carling would lead England in the 1991 World Cup (still three years down the road) which indicated that both Cooke's and Carling's careers were on the line together. Cooke actually qualified his forecast with a proviso about Carling maintaining his international form in order to justify his position. But such was the effect of the announcement that nobody cared about the small print. 'I made it clear to Will that we expected him to captain the side throughout the season,' said Cooke at the time. 'We had had a succession of short-term captaincies. The feeling was that we had to establish an England captain who, though it was early for him, would take us through the next three seasons to the World Cup.'

Behind the scenes, however, Cooke and Carling did have doubts. It was a giant step into the unknown. It was England coach Roger Uttley who, once he had mulled over Cooke's suggestion, instinctively realised England were on to a winner. Cooke and Uttley were determined to bring stability to the England set-up. But the captaincy was proving a stubborn problem, especially to Cooke. Much of his reputation up north had been built on player-loyalty but, after six months of 1988, Cooke had a credibility problem. His first four attempts at picking an England captain had ended in failure. He could not afford another mistake with number five.

COOKE
Nigel Melville had been my long-term choice. Nigel was an automatic selection at scrum-half and had a good attitude. He had taken over when Mike Harrison was dropped midway through the 1988 championship. Mike had done a great job for Yorkshire, the North and England. Telling him he was dropped was the hardest thing I've ever done. But Nigel only lasted one and a half games before a serious leg injury against Ireland finished him. John Orwin took over at half-time and was then put in charge of the Australia tour that summer. I was buying time so I could identify the man who would do the job for England.

Suggestions that I had Will earmarked for the job even before he made the England side or went on that Australian tour are all wrong. But, after Australia, Will stood out. I kept those thoughts to myself for a few weeks to work it out in my mind, then tested the water with Roger [Uttley] and John [Elliott]. Of the others, I didn't consider Brian Moore or Simon Halliday serious contenders, Peter Winterbottom was not playing for England at the time, Wade Dooley was not a captain, and Dean Richards would not have been comfortable with the job. It boiled down to Will or Rob Andrew. Rob was the more obvious choice, but he had just returned to the side and was having enough trouble with his own game. I couldn't give him that extra pressure.

Will had precocious talent, and so much confidence. Maybe he could grow into the job, I thought. That would take the weight off Rob. But I had doubts, lots of them. Will was so young and inexperienced. Here I was, about to thrust him into one of the most demanding jobs in sport. Was I going to ruin one of the best young players we had in England? I knew he wasn't going to be an instant success. I told him to concentrate on his own performance as a player. I said captaincy was a collective effort.

Will knew he wasn't on a match-by-match trial. He had a chance to grow into the job. Will was being offered the opportunity to lead England into the next World Cup. That wasn't an automatic guarantee, but he was the man we wanted. And he was made aware of that.

UTTLEY

Geoff phoned me and asked, 'What about Will?' I knew what he was on about. The captaincy was our big crisis after the summer tour. We could not duck the issue. Time had run out. Australia were due straight back, and we couldn't wait. Once Geoff had set his criteria – 'Automatic selection, good attitude' – there was only one choice for me. There was no guarantee Rob Andrew was going to hang on to his place. Yes, in 1993, you can look back and say that we could have made Brian Moore, Rob Andrew or Peter Winterbottom captain instead. But when the choice was made, they were not in the frame.

If it had been a year later, I'm sure Rob would have got the job. In many ways, Rob was much closer to Geoff. Rob was known as 'Squeaky Clean' in the squad. He was the player regarded as 'Son of Geoff' – much more than Will. He would have been easier to get along with. Rob's much easier to talk with. Will, for better or worse, has the facility to make me feel uncomfortable. But he was definitely the man for the job in

1988. I had no doubts about him coping. Will had the mental capacity, that was obvious. He was the one man in the side who would relish the challenge.

Captaincy was always a problem when I was playing. England captains had little feeling of support. The captain was the link between the selectors and the players, but he was never officially recognised as such. It was always the players who carried the can. Geoff and I decided we had to work in concert with the players. The players were very low when Geoff and I took over. Mickey Harrison had taken too many psychological knocks, then Nigel Melville got injured. The Aussie tour fell apart, so we had to look for someone new – that man was Will Carling.

Will Carling was oblivious to all these discussions, blissfully unaware that his life was about to change for ever. Carling was actually making his own career decisions around the same time that Cooke was considering his credentials as captain. Carling had been distraught to discover that his first year in the Army would cost him his England place. As much as Carling had set his heart on going to Sandhurst, the outcome of that conflict of interests was never in doubt. In September 1988, he bought himself out of the Army. The following month Carling was named as the youngest England rugby captain for 57 years, still two months short of his 23rd birthday. He was the 10th England captain since Bill Beaumont, who had led England a record 21 times before retiring on health grounds in 1982.

Carling never dreamed he would be Cooke's answer to England's leadership problems. He was just settling into his first job, with Mobil, and looking forward to his first full season as an England player. The first hint that something was up came when he visited his parents' house, to be told that Cooke had rung and would like his call returned. Carling braced himself. Suddenly, leaving the Army did not seem such a sensible move. Cooke was bad news. Uttley was the communicator of good tidings in the England set-up; Cooke, because he felt that the man at the top should have the tough jobs, was the one to tell players they were out of the team. No player, however obvious a choice he appears to the rest of the world, feels totally secure. Politics have always played a part in team selection. Carling had been reasonably happy with his first international year thus far. But England were well served for talent in the centre. Worryingly, he realised that the need to find a new England leader might have cost him his place, with an outsider brought in. Many would have deferred the phone call, popping out to the pub to find the inspiration to tell the England team manager exactly what they thought of his treatment of such a dedicated and loyal player. But that's not Carling's style. Dutch courage wasn't the answer. Nor was there any point in delaying the inevitable. Carling made the call, prepared with his 'disappointed, what have I done wrong, but I'll fight hard to get back' speech.

Minutes later, he was scribbling a message in relief to his mum and brother: 'I am the captain.' He tried to take in the implications of Cooke's message. News of Carling's promotion was embargoed until Sunday morning, which gave him some breathing space, and also some worry: how would the rest of the side respond to the youngest member calling the shots? But Carling was already working out what was required and how he was going to cope with the challenge. The next 48 hours were tough, but he resisted making a fortune on the numerous bets that were being laid on the next England captain. Only Australians or someone with inside information would have been interested in the long odds being offered on Will Carling being that man.

Carling's first test came in the players' room that Saturday night. The players knew one of their number had been told that he was the new captain, but nobody was letting on. It was the first sign that Cooke had chosen well. Before making the announcement, Cooke stressed that the selectors had gone for someone who would be a fixture in the side and would still be around for the 1991 World Cup. Rory Underwood remembers audible gasps round the room when Carling's name was mentioned.

Rob Andrew, who was top of most of the players' guess lists, reflected the mood of the England party that night. 'It was a brave decision by Geoff. Will may not have been around for long, but he was already established in the team. We knew he was going to be around for a long time, and nobody doubted his right to be there. It was no secret that the England captaincy was a problem that had to be confronted. Geoff was looking for someone to do the job long-term. Nigel [Melville] had been his first choice. With Nigel gone, he plumped for Will because of what he'd seen of his character and the strength of that character. I was just finding my feet again. Geoff saw that he could mould a side around Will. No one said, "Christ, what's going on here?" behind Will's back. There was no dissent. I'm sure a few felt "rather him than me". He had our full backing. Will had made the most of his rugby opportunities so far. I saw no reason to doubt that he would not seize this chance.'

CARLING

It was a hell of a shock, completely out of the blue. I'd only just started playing for England. Even now I wonder about it. I kept getting cards from friends wondering whether the selectors had lost their senses. It was an amazing thing for Cookie to link me with the World Cup like that. I had not really felt that I was an established member of the side. I'd played one Five Nations match, the Millennium game in Dublin, and two games on tour. There was no time to say I was part of the set-up. Had I stayed with the Army, my life would have been totally different. That's why I think I'm a lucky person. People say I got the captaincy much too early, but I wouldn't have had it any other way. One day when all my rugby is behind me, I'm going to sit down with Geoff Cooke. And, after the right amount of alcoholic influence, I'm going to try and get a straight answer to the most puzzling question of all – 'Why the hell did you pick me, Geoff?'

In many ways my whole rugby career has been a bed of roses, the way it's gone along; it's been very easy. Often I wander along and wonder why all this has happened to me. I view it simply as right place, right time. I can't tell you why I'm a better player than someone else – why I have played for England and another centre hasn't. That doesn't mean I'm inferior; I don't worry about who I'm playing, I know I can beat them on the day. But I would never say I'm better than so-and-so. I got picked for the North when I was still at university. Other centres around included Bryan Barley, Kevin Simms, John Buckton and Fran Clough. Why the hell did Cookie pick me ahead of them?

People say I was mad to give up my Army career when I might still be dropped by England. I believe you have got to be positive. I was looking to stay in the England side. When dilemmas come along, I look at them as an opportunity rather than a problem.

I struggled to keep it quiet. I went to watch the Quins play at Richmond. All the talk in the bar was about the new England captain. I listened to our forwards mentioning all the names, except one: mine.

The squad were told by Geoff on the Saturday night that I would be captain, although the team for the Australia game wasn't announced until the next morning. I'd been waiting for two days for their reaction. I understand there were one or two bemused faces. I don't know. I couldn't see; I was staring at the floor. There was certainly a heavy silence. That's all they were told. I was the youngest person there, just wondering how they were going to react. But it was rather subdued.

They all came offering congratulations. I don't know whether some felt sorry for me at such an early stage in my England career. Being captain was just about the quickest way of going out of the side at the time. Again, I looked at it positively. I thought I had the potential to do the job and I wanted to be involved in the process. Maybe I could influence a little bit of what happens. My view was to give it a shot. Again, if it went wrong, then at least I'd have had a go. I didn't want to look back and think I chickened out. It was the same with my first cap. I wanted to give it a go, rather than be safe. What's the point of hiding in the ranks and going with the tide? I want to get involved. If it doesn't work out, fine. If the job lasted for five minutes and I was thrown out, that's how it was meant to be. It's no good looking back in 20 years and wondering, 'If only'. The World Cup certainly wasn't part of my game plan that weekend, though. All my rugby future was tied up in that Australia game, which was less than a week away.

Chapter 3

Dream Start

Did England deliver – did they ever!

STEPHEN JONES, *Sunday Times*

The rugby press, who pride themselves on being able to tap the Rugby Football Union's jungle telegraph, were as ignorant of Cooke's intentions as the England players were. The numerous alternatives being touted revealed that the new team manager was not considered to have an automatic choice. Carling had promise as a player, but had been in the England set-up for only a few months. His captaincy experience was extremely limited. Although Nigel Melville had made his debut as both player and captain four years earlier, also against the Australians, Melville had always had 'future England captain' stamped all over him.

Stephen Jones, the astute rugby correspondent of the *Sunday Times*, did not attend that press conference when Carling's appointment was announced. On the telephone, he was asked to identify the new captain from England's assembled squad. Carling's name was his 13th offering.

Geoff Cooke's introduction of Carling could not have come at a better time. Despite a poor World Cup in 1987, an average 1988 Five Nations championship and a disastrous summer tour Down Under, English rugby was currently on a high. Three of the four Divisional

23

sides had inflicted stirring defeats on the touring Australians. Actually, Stephen Jones had been spot-on in his column that morning: 'The key does not chiefly lie in the identities of the men they announce today – it lies in the attitude which Geoff Cooke and his coaches can instil in the chosen ones. For a start they have to pass on the new mood – the pace, the counter-attack, the green light for speculation. In the past eight seasons, England have tried to play through their forwards and failed utterly.'

London, under coach Dick Best, had set the tone with a dazzling 21–10 victory over the Wallabies at Twickenham. The North then kept up the pressure with a 15–9 success at Otley four days later, Carling's run setting up scrum-half Dewi Morris's winning try in the dying minutes. The South-West were the other Divisional winners. For the international, Australia's coach Bob Dwyer hurriedly sent for Michael Lynagh, who had originally been unavailable. An injury to centre Paul Cornish was the official reason, but the tourists were in such disarray that Lynagh would have been bounding up the aircraft steps if the baggage man had cut himself shaving. After Otley, when Australia gave away 22 penalties, Dwyer lamented, 'Much of our play was absolute rubbish.'

Cooke's selection of the North's Morris epitomised England's new courage. London's Andrew Harriman and lock Paul Ackford displayed respectively the pace and quality that had exposed Australia, and that trio were the new England caps. Ironically, none had been born in England: Harriman was the son of a chief from Lagos, and was the first prince to play for England since the Russian, Obolensky, in 1936; Hanover was Ackford's birthplace, while Morris was a Welshman from Crickhowell. His rise had been as unexpected as Carling's elevation to the captaincy. With Melville out of the reckoning and Bristol's Richard Harding, captain in the international in Fiji that summer, reckoned to be too old at 35, the spotlight had fallen again on Richard Hill. The Bath scrum-half had been England's captain the previous year, but had lost his job and been suspended for one match, along with Wade Dooley, Gareth Chilcott and Graham Dawe, after a bruising match in Cardiff. Hill's chance of a recall against Australia disappeared the second he punched Harlequins scrum-half Richard Moon in an early season match at Twickenham and was sent off by Welsh referee Gareth Simmonds. At the same time, the North were playing an International XV at Gateshead, and Morris, who had just joined Liverpool St Helens from Winnington Park, was making his big-time debut. In a spectacular two months, Morris went from junior to senior rugby and played for the North, England B and then the full England side.

Cooke had made seven changes in all from the England team that had beaten Fiji 25–12 that summer. Out went Harding, Chilcott, Barrie Evans, Bryan Barley, Stuart Barnes, Nigel Redman and Gary Rees. Cooke stated, 'In case of doubt, fitness has proved a factor in selection. Character and commitment have been other areas we have taken into consideration.'

Carling was careful to make his first public utterance in charge positive and thoughtful: 'Although we have three new caps in the side, there is a lot of experience. I have to see that we gel and get it mentally right. I'm not getting carried away because we have not seen the full Australian Test team yet. They are dangerous and they must win the international to make their tour a success. But I think we will win. They look very vulnerable when you run the ball at them.'

The press made much of Carling's officer class. The player who had taken England to Australia, John Orwin, had been a corporal in the RAF. Most of the Carling headlines were of a military nature. Cooke's bold decision was applauded by the rugby writers, while judgement on Carling was reserved. They concluded, quite rightly, that, for the time being anyway, Cooke would be calling the shots. *Today*'s Tony Roche, who got to know Carling well, admits: 'I was absolutely gobsmacked, along with everyone else, when Geoff made the announcement. The thought had never entered my head. But Will's a real natural loner. And that has to be a good quality if you are to cope with the job. I knew he'd live with the pressure.'

Carling's first week in charge flew past, although celebrations were curtailed by the closeness of the match. Telegrams and cards poured in from relations and family, school and university friends. It was easy to spot those who got on with him best: those messages were full of light-hearted abuse and queries about the sanity of those in charge of English rugby. Twickenham internationals were still a relatively new experience to Carling, but the place had played a full part in his rugby dreams since the age of 6. Those dreams had never involved him as England captain, though. Carling was entering new territory, even in his mind. Cooke, without wanting to undermine the new man, tried to ease his burden; he had no need. Carling had already considered the problems of a young leader getting the best out of an experienced squad. That was exactly what his Army duties would have required.

And Carling had given the subject much thought during his student days.

Cooke watched him closely. 'He didn't try to impose himself. There was no "I am the captain: we're doing it this way." One of Will's strengths is that he can relate to different people. He adopted a low-key approach straight away. Senior players were asked, "What do you think?" I was amazed by the way he handled it.'

Cooke had no cause to worry. The day could not have gone better if Carling had scripted it himself. England responded to the Divisional sides' adventurous approach, and the Twickenham crowd, so often inhibited and reserved, too often disappointed, were for once seduced by the emotion of their national side's display. Five years on, that one-night stand has become a full-blown affair with the rugby team. Twickenham now has become as intimidating to visitors as Murrayfield, the Arms Park, Lansdowne Road and the Parc des Princes. Before the Carling era, most opponents thought Twickenham was the next best thing to playing at home. Now it has English clout, on the field and in the towering stands. That pride can be traced back to Guy Fawkes Day, 1988.

'Did England deliver – did they ever!' was the verdict of Stephen Jones. It was a dream day for England and the new captain. Carling, virtually unknown a week earlier, had become a national hero. The new skipper was given a rousing ovation by an ecstatic Twickenham when forced off by concussion. His last act had been to make the game safe, putting Simon Halliday clear for the winning try before being taken out by a late tackle. It was a struggle to get Carling to leave centre-stage. England physio Kevin Murphy was fighting a losing battle before the RFU doctor Ben Gilfeather appeared and the captain was led away.

But the job was done. What a professional job it was, too. England had trailed twice, the second time by 13–9 early in the second half after a David Campese try. But two quick tries from Rory Underwood took England back in front before Australia closed the gap to 3 points; then Halliday's try sealed this pulsating match by 28–19. The Australians had played a full part, but England's gambles all worked. The bold approach came off, and Morris scored a debut try in the first half after Andy Robinson had charged down Lynagh's kick. Flanker Robinson, first capped in the summer, was magnificent; Dean Richards was his usual tower of strength at No. 8; Ackford, after a decade on the fringes, took full advantage of this first

26

international chance. More important, the team showed character, held its nerve when other England sides would have buckled. It was too early for Carling to have had that effect, though. It was down to the confidence and pride instilled by Cooke and Uttley.

Uttley actually missed the match. His duties at Harrow School required him to wander up the touchline during the 1st XV's home game against Wellington instead. Well, Rugby Union is an amateur game, and Uttley was the director of physical education there. The strange thing is that the Harrow headmaster at the time was Ian Beer, a member of the Rugby Football Union's executive. And it was Beer who had prevented Uttley becoming England coach a few years earlier when he had explained that Uttley could not combine both jobs. Fair enough, but maybe Uttley would have preferred to make up his own mind. He was never given the choice, only learning of his candidature after another coach had been appointed. Uttley was also refused time off from Harrow for England's tour to Australia in 1988. The B team's coaches, Alan Davies and David Robinson, went instead.

Uttley was disappointed to leave the squad at 1 o'clock before the match and head back to Harrow. But he has never needed to be reminded about his responsibilities, where his duties lie. Uttley took his 'punishment' like a man, without grumbling, but was heartbroken to be abandoning his lads. Well, not totally: a small transistor was hidden in his anorak as he patrolled the school touchline. Who says you can't be in two places at once? Fortunately, the school match – which ended in defeat for Harrow – finished early, and parents gathered round Uttley for Carling's *coup de grâce*. Even now, Uttley rarely remembers feeling so helpless.

UTTLEY
It was the most bizarre afternoon of my life. I didn't think it would be so strange, but it was a bit schizophrenic, dealing with senior players and then coming back to younger lads who need much more attention. I was amazed how draining it was. It was so important to win that game in the way we did. It was a big, big psychological barrier. We shattered the myth of antipodean invincibility. We had to be sensible – we expected to win. But the way the boys dealt with the pressure gave everyone a boost. They kept their faith when they were behind. England were shown the way by the London Division and caught the

Australians out of their season. We didn't beat them by much. But it's the wins that are important – not the quality. England came through in the last quarter. That's the sign of a good side.

COOKE
It was the first sign that we had begun to turn the corner. Now we could start the next phase. The game ran for us. We had planned carefully, and you could see the benefit of the collective approach. We gave the Aussies a hard time in England. They were apprehensive at Twickenham, and we took our chances. We didn't in the World Cup final three years later, and that's why we lost. But that first game was an important start for Will. It was a team effort for all to see, but he played a full part and the Twickenham crowd had a captain to identify with, probably for the first time since Bill Beaumont.

The television coverage had made Carling a celebrity. Yet the full impact of his leadership had been missed by the cameras. After Campese's interception try, Carling had gathered his team under the posts. Beforehand, the new captain had stated: 'On the evidence of the Wallabies' games so far, it seems that the best plan is to run at them, where they appear most vulnerable. That doesn't mean waiting until the last 20 minutes when legs are weary, but throughout the game, even at the risk of making mistakes.' Under the posts, Carling was more emphatic. 'I told them not to panic. That we had agreed beforehand that, if we were going to play an expansive game, things could go wrong. We were disappointed, but I felt it would come. We had to keep our cool and keep on attacking. It might have looked like I was reading the riot act. But you've got to make your points pretty forcefully in the middle of an international to have any impact.'

If the captaincy had come as a shock to Carling, so much more so did the reaction to the victory over Australia. As is the way with England sporting triumphs, this impressive performance was seen to cure all ills, erasing several years of disappointment and unfulfilled potential. Carling knew better. The captaincy, form permitting, was his for the next three years. He had still to make his mark, though. 'At the time, and even looking back now, I know my contribution to that Australian success as captain was negligible. It couldn't be otherwise. Geoff Cooke told me to concentrate on my own performance. He and Roger were in charge. What could I do in six days? If I made any impact, it was on the field, making sure we stuck to our original plan.'

After the match, Cooke warned everyone not to get carried away by the result. The press, as usual, made their own minds up. The *Daily Mail*'s Terry O'Connor didn't hold back: 'England conjured up more movement than I've seen in 40 years of rugby. Skipper Will Carling symbolised the new adventurous spirit of English rugby when he smashed aside two defenders to create a final try before being floored by a late tackle at the climax of a magical Twickenham autumn day.'

Today's Tony Roche went even further: 'England cast off the dark protective cloak which has enshrouded their game for seven years.'

Finally, the ultimate: a press apology. John Mason, of the *Daily Telegraph*, admitted 'delightfully, that I was wrong that Morris had come in too early.'

With journalists admitting the errors of their ways, Cooke knew he had got something right. But England's team manager realised better than anyone that getting carried away by this one performance would be the biggest mistake of all. Still, Carling and England had taken an impressive first step towards the 1991 World Cup. Australian coach Bob Dwyer said as much, and the touring captain Nick Farr-Jones made England favourites for the 1989 Five Nations championship.

After only a week in the job, Will Carling had become everyone's favourite and darling.

Chapter 4

You're Our Captain, Will

It was a hell of a shock, probably worse than being made captain. There was now this line between me and the players. Not them and us. But me and them. Whatever they might say, they expected me to set the standards, to behave in a certain way. And that was a terrible realisation for me at that age. I couldn't be one of the boys any more.

WILL CARLING

Overnight, Will Carling had become the symbol of England's new rugby pride. Most sporting heroes, even those as genuine as George Best and Ian Botham, have a probationary period. Not Carling. England's captain became public property in a way no other rugby player had experienced. Gareth Edwards was the first British rugby superstar; the first to attract attention outside the confines of rugby and sport. Bill Beaumont was to become just as famous but, like Edwards, most of the adulation came at the end of his career. Beaumont's exposure has been maintained by regular appearances on the BBC's quiz programme 'Question of Sport'. It is Beaumont's captaincy of that team rather than of the England rugby side that has made him such a familiar face.

Six days into the captaincy, Carling was already on his way to becoming the most popular rugby player of all time. The success of the 1991 World Cup was to seal his fate. Rugby, after decades of

31

being held back and protected by its own governing bodies, at last assumed its place on the world's sporting stage. David Campese, to the rugby fraternity, reflects rugby's new status, travelling the globe and making a fortune out of playing the game. But, to the world at large, Will Carling is the face of Rugby Union.

England's new rugby hero had been concussed. Initially, Carling claimed it was just a bang on the head. But, eventually, he had to accept three weeks out of the game because of the RFU's safety guidelines. Carling took advantage of the enforced rest to contemplate the implications of England's win. That meant missing the Barbarians' end-of-tour fixture with Australia, as well as sitting out the Harlequins' next three Courage League matches.

The Wallabies found their form in the second half of the tour. They beat Scotland 32–13 and the Barbarians 40–22, Campese crossing for two tries in both games. The tour verdicts made good reading for England: the tourists lost four of their thirteen matches in Britain, all in England. Australia's coach Bob Dwyer was diplomatic in the face of demands for his prediction of the outcome of the England-Scotland game, which would open the 1989 Five Nations championship: 'Well, I think the Calcutta Cup will end up in much better shape than last year' – referring to the damage inflicted on the oldest rugby trophy in post-match revelry the previous season!

The Aussies still believe that England had caught them cold. 'I didn't realise that six weeks out of the game would have had such an effect on us,' admitted Dwyer. 'I think they were very lucky to have had a very positive coach [Dick Best] for the London Division in the first game. England may not have been so inclined to play the way they did had the Divisional approach gone astray.' Very true, but an obviously superficial observation from one of rugby's most astute thinkers. The Australian coach has always been a realist; his comments were directed forwards to the World Cup rather than backwards to this tour. One of his favourite ploys is to question the opposition's tactical style, so as to instil doubts within that team.

Fortunately, England had themselves uncovered a manager of some strength in Geoff Cooke. His job has not been easy simply because he has had great players and, therefore, a great team at his disposal. England have always had great players. The All Blacks and the Springboks realised long ago that, if England ever harnessed that talent, the rugby world would have a serious northern hemisphere challenger.

But producing a winning team has never been a high priority at Twickenham. The Rugby Football Union do not care that much for the players. They see them as a necessary nuisance in their quest to maintain this 'great amateur game of ours'. And they are treated accordingly. England had more world-class forward talent to choose from during the late 1970s than was available during the two back-to-back Grand Slams in 1991 and 1992. Unfortunately, the system designed to bring out the best in them at international level was almost non-existent. Occasionally, because of the law of averages or, more likely, the dedication of a group of single-minded players fed up of being ridiculed, England got it right. But that was often on tour, when the influences of Twickenham were furthest away.

Many have tried to beat the system. Don Quixote had more chance tilting at those windmills. Good men not only failed, but were left shattered by the experience. Few of the national coaches lasted the course. All pleaded the need for change, for a more streamlined, competitive way forward. The RFU are not good listeners. But, finally, they could not ignore the rest of the world. Or the 1987 World Cup. England's standing was now official: seventh in the world, which would be their seeding for the next World Cup in 1991. Despite honest preparations, England had been bundled out of the tournament by Wales, of all adversaries, in the quarter-final.

That failure brought Cooke to the fore. Mike Weston was actually appointed to carry on as manager after the World Cup, but resigned when the coach, Martin Green, was sacked. Cooke, who admits that the height of his ambition had been to become an England selector, was now handed more responsibility and control over the England national side than anyone before him. 'I wasn't a well-known figure outside the north,' recalls Cooke. 'And I hadn't played international rugby. There's always a credibility gap when that's the case. How can you relate to the players if you don't know what they are going through? Australia's Bob Dwyer and others have since laid that myth to rest, although it didn't matter in my case. My partner in crime, Roger Uttley, had been there, done it and done it well for England and the British Lions. Roger and I got on. We complemented each other.

'Mike Weston did a hell of a lot, and I don't believe that Mike has had the credit for the groundwork he did. It was Mike Weston who started the cycle of change. I followed him at the North. He was the chairman there when I was first involved. I knew his contribution.

People forget that he was reappointed after the World Cup, but resigned on a point of principle.'

Cooke had spent a lifetime in sport and local government, and those experiences were to prove invaluable. He identified the two areas where compromise was fatal: management and selection. 'If I failed, then it was going to be my failure. I wasn't going to carry the can for anyone else, for a failure that wasn't mine. Management is about accountability. Too often that's not the case. And our selection policy had to be right. That had been England's biggest problem. For a variety of reasons, it was always being botched. There was a huge fear of failure, no stability. No one knew what was going on. Mike Davis, who won the 1980 Grand Slam in his first season in charge, started to get things on track. But, as the results tailed off, so did the stability.'

Cooke's good intentions were immediately put to the test. England lost the opening two games of the 1988 Five Nations championship, and the heat was on. A scrappy win at Murrayfield eased that pressure, and Chris Oti's three tries against Ireland, then the Millennium win in Dublin gave Cooke a satisfactory end to the season. But the Australian tour that summer seemed to leave him and England back where they had started. Not quite, though. Cooke's skill as a selector was already having an effect. Jeff Probyn, Will Carling, Mickey Skinner, Andy Robinson and Chris Oti had all made their debuts under the new regime. And Dewi Morris and Paul Ackford then came in for the Australia game in the autumn. Cooke's choices were made carefully: character, ability and the potential to fit in, as well as the ability to play international rugby, were all considered. Cooke knew that mistakes in that department would leave him vulnerable to the Twickenham establishment.

The captaincy was the most crucial issue of all, and that Australian win would benefit his new choice. It meant that Carling's honeymoon period in the job would be extended to cover the 1989 Five Nations championship, for which England's victory had earned them the dubious title of favourites. England sat out the first international Saturday, which is not the preferred way of starting the championship for most rugby coaches. They consider that, win or lose, their opponents have the benefit of a game under their belts, making them more difficult to beat.

Cooke and Uttley planned their campaign, with Carling consulted for the first time. Carling had worked under Cooke with the North. His methods were familiar. England did away with a trial match, and the management instead used the Divisional Championship to pick a 25-man squad for a weekend trip to the Algarve in January.

Two of the most exciting players of the post-war era dominated the pre-championship news. Jonathan Davies turned professional with Widnes just two days before Wales left for their squad gathering in Valencia. That was also a blow to the British Lions. As captain of his country, Davies was favourite to lead the party that summer to Australia.

The other player was Pierre Villepreux. The former French international full-back had been invited along to England's squad session in Portugal by the RFU's technical administrator, Don Rutherford. Villepreux, recently rejected as French coach, accepted. Immediately, Anglo-French relations were strained. The French Fédération felt that the invitation should have been channelled through them. The RFU restored the *entente cordiale* with an apology that stated, 'It might have been remiss of us not to notify the FFR.' Villepreux cast his eye over the new England captain. 'Carling is fast and has good vision. He is an interesting boy.'

Carling was looking forward to his first championship in charge. After appearing for the North in the Divisional Championship and showing his goal-kicking prowess when fly-half David Pears was injured, a couple of nagging doubts had clouded his preparation, both of which were to materialise and affect England's challenge. Carling was worried first because expectations were so high. The win over Australia had been a fine performance, but it was one game. Yet, on the strength of it, talk of Grand Slams was being bandied about. Carling knew it was the kiss of death.

Carling's other problem concerned his fitness, particularly his left shin. Shin splints was diagnosed, and rest was the recommended cure. The only person more distraught than Carling about the news was Cooke. His captaincy choices appeared to be jinxed. Carling was prepared to stand down if necessary, no matter how big a disappointment that would have been. But he made the decision to carry on playing, although the condition could not be hidden from the press. Carling helped the Quins to a Cup victory at Rugby the week before the Calcutta Cup, but was unable to take a full part in England's subsequent squad session at Twickenham. The seriousness of the injury was played down at the press conference that afternoon.

Scotland had won their opening championship game against Wales 23–7, but England were still firm favourites for the Twickenham

35

Calcutta Cup. England made two changes from the Australia game. Mike Teague, a Gloucester stalwart for a decade, was recalled on the blind-side flank at the expense of Bath's David Egerton. Teague had toured South Africa and New Zealand in the mid-1980s, winning three caps. And a knee operation cost Andy Harriman his place, so Chris Oti returned on the wing.

There has never been much love lost between England and Scotland on the rugby field, as in most other fields. Now the officials were at each others' throats. The Calcutta Cup has never caused such arguments and long-term consequences as followed its battering in Edinburgh a year earlier. England's Dean Richards missed the subsequent Millennium game in Dublin because of his part in the affair, while John Jeffrey was dealt with more harshly by the Scottish Rugby Union and was not selected for his country's summer tour. The SRU, not for the first time, occupied the high moral ground and declared that Richards's punishment had not been severe enough for the £1,000 damage. 'If you put four bottles of Scotch on the table before a dinner, then it's going to create massive mayhem,' retorts Roger Uttley. 'The next morning, I got a phone call from the RFU's Roger Godfrey. He said, "I'm just leaving. There seems to be some problem with the Calcutta Cup. Can you sort it out?" Some problem? He wasn't wrong there.' The repercussions were to rumble on until the 1991 World Cup.

England retained the Calcutta Cup in 1989. But only just. The 12–12 draw was a great disappointment; the excitement and adventure of the Australia match had vanished. The Scots set out to frustrate England and left Cooke in a similar state: 'They did what they came to do – not a lot,' was the manager's initial verdict. England could also point the finger at French referee Guy Maurette, and not only for missing a blatant offside when John Jeffrey hacked on for the game's only try. But England really had only themselves to blame. Rob Andrew and full-back Jonathan Webb missed seven kicks out of 11, allowing Scotland's indiscretions to go unpunished. Andy Robinson gave his worst international performance to date, deciding to chase after Scotland's captain Finlay Calder instead of the ball. England's inability to raise the game out of the mire and cope with the persistent Scottish infringements was evidence that Uttley and Cooke still had much work to do.

Carling was disappointed with both the performance and the result. There would be no Grand Slam or Triple Crown in his first season as captain. The honeymoon had ended as abruptly as it had begun.

CARLING
The media had really got behind us after that Aussie win. They felt English rugby was going somewhere. I was staggered how it all changed after that draw with Scotland. They really got stuck in. Before the Irish game, I told them that I thought some of the criticism was harsh and not merited. Nobody said a word and they wandered off.

The *London Evening Standard*'s Chris Jones stayed behind and said: 'Big mistake.'

'What big mistake?'

'Criticising the press.'

'I hardly call that criticism.'

'Well, they won't take kindly to it.'

'Chris, they criticise players in front of millions and we have to take that. I'm just passing on some thoughts.'

'I'm just telling you how it is.'

He was right. You can't win. That's when I learnt my first lesson.

It was the first of three lessons for Carling that weekend. The second came the night before the game as the backs relaxed. 'The backs often behave a bit childishly,' says Rob Andrew. 'It's our way of easing the tension. Will's usually in the middle of the shaving-foam or talc fights. That's very much him. Sometimes he finds it hard to suppress those instincts. But being boisterous can sometimes lead to conflict. The backs are much more relaxed than the forwards. The big men get keyed up for the physical battle to come. If you catch a forward at the wrong moment, there can be trouble. Will received a terrible rollicking from Dean Richards, our pack leader in Dublin, for messing about. But it's just Will's way of easing the tension. It shouldn't imply that he doesn't take his rugby enormously seriously.'

Carling did show more authority in England's impressive 16–3 victory in Dublin. The game turned when England took a tap-penalty midway through the second half, and Brian Moore scored. 'Rob [Andrew] wanted to kick it,' said Carling. 'But I felt the forwards were coming on to their best phase and that it was wiser to run it.' It was an important moment for the captain.

* * *

CARLING

Beating Australia had been like a dream. This was for real. After the draw with Scotland, it was a relief to go to Dublin and win. I was elated to beat the Irish. I felt I had arrived as an international captain, and now I could really celebrate. I got absolutely hammered at the dinner that night. The captains always have to make speeches, but I could hardly open my mouth. It was a complete disaster, but I wasn't worried. I could see the rest of the lads laughing. I thought they would think this was absolutely hilarious. A few days later I found out I'd made yet another mistake when I had lunch with Rob.

He said to me: 'By the way, the feedback I've had is that the lads were really surprised at your behaviour on Saturday night.'

'What do you mean?'

'Well, for a start, you were out of your box.'

'So were they.'

'That's not the point, Will. You're their captain.'

'Rob, I'm just 23 years old.'

It was a hell of a shock, probably bigger than being made captain. I was now expected to behave in a certain way. I couldn't enjoy myself. That's when it dawned on me that I couldn't really let go. There was now this line between me and the players. Not them and us. Me and them. Whatever they might say, they expected me – and I knew it – to set the standards, to behave in a certain way. And that was a terrible realisation for one so young. To have all those old guys expecting that. I couldn't be one of the boys any more.

It was a situation Will Carling had been used to at school. He had never expected it to have such an effect on his career as an England rugby player.

Chapter 5

The Old School Tie

I wonder now why I was a bully. I had been beaten up by my own brother, so I thought I would get my own back. 'Do this or I'll beat you up.' I stopped one day when I turned on someone with my usual threat. I saw this look of fear in his eye. I realised this was not the way to treat people.

WILL CARLING

Much has been made of Carling's upbringing. How the Army and the lonely boarding public school background moulded a character of privilege, a leader with a stiff upper lip, arrogance and aloofness. Carling has never denied that it was a privilege to attend Sedbergh School, a famous rugby nursery. But he laughs at those who paint the picture of the abandoned child suffering hardship at an institution resembling Dotheboys Hall. Neglect is not the way of the Carling family. The Carling boys, Will and elder brother Marcus, are part of a close-knit unit, and Will is not afraid to display the affection that genuinely exists between them. His family has provided him with valuable support and refuge during times of strain.

Carling discovered his love of rugby at Terra Nova prep school. Even then, he was a player of distinction, a star for the future – even an international one. Success at school, however, whether scholastic

39

or sporting, can come at a price. Resentment and jealousy are fairly common, and Carling did not have to be at Sedbergh to experience that. His problem was that his team-mates were not his class-mates, for his prowess on the rugby field took him ahead of himself. That way Carling learnt to live a rugby life alone, away from the team. But that role is not alien to his nature. He is comfortable as a man apart. His basic nature would have led him in that direction anyway. For that reason, Carling's schooldays were not an ordeal, despite the separation from his parents.

Unfamiliar surroundings were part of Carling's childhood. Bill, his father, was a lieutenant-colonel in the Air Corps. His own distinguished rugby career was played out with Cardiff, Bath, Blackheath and Cornwall, and the burly prop was picked for an England trial. Tours of duty abroad took the Carlings to Hong Kong and the Far East and, in all, they averaged almost an address a year for all of Bill's 25 years in the service. He was stationed at Warminster when the two boys were born. Marcus and Will were born in the same maternity bed in Bradford-on-Avon in Wiltshire. William David Charles Carling, weighing 7lb 15oz, arrived 19 months after his brother.

The younger Carling ate and slept. And ate and slept. His mother Pam was happy with that. 'William was incredibly placid. I used to forget about him. It would be the middle of the after-noon, and I would suddenly realise that I'd forgotten to give Willie his lunch. He would never remind me by crying or screaming. And, as you can see by the photographs, he was a baby who liked his lunch.'

Carling spent his first three school years at Montgomery Infants in Colchester. His father was then posted abroad, and Will joined his brother (Carling i and Carling ii) at the Terra Nova School in Cheshire. The choice was made because his grandparents lived nearby. By the time he left there at 13 in 1979, Will Carling's sporting career was up and running. He was a crack shot in the rifle team, an off-spinner and hard-hitting middle-order batsman at cricket, a record-breaking long jumper and runner and, eventually, a sniping fly-half on the rugby field. As he thinned out, the young Carling moved from hooker back through the scrum to the comparative safety of the backs.

The competitive edge was apparent from an early age. 'Pam was watching him in a prep school cricket match,' remembers Bill

Carling. 'Willie was given out. He was not happy and stormed off in a fury making a scene. His bat was hurled away in anger. I was away. But Pam was having none of that. She went straight into the pavilion and a clump around the ear quietened him down. He never did it again. Willie hasn't lost that fury. He has learnt to control it.'

His size created problems in his prep school-days, and Will Carling got the reputation for being a bully. 'It's not a pleasant activity to look back upon. You wonder why you do it. I had been beaten up by my own brother, so I thought it was about time that I got my own back. It wasn't, "Give me money or I'll beat you up" – it was, "Do this or I'll beat you up." Not much of a difference, I suppose. I stopped one day. I turned on someone and made my usual threat. I saw this look of fear in his eye. I realised that this was not the way to treat people.' Carling's fondest memories of Terra Nova concern his rugby and the Danish matrons. 'Even then, I appreciated them. Then a maths master ran off with one of them. I was distraught.'

Carling's instinct for self-preservation was evident at age 13. 'Traditionally, those about to leave school go for a swim in the out-of-bounds pool. The skill is not in going for the swim, it's in not getting caught. You escape by running up the side of the wood and back into house. I was leading this charge. Then I got the feeling that this was not a good idea. I dropped to the back just as the masters appeared in front of us. The rest were rounded up. I scarpered through the wood, up the back fire escape and into bed, just before the master appeared. That might be cited as an example of me looking after No. 1. Maybe. I just did what I thought was best.'

His headmaster, Andrew Keith, said goodbye with a warning. 'He has dominated much of Terra Nova life for a fair amount of time, and much of our sporting and artistic success is due to him. I hope that William can make the adjustment from being master of all he surveys to being just another lowly new boy with the right degree of humour and humility.'

Even at Terra Nova, Carling had found himself on the sporting field with his elders, sometimes his brother. That was to continue at Sedbergh, a school with a great rugby tradition. Carling arrived in 1979 as the school celebrated 100 years of rugby. Eleven former pupils have played for England, including three captains (Wavell Wakefield, John Spencer, and now Carling), sixteen for Scotland and two for Ireland. Sedbergh's 'brown shirts' are no less famous or feared than Oswald Mosley's were; the Sedbergh 1st XV colours have certainly been longer-lasting and worn with more distinction. With the jersey came the brown blazer, the object of all those with rugby ambitions. Carling went into the Sedbergh record books when his entry into the 1st XV as a fifth former denied an established 'Brown Blazer' his place. For his final two years, W. D. C. Carling was a regular in the England Schools team, and captain in his last season.

Carling's week in the winter revolved around rugby. 'We trained on Mondays and Tuesdays. Wednesday was practice-game time. Another short session followed on Thursday, while Friday was spent getting ready for the match. I cleaned my boots, stuffed them with newspaper – the *Telegraph* was all we were allowed to read – and polished them. Then the match. That's how I spent my five years there, with a little work fitted in.' That is slightly modest: Carling passed A levels in geography, economics and English, and was destined for Durham University after a year's break.

Carling's softer side manifested itself in his poetry and sketching at school. He had arrived at Sedbergh on an art scholarship. The poetry was a passing phase although a couple – 'Love' and 'Mutual Evolution' – made the school magazine. As with most adolescent ramblings, he would rather they stayed there. The sketching is still part of his relaxation, however. He claims no great skill or insight, just enjoyment and, occasionally, the satisfaction of a task accomplished well.

Carling's first year was spent in a dormitory, then he moved to Winder House and his own room. Winder House was where his brother was also domiciled. Marcus was something of a rebel, and there was talk of splitting them up. But they stayed together. The house, where Will Carling was head in his final year, has one drawback: it is the furthest one away from the centre of school, two-thirds of a mile, a journey made six times a day.

Carling remembers how bleak the Yorkshire moors can be in the middle of winter. On one camping trip, when he was 14, Carling's trust in his own instincts was reinforced.

CARLING
Half a dozen of us were on the moors, getting from A to B with the help of maps. Suddenly, this blizzard descended, and all the landmarks disappeared. There was no master with us. We had to decide quickly which way to go for safety. Eventually, after a discussion, we decided to go one way. But I wasn't happy. I knew

it was in the wrong direction. The lads said we'd taken a majority decision. 'Fair enough. But I'm going this way.' I didn't just storm off. I explained my reasons. They came round, and we were back within half an hour. Two of the group had hypothermia. I've never been so cold in my life. We had lost all our equipment.

We had looked at the maps. I just couldn't go with the crowd. I reasoned with them. But I would have gone off on my own if I hadn't persuaded them. I've got to trust my instincts.

Some of Carling's days at Sedbergh were spent drinking. The school's traditional drinking club is called 'The Epicure'.

CARLING
Acceptance is by word of mouth. One lower sixth former is voted in by the year above. Then he recruits a dozen from his year. We used a room in a restaurant in town. You'd wander up some rickety old stairs and serve yourself. It was all done on trust . . . and on a slate. You'd settle up every couple of weeks. I'm sure the masters knew what was going on. But it was all part of your education. Had the breathalyser been used at house prayers, then quite a few school and house prefects would have been in trouble. All you could smell was beer and mints. I didn't go every day, but I was a regular at the weekends. Nobody ever refused if they were asked to join the 'Epi'.

Tradition was a big part of life at Sedbergh. The Wilson Run had been taking place since 1881. Originally a paper chase, the tough cross-country course was not to Carling's liking. Although one of the school's top athletes, he finished 125th with a time just inside one hour and 45 minutes. Since Carling left, the record has been broken for the first time this century and now stands at one hour, eight seconds.

Carling's rugby ability singled him out at Sedbergh, even in an outstanding side. Every school year has its sporting stars, but Carling was a star outside his year. He played for the year above throughout until the sixth form. When he was captain of the Colts XV, Richard Mowbray, the master in charge, made this assessment. 'The success of the XV this term has been largely due to [Carling's] great maturity. As a player with impressive individual skills, particularly in his timing and awareness of space around him, his own performances have been quite outstanding. However, it has been his character which has most impressed me this term. Despite their record, the XV are not a team of world-beaters. William's leadership, encouragement and example have brought the best out of the players around him. Their respect for him is considerable. It has been a genuine privilege to work with such a gifted but self-effacing young man. People like William make education such a pleasure.'

Carling moved to full-back and took over the 1st XV goal-kicking duties in his final year, scoring 13 tries and over 100 points. *Rugby World* magazine voted Sedbergh School of the Month for November 1983, and Carling received the pennant from old boy and former England captain John Spencer. Carling had been in the 1st XV the previous year when Andrew Harle received the same award for October 1982. Even then he was set apart. His achievements brought him representative honours and trips with Yorkshire, the North and England. He missed the 1st XV's tour to British Columbia the following April because of the England matches, although his compensation was to lead Yorkshire Schools to Zimbabwe in July and August 1984. They lost one game, but beat both Zimbabwe U19 and Zimbabwe Schools.

Brooke Dawse, who taught Carling classics at Sedbergh in the fourth form, was a Yorkshire Schools selector and managed his first tour as captain.

DAWSE
The first time I really noticed him was when he made a superb break against Blackrock College. Opposite him that day was Brendan Mullin, later to play for Ireland and the British Lions. The team was outstanding in his final year. There was a buffet lunch for the parents before the match against Loretto, and we arrived a few minutes late. Sedbergh were already 24–0 up. I remember thinking John Spencer and Alastair Biggar were quite good; I thought the same of Will Carling, though you are never quite sure. I remember his first Yorkshire trial. One of the other selectors came up to me and asked: 'Is there really something to this lad?' Yes, there was. The interesting thing about him was, as he went up, the bigger the challenge, the better he got.

I was very impressed with him as captain in Zimbabwe. We had one problem, and he sorted it out very quickly. The lads went on the Booze Cruise when we visited Victoria Falls.

Basically, it's just a floating bar, and some of them drank too much. Last thing at night, there was some damage, about £10 worth. It needed to be nipped in the bud. Will sorted it out, got the money to pay for repairs, and I gave them a two-minute lecture. Will was super. He backed me up 100 per cent.

Willie was nearly in tears when we lost our only game to a late dropped goal. I reminded him that he had just taken part in a marvellous game of rugby. My lasting memory of the tour was the lads singing to their hosts on the tarmac of Harare Airport before we flew home. Will likes coming back to Sedbergh, but doesn't like the red carpet or a fuss being made.

Strangely, Carling captained England Schools before he led Sedbergh. His first year with the national team was alongside the captain, Kevin Simms, who was to partner him on his debut for the senior side in Paris. Here, Carling experienced his first Grand Slam failure, seven years before the Murrayfield heartache. England had beaten Ireland, France and Scotland, but lost 13–12 to Wales, and Carling was denied a match-winning try in the last minute when Robert Jones, later a British Lions colleague, tackled him into the corner flag. Later that same season, he celebrated his first and only appearance for Andover, in their 15–7 victory over Old Crickladians, with a try at Middle Wallop. His dad was based locally, and Carling had gone along to watch.

Carling was England Schools captain in 1984. He was not ready for another Welsh defeat. He was given permission to take the squad to the cinema the night before the game: they went to a pub instead. Not for a piss-up, but to get the players feeling together. This was an early example of Carling's diligence in the role of leader. England beat the Welsh, again with Jones at scrum-half, by 18–0. Defeat in Belfast followed, then Carling scored a try as England won in the last minute in France. Carling had taken his captaincy duties seriously, but thought little more of it. As far as he was concerned, this experience on the rugby field would be a valuable help when he went into the Army.

Carling's captaincy career did not make the record books at Sedbergh, however. Made captain of the 1st XV for two games in his final Lent term, those two defeats were the last time Carling was put in charge of a rugby side on home soil before he led England out against Australia at Twickenham in late 1988.

* * *

CARLING
My record as captain was the worst at Sedbergh in recent years. Played two, lost two. We lost to the Anti-Assassins and the Luddites. I hear that Sedbergh has changed. It used to be very outdoors-orientated. I believe that it's become very traditional in terms of learning. In my day, it was more middle-of-the-road and provided a more rounded education, which produced fairly well-rounded citizens. Would I send my son there? I'd wait and see what he was like. That sort of life doesn't suit everyone. I wouldn't put his name down for anywhere just as a matter of course.

I enjoyed myself there. It wasn't something I think has affected me detrimentally in any way. Going away like that, you make very close friendships. Friendships which have stood the test of time. I never felt abandoned. The school can be a very intense community. In my own year, I felt I was watched all the time, because rugby was what it was all about up there.

His time at Sedbergh, as at Terra Nova, is obviously remembered with great affection. He enjoyed the outdoor life. Despite his lack of daily contact with his parents, Carling never felt unloved. As with most people, certain sides of his character were exposed and corrected at school. The bullying stopped abruptly without outside influence. That display of petulance on the sports field was dealt with effectively by his mother. His intolerance of others has never quite disappeared, but he has learnt to control his annoyance at other people's dithering. The arrogant schoolboy was an imagining. Carling took pride in his rugby success, but circumstances dictated an otherwise low-key approach.

John Morris, his tutor at Sedbergh, was in charge of cricket and assistant at rugby. 'Will was a very good cricketer and was in the 1st XI for three years. It was always obvious that rugby would win, but he would have made a very good club cricketer. Will was a brilliant cover-point. I always found him a great man for the team, who enjoyed the success of others. That's very important. Marcus was a joker, very amusing. Any chink in a master's armour, and Marcus would find it. That made him something of a nuisance. Any worries that Marcus might lead Will astray were soon gone. Will went his own way, and it was Marcus who rather had to live in the shadow of his younger brother. That's never easy.

'There were and are certain contradictions about Will. He is very sensitive, rather shy. But a very confident sportsman. I remember a TV close-up of him in the tunnel before coming out for his first England cap. This was going to be no nerve-racking experience; Will just wanted to get out there and play. He was lucky that he found some kindred spirits here. Will's group were all very gifted. I think he still feels secure here. Will came with his girlfriend and stayed the week after the World Cup in 1991. The school is certainly proud of the image he projects.'

Carling's final school rugby report stated: 'A captain's contribution often sets the tone for the rest of the team, and William must take much of the credit for the thoroughly pleasant and level-headed atmosphere to be found around Buskholme. It is difficult to weigh his value to us except to say that his freshness and enthusiasm and sheer class have been watched and enjoyed by a lot of youngsters and, hopefully, new standards have been set for the years ahead. On a more personal level, I have been much impressed by his increasing maturity and sound judgement, both in rugby matters and elsewhere, and I am not surprised that both Yorkshire and England have acknowledged his qualities. He will need to steel himself for a carefully organised few months ahead, so that he can move on to Durham with some respectable grades and his head high. I wish him all strength.' This final verdict came from the master in charge of the 1st XV, Kerry Wedd.

As ever, a qualification among the gushing phrases. Maybe some masters and pupils thought Carling was heading for a fall. Surely, nobody can be that good. Schoolboy rugby stars are six a penny, and Carling might be another who would fall by the wayside. The England Schools system is not designed to find the best, just the best from a few select institutions. Carling had made his mark, but he was about to disappear off the scene for a couple of years. And, at the end of that time, Carling wondered whether there was any point in continuing with his rugby career.

Chapter 6

Sedbergh to Durham Via Moomba

The room was one of the most remarkable I've ever been in. The ceiling was covered in mirrors, and occupying most of the floor was a huge waterbed. The first thing I did was jam a chair under the door handle. I switched on the TV. But there was no escape. The only viewing available was on the nine hard-core porn channels. I didn't get much sleep.

WILL CARLING

Carling's Army future was much more in focus than his rugby career when he left Sedbergh. To start with, he followed his brother. Marcus had taken a year off after school to go round the world before attending Lancaster University. Younger brother did the same, having appeared before the Regular Commissions Board first. Like father and brother before him, Will Carling would be heading for the Royal Regiment of Wales on his return.

His grandparents provided the round-the-world ticket, along with £100 of spending money. Nowadays, when his mum looks at his picture, rucksack on back, ready to take on the world, she thinks he looks so young and innocent. But she knew then that her younger son was a self-sufficient soul and kept her worries to herself.

Carling's route took him to Hong Kong, Singapore, Australia, New Zealand, Hawaii, Los Angeles and New York. The Carlings'

49

connections, both Army and school, meant that most cities accommodated at least one family or friend who could keep an eye on him. Australia was the place he enjoyed most and, ironically, that country has continued to play a major part in his sporting life.

CARLING
I worked in the Australian desert at Moomba, near Alice Springs, as a surveyor of pipe corrosion. It was a male-only refinery. The money was fantastic, over £100 a day. I did two stints there, three weeks on and one off. The locals were classic Aussies – real Crocodile Dundees. And I was the typical Pom. There wasn't much to do except play cards and drink. Poker and pontoon were the games. And it was just as well I was being paid a lot because I lost a lot. I've never eaten so much in my life. With the heat, all you could eat was meat, sometimes five steaks in a day. When I came back from my trip I was over 14½st.

Carling spent his first week off in Adelaide, then continued his trip in Perth after his second spell at Moomba. He found a bar with a TV to watch the 1984 England-Australia match at Twickenham. Nigel Melville and Stuart Barnes were making their England debuts, the former as captain. England were well beaten, 19–3. While the Aussies were cheering in the bar, Carling enjoyed a drink with a Scotsman who had wandered in. The conversation took a strange turn when the newcomer said that his brothers were going to play for Scotland.
    'Yeah. And I'm going to play for England.'
    'Who are you?'
    'I'm Will Carling.'
    'Never heard of you.'
    'Who are your brothers?'
    'Gavin and Scott Hastings.'
    'Never heard of them!'
    Gavin Hastings and Carling have had a good laugh about it since. As bar-room chat, it was less inflated by alcohol than most.
    Carling liked the sun and the atmosphere of Australia. He worked as a welder and driver without a licence in Perth, sold paintings in Sydney, and served in a sandwich shop in Melbourne. Then he hitch-hiked around New Zealand, discovering when he returned home that he had slept on exactly the same bench in Rotorua that Marcus had

used two years earlier. The future second lieutenant showed a certain naïvety when arriving in Los Angeles, however.

CARLING
It was two in the morning, so I decided not to ring the friend I was due to be staying with. Instead, I hopped on to a bus and headed downtown to find a motel. When I got off the bus, I realised that this was probably not the safest place to be. I dived into the nearest hotel and asked for a room. I was asked, 'How long for?' I said just one night. 'No, how many hours, I mean!' The room was one of the most remarkable I've ever been in. The ceiling was covered in mirrors, and occupying most of the floor was a huge waterbed. The first thing I did was jam a chair under the door handle. I switched on the TV. But there was no escape. The only viewing available was on the nine hard-core porn channels. I didn't get much sleep. First thing next morning, I rang my mate to come and get me.

At least Carling was sensible enough not to try the white stuff offered to him when he reached New York. The police did appear, though, when he went jay-walking in the city. Carling kept walking. Only when the policeman put a hand on his gun did the Englishman halt. Then he received the caution and lecture normally reserved for ignorant foreigners.

Carling's year away taught him a lot. 'In the school environment, I was the top dog. Now I was just a young, immature lad. Nobody knew who I was. It was great. I didn't play one game of rugby. I did nothing at all on that year off.' Carling finished it at a holiday camp in Newquay, working with his brother in a bar; he still rates himself a mean cocktail maker. The rugby was back in view, though, and he began training in Cornwall for his first term at Durham in autumn 1985.

Carling was destined for Hatfield College, which was then an all-male, sporting institution. Newcomers are allocated rooms to share with another student. Will Fawcett was worried when he examined Carling's kit: the Army boots led him to think he was sharing with a skinhead. 'There are certain first-night nerves before you discover what your room-mate is going to be like. Will's kit did not fill me with confidence. But after the sherry reception that night, I realised there would be no problem. Hatfield is full of rugby types. We had a bloody good laugh boozing and doing all the other extra-curricular activities that year. I warmed to Will very quickly.'

That first year was a happy time for Carling. He was a minor celebrity. The rugby club had a healthy reputation on and off the field, and was a close-knit community. Carling's small circle of friends come from school and university: Andrew Harle and Alex Hambly were with him at both Sedbergh and Durham. These friends remain fiercely loyal.

Yet the remarkable thing about the former England Schools captain's first year at university, in view of subsequent events, is that he felt his rugby career was going nowhere. Fawcett explains: 'Will arrived as a heralded name. He was one of only two freshmen in the side. He imagined that he would play where he had for England Schools, in the centre. He was hacked off about playing full-back. Will made a comment to me early on: if he was going to play for England, it would be in the next couple of years. I thought he was joking. But that is effectively what happened.'

CARLING

That first year was spent at full-back, where I'd played in my final season at Sedbergh. I hated every minute of it. When the ball came to me, our coach Ted Wood told me to kick it, not to run. It used to drive me mad; I had Chris Oti on one wing. It just wasn't me. I had come from the idealistic world of schools rugby, where you run all the time. Suddenly, I was stuck at full-back. All I got was high balls and Blaydon rugby club kicking hell out of a student. And I was told to kick it. We had Alex Hambly at centre, and a good university back-line. That's what student rugby is all about: you get hammered up front, then try and run the feet off them in the backs. But, no, Ted was having none of that. At the end of that first season, I thought if this is senior rugby, you can keep it. I didn't train all summer, then I went back to Sedbergh to play in an old boys' game. It was a great game, so I thought I'd give it another go. I'm not saying I would have quit, but I was seriously hacked off. It was a major problem at the time.

I talked to dad, Alex [Hambly] and Andrew [Harle]. They all said, 'Bide your time. Don't stop. Enjoy it. Play for fun.' I had had a lot of success at schoolboy level. Probably I was expecting too much to happen for me in that first year, and I was frustrated.

52

My England Schools partner Kevin Simms had been capped during my year abroad, and I was thinking I might be next. But absolutely nothing was going to happen to me at full-back in that university side. You think you are forgotten. Where's it all gone? I didn't know what I should be doing, who I should be playing for. That was the major thing. Should I be playing for the university, getting into the university side and being seen that way? Or should I be playing for a club, getting into a county and Divisional side?

I've had a few words with Ted Wood since. He's never given me an explanation other than: 'That made you what you are today.' I had no objection to playing full-back. You can't expect to walk into sides. But being expected to kick it every time was heart-breaking. I had spent my last school year at full-back, and I quite enjoyed it. You get more freedom than in the centre. But I can't say that I relished standing under the high ball. After two years at full-back, I thought it better to stick with what I knew.

Fortunately, the social side of Durham more than compensated. Carling really let his hair down in that first year. That was just as well: his rugby career was about to take off again. Sadly, the youngster had to cut himself off from university life as he aimed for World Cup glory.

Chapter 7

World Cup Woe

When I first saw him for Durham County, I had the same feeling as when I saw Rory Underwood for the first time. The guy had it. I didn't need any further proof that here was someone the North should be promoting.

GEOFF COOKE

Will Carling's career was transformed after an outstanding performance for Durham against Lancashire at West Hartlepool in the County Championship in autumn 1986. Durham lost by a point; Carling had certainly made one. North selectors Geoff Cooke and Dave Robinson were in attendance, and they decided that Carling's talent would serve their side well. His frustration from the previous winter then exploded in a series of devastating displays that helped the North to the Thorn-EMI Divisional Championship title, and Carling went from nowhere to the fringe of international honours in less than a month.

COOKE
I'd heard his name mentioned when he was playing for Yorkshire and England Schools. He was billed as a 'lad who's a bit special', though I didn't hear anything that marked him above being just a 'good prospect'. The first time I met him I was dining

with Ted Wood, coach of the university, and Will came by. 'Hello' was the extent of our conversation. A very quiet guy. He obviously had ability and an outward confidence in that ability. Really, though, he was just a young player with stars in his eyes. But when I first saw him for Durham County, I had the same feeling as when I saw Rory [Underwood] for the first time. The guy had it. I didn't need any further proof that here was someone the North should be promoting.

Stephen Jones, the *Sunday Times* rugby correspondent, saw his Divisional debut. The headline read: 'Carling turns into North ace of clubs.' Underneath, Jones wrote, 'And the North also discovered a meteor in Will Carling, their young centre.' 'Carling the North Star' was the *Mail on Sunday*'s heading. Mike Weston, then chairman of the England selectors, was quoted as saying, 'He obviously made a very favourable impact against the South-West. I will be interested to see if he can build on that. His emergence shows that, in forward-dominated matches, the opportunities are still there for eager young backs to show their worth.'

The *Sunday Telegraph*'s John Reason talked to former England captain Peter Dixon, who was helping Ted Wood coach Durham University. Dixon had no idea of Carling's frustration in his first season. 'He played full-back for us last year and did exceptionally well. He is a safe fielder and, when he comes into the line, he really hits it and puts some pace on the ball. He kicks a long way, passes well, and as a tackler he reminds me of an American footballer. I still can't decide which is his best position, because he has such a good head for the game. But, as a full-back, he made so much space for Chris Oti on the wing last season that Chris was worth 6 points to us without fail in every match. They are the sort of lads who would really shake up the first team if they played in an England trial.'

The North's back-line was full of running. Fly-half Rob Andrew had already played for England, along with Carling's threequarter colleagues, Rory Underwood, Mike Harrison and Kevin Simms. The North finished their campaign with a six-try demolition of London but, suddenly, Carling was looking towards Wales. Because of his father's playing days with Cardiff, the youngster on a Royal Regiment of Wales scholarship had been in touch with London Welsh and planned to play for them in the Christmas holidays. The Welsh were keen to emphasise his eligibility for Wales, so England moved fast. A fortnight later, Carling was one of the Rest centres in the final England trial. December finished with Carling a new Barbarian. A week later, he was the William Younger Rugby Player of the Month.

ANDREW

I first got to know him when he was picked for the Divisional Championship in 1986. He was rather quiet. That surprised me, because the word had gone round that Will Carling was going to be the greatest thing since sliced bread. Will didn't blow his own trumpet, though. There was a steely determination. He didn't feel the need to shout from the roof-tops. Immediately, you could see why he'd been brought in: his power and pace. He didn't have the electrifying burst of the Underwoods or Jerry [Guscott], but he had the power to break through tackles. The Divisional side is half-way to an England cap, and I had little doubt that Will would be an England player before too long. Several of us were in the squad already. He was just like the rest of us: a young bloke who enjoyed playing rugby.

At this time, Mike Weston advised him it was time for a change, and he dangled a very big carrot in front of Carling: a place in the England squad for the first-ever World Cup in Australia and New Zealand that summer. Weston told him that he needed club experience – and not at London Welsh! But the club he suggested was not on Carling's doorstep. It was the Harlequins, who trained and played a mere 250-plus miles down the road from Carling's university base. Carling did not argue. Nor has he ever asked why it was necessary for him to travel almost the length of the country several times a week in search of a first cap. Carling would leave Durham for training at 3 o'clock in the afternoon, and arrive back on the last train at 3 o'clock in the morning.

Not surprisingly, that was the beginning of the end of Carling's studies. He also disappeared from the bulk of the university social life.

CARLING

My season took off after that Durham game at West Hartlepool. I made three or four outside breaks. I didn't even know the North selectors were watching. It was the right game at the right time, and that's down to luck. I'm not even sure they had ever seen me before. It was an important break, especially as I'd been considering packing it in only a few months earlier. I felt my rugby career had been in limbo for a couple of seasons. The year travelling had been my own decision; but the year at full-back had been a waste of time. I didn't feel as if I had played. Quitting was not the answer. I knew deep down that I still wanted to play rugby. A few months later, I was lining up for a final trial at Twickenham with the best English rugby players. Playing for England had been my long-term aim, and I had allowed myself to be distracted. It was a valuable lesson so early on.

Simon Halliday and Jamie Salmon were the senior centres in the England trial, although Simms partnered Salmon in the Five Nations championship before he was replaced by Halliday in the final game, when England denied Scotland the Triple Crown by winning 21–12 at Twickenham. Mike Harrison had taken over as skipper from Richard Hill after the 19–12 defeat in Cardiff; Hill was one of four England players to be disciplined following the violence in that match. The Calcutta Cup victory saved England from a championship whitewash and gave them renewed hope as they set off for the 1987 World Cup.

Carling's position as a nearly-man was confirmed throughout the rest of the season. Durham won the UAU championship, overcoming Bristol and Jonathan Webb in the final at Twickenham, and four days later Carling was back at HQ playing for the Army. His four Barbarians appearances included the traditional Easter Saturday fixture with Cardiff, one of his early televised performances. Carling linked well with Martin Offiah, their only match together before the winger turned professional with Widnes. Fran Clough, who had played for England the previous year, was Carling's partner in England B's 22–9 win over France at Bath. After that, the World Cup campaign would have crowned Carling's season. But it was Clough the selectors plumped for along with Salmon and Simms.

CARLING
I really believed I was going to the World Cup. I know I had not played for England, but all the signs had been promising. When the chairman gives you the nod, you tend to accept it. It was a shock to be left out. Nobody said anything. I had to go asking for an explanation, and they said I was too tired! I was only too tired because I'd been travelling 1,500 miles a week in my spare time

at their request. It was a real kick in the teeth. Players have been treated far worse than that, but it was my first contact with England. No wonder players moan about selectors.

Chapter 8

One of the Lads, Briefly

After Orwin had told us he was out of the Test with a calf injury, we asked him which leg it was. He turned to Geoff Cooke, who was some distance away, and shouted: 'Which leg was it, again, Geoff?'

TONY ROCHE, *Today*

England's poor World Cup showing in 1987 catapulted Geoff Cooke into the team manager's position. No single person has ever been given such accountable responsibility for the England rugby side. Roger Uttley's appointment as coach gave Cooke a valuable right-hand man with a proven track record, but any early thoughts that Uttley would be in charge were quickly dispelled by Cooke. When asked about who would get his way if there was a selection dispute, Cooke was perplexed by the question: 'Why, me, of course.' Not that Cooke was planning any collisions with Uttley. The pair were determined to get English rugby back on course together.

Carling spent part of that 1987 summer on exercise with the Army in Germany. Back at Durham, final exams were looming, but the psychology student had lost interest in his course. The long, arduous train trips to London for training and playing with the Harlequins had taken their toll. While a World Cup place remained the carrot, the journey had not seemed so tedious. December brought some relief, with the Divisional Championship reducing his travel time. Carling

61

was paired with John Buckton in the centre as the North took the title again, and those performances earned him another place in the junior side alongside Kevin Simms for the England trial at the start of 1988. Now Carling was just one step away from his rugby dream. A few days later that dream came true: injuries to the centres who had played in the senior side, Simon Halliday and Buckton, meant promotion for Carling and Simms for the 1988 Five Nations opener in Paris.

Carling was enjoying his Christmas vacation at home when the news came through. 'Obviously, I knew I was in the frame because I'd played in the trial. But you assume nothing. There are too many stories of players who got even closer than me to an England cap, but never played. It was still a shock. It was great for the family. I know it meant such a lot to them. Of course, there were the customary celebrations and over-indulgence.' Carling then had the media beating a path to his door. Little was known of him. Carling is not comfortable talking about himself and, even initially, he came across as reserved and cold. Jeff Probyn and Mick Skinner were the other new caps in a side which contained just six survivors from the World Cup quarter-final against Wales. Nigel Melville was recalled at scrum-half, with Mike Harrison remaining as captain. England were given no chance: France, World Cup-finalists, were on home territory against a rugby nation in disarray.

Carling was determined to enjoy himself, and even Roger Uttley was surprised by the newcomer's confidence. 'I first came across him when I was coaching London,' remembers Uttley. 'We played the North at Wasps. We had Martin Offiah on the wing, but got blitzed. I'd heard of this Will Carling and knew he was highly rated, a very strong centre. Even in a field of 30 that day, he stood out. The new players usually travel into Paris to take a close-hand look at the Parc des Princes. Will was there only a matter of minutes. He had a quick look and then disappeared into Paris to see a friend. That level of independence before a first cap was very striking.'

Cooke was happy that his choice felt so assured. 'Our biggest problem and highest priority was the lack of confidence. We went to France totally written off. I was amazed at the players wanting to be told what to do. I remember saying to Roger: 'These guys are unhappy because nobody is telling them how to play.' 'These guys' were England's best rugby internationals, but they had no confidence. Before the French game, we made sure there was no reference to the negative side. There were no English papers or TV. The players always spend a lot of time together in France; we insisted all their talk was positive. England have always been good at winning the ball, but not so good at using it. There was a great feeling of them and us, between the players and officialdom. Roger and I worked hard that season to break that down.'

France recorded the expected victory, and so Carling's England career began in defeat. It was a travesty. The visitors should have won after stunning the French pack with a determined display. England led 9–3, but lost the advantage in the final 10 minutes. Webb was unlucky to be adjudged to have knocked the ball forward by Irish referee Owen Doyle, and the resulting scrum led to France's second penalty goal. Three minutes later, Blanco counter-attacked, and England's defence got in a tangle trying to clear the chip ahead. Dean Richards tried to pick it up, Harrison tried to fall on the ball. Laurent Rodriguez just got his toe to it and won the chase to the line to give France the lead for the first time by 10–9. The final whistle went with Carling holding the ball on the ground, but that was immediately wrenched from his grasp by French flanker Eric Champ. Carling and Philippe Sella, his opposite number, agreed to swap jerseys in the tunnel.

The new centre had certainly made an impression. Carling made a searing break on the outside in the opening minute, but Pierre Berbizier got his hands to the youngster's pass and the chance had gone. Bill Beaumont commented on the television: 'Carling must be kicking himself.' But Carling had been waiting for either Simms or Harrison to come inside, and Berbizier had shadowed his man well. Simms should have scored himself midway through the first half. Rory Underwood was brought down after the ball had gone along the England back-line; Carling swooped and went up the left touchline, then passed inside to Simms. The centre was tackled and passed back just as it became apparent that his momentum would have carried him over the line. Skinner still claimed the touchdown and probably did score, but referee Doyle had been bowled over in the rush for the ball. Skinner was obviously still thinking about the try when he allowed the ball to squirt out of the side of the scrum that followed and France cleared the danger.

Since the pre-match publicity had portrayed England as lambs to the slaughter, their performance was praised to the rafters. Uttley was not happy, though. It was another example of winning possession, but not the match. John Orwin, England's pack leader, summed it up: 'I've never been so disappointed in my life. We certainly put the effort in up front. We managed to get sufficient ball for the backs to use. But if you don't score the points, you don't win the game.' Harrison, the skipper, knew a great chance had been missed. 'France had one chance. And they took it. There are some very sick players in the dressing-room. I'm disappointed we haven't got the result we desperately need to give us confidence.'

Paris, even in defeat, is not a bad place to start your international career. Carling had been determined to soak up all the atmosphere and enjoy his first cap. That he did. Just because England had been beaten, Carling was not going to miss out on the delights that the Paris night and early morning has to offer.

There are further benefits in winning your first cap abroad, not least that it allows another debut at Twickenham. Carling then had three weeks to wait for the visit of Wales. He was now an even bigger celebrity at Durham University, but had little time to enjoy the status. For all that Carling was enjoying his rugby, defeat by Wales had the new management team worried and looking at changes. The scoreboard was bare at half-time, but two tries from Adrian Hadley separated the teams in the second half. Wales had fielded four fly-halves: skipper Jonathan Davies, Tony Clement at full-back, and Bleddyn Bowen and Mark Ring in the centre. And it was Davies and Five Nations newcomer Clement who brought the match to life. Carling saw a lot less of the ball than he had in Paris. Defence was the order of the day. The 11–3 defeat hit him harder this time. Carling felt dejected walking off after his first championship match at Twickenham with Welsh cheers ringing in his ears. Two defeats in a row had not been part of Cooke's master plan either, and the pressure was on.

Carling's co-centre was dropped for the trip to Scotland, along with the captain and fly-half. Halliday came in for Simms, Melville replaced Harrison as captain, and Chris Oti, a former Durham colleague of Carling, was the new wing, while Rob Andrew returned at No. 10 for Les Cusworth. Uttley and Cooke had laid the blame for the defeats fairly on the shoulders of the backs. Scotland were firm favourites to regain the Calcutta Cup. But the first half was pointless and tedious, and the exchanges were no more enthralling after the interval. To England's great relief, two Webb penalties and an

Andrew dropped goal gave them victory by 9–6 in one of the dullest, drabbest games for many a year. Carling was having nothing of that, however. 'It was such a fantastic feeling – my first international win. I know it was boring and pretty close. But we had lost the first two, and this was an away game. Some of the lads looked a bit disappointed as they trooped off. I was ecstatic. In the dressing-room, Rory looked really down. "That was terrible," he moaned. "Rory, hang on," I said. "This was my first international win." I suppose if I played in a game like that today, I might feel the same as Rory. But then – wow. Edinburgh, watch out.'

Edinburgh 1988 holds a special place in Carling's memory for another reason. 'It's the only time I've ever seen Geoff Cooke lose it. Geoff's a very level-headed man. But England had lost his first two championship games in charge. His judgement and ability were being questioned. The backs were going through their drills in training and making a right mess of it. Even with five attackers taking on two defenders, we couldn't get past. Balls were being dropped. It was so pathetic, it was sad. Geoff really blew his top. I don't blame him, but it wasn't Geoff's style. The pressure had got to him. I remember looking back at him as we left the field. I couldn't believe he was so uptight.'

Ireland's visit to Twickenham saw another slow start, with the away side leading 3–0 at half-time. England's championship matches produced 86 points in 1988. Yet the only first-half scores in those games were two penalties and a dropped goal. England's season looked like ending in further disarray when skipper Melville was stretchered off at the interval with the ankle injury that effectively finished his England career. Richard Harding was the replacement scrum-half, while Orwin took over the running of the side. Harding decided to get England's backs moving: within 40 minutes England had scored six tries, five to wingers Oti (three) and Underwood, as Ireland were crushed 35–3. That try avalanche helped the crowd find its voice. For the first time, the strains of *Swing Low, Sweet Chariot* echoed around Twickenham.

COOKE

I hadn't really known what to expect when I took over. I was amazed at the players' lack of confidence. And at the lack of basic skills. That sort of coaching should be finished by the time you get to international level, but there were so many things they couldn't do. I was wasting time at sessions teaching skills. And it was also obvious that they hadn't thought about the game in any great depth.

We had to win at Murrayfield; I make no excuses for our dour performance. After two defeats, we had no alternative. But we finished on a high note. That showed that it's silly little things, sometimes. Ireland kicked off the second half straight into touch, and that started the change. We were 3–0 down. Suddenly, Harding, who'd just come on, moved the ball and Rory was away for Gary Rees to score. Everyone had been upset at losing Nigel. The emotion had been built up because of that. And Corky [Richard Harding] released it. Then we just started running. And the crowd started singing *Sweet Chariot*.

Most of the attention that afternoon had been focused on Cardiff, where Wales failed to achieve their first Grand Slam for a decade when they lost 10–9 to France. The Twickenham contest was regarded very much as second division. That did not bother Carling. This was much more like it. And the season then offered a little bonus, a trip to Dublin for the Millennium match. England won that, too, by 21–10. After the encounter, Carling was looked after by Ireland's Paul Dean and Michael Kiernan to such an extent that he still has no idea where he went, what he did and when he finished.

The extra international, plus Harlequins' Cup run and the Inter-Services tournament, were playing havoc with his university work. Eventually, Carling had to make some concessions after he was picked to tour Australia with England in the summer. He had hoped to sit his exams after the trip, and the RFU did make representations to the university on his behalf. But to no avail. Carling was forced to fulfil his academic obligations and then fly out after the first Test against Australia. That allowed England to take Halliday, who had not otherwise been available, for the first part of the tour.

Meanwhile, Carling's winning season continued. The Army beat the RAF at Twickenham to take their first Inter-Services title for five years. Then Harlequins became the first London club to win the Cup, overcoming Bristol 28–22 in a thrilling John Player Special final. Carling scored two tries to climax a remarkable first full season of first-class rugby. 'The final was just an extension of my dream season. Everything seemed to be going my way: England had won three in a row; the Quins were going well. We went out there to run, to counter-attack, and run again. Conditions were ideal, and it worked. There are just times when the ball runs your way. This was one of them for me.'

That was to come to a sudden halt when he arrived in Australia. England's tour was falling apart. Uttley had been unavailable for the trip, and he was replaced by England B coaches Alan Davies and David Robinson. Then the players had problems with their boots. Cooke claimed, 'Almost all the 26 members of the squad are unhappy with the Nike-made footwear.' Over 12,000 miles away, Dudley Wood at the RFU was more reassuring. 'The suitability of Nike boots, which have been used for two full seasons, is not in question.' Cooke countered: 'It was the last thing we needed. You expect injuries caused by playing and training, but not by equipment. I am upset because the players are complaining and naturally they cannot concentrate fully on the work they should be putting into practice. Imagine a top footballer, tennis player, golfer or boxer complaining that his footwear hurts before he faces the opposition.' Nigel Redman's feet were a mass of blisters, and all the studs on one boot had come off in the opening match. Others also complained that their boots did not fit. The Nike boots used during the World Cup the previous summer had not been rated highly, either. But, to the RFU, a pair of rugby boots is a pair of rugby boots. Cooke later apologised to the press after his initial complaints that the tour manager had been let down by the media.

Cooke had reason to be grateful to the press on the tour. Had they reported all the goings-on, then it would not have been just Davies and Robinson whose England futures were permanently damaged. No one in authority would have survived. The tourists spent some of the first week at Mackay in Queensland. After one of the traditional players' court sessions, John Bentley refused to pay his fine. He was taken, tied to a palm tree, told to drink and sing a song by Charles Aznavour. Most of the players were rather the worse for wear. Yet nobody quite believed it when the England captain John Orwin appeared from behind the tree and relieved himself down Bentley's back. It surprised nobody when Bentley signed up for Rugby League shortly after returning to England.

England lost the first Test 22–16, after leading by 13 points. Carling arrived two days later. He wasn't expecting the red-carpet treatment; it was just as well. When he pitched up at the Illawarra Steelers Hotel, just south of Sydney, the tour captain greeted him with: 'Where the f****** hell have you been?' Carling found himself duty boy that day.

The hotel service had been very poor, and an Army officer was just the man to get things running smoothly. Or so it seemed. Everyone's dinner arrived two hours late, with Carling protesting: 'It was a good system, but they've messed it up.' Carling had little time to adjust. He regained his international shirt, but England were well beaten 28–8 in the second Test. Meanwhile, Wales, the Triple Crown champions, were having an even tougher time in New Zealand, where they lost the Tests by the humiliating margins of 52–3 and 54–9.

Cooke was worried. It was not so much the defeats, more the way in which the spirit and progress made during the championship had disintegrated before his eyes. England moved on to Fiji, where they won the Test 25–12 with Harding as captain. Orwin had originally been named in the team, but withdrew with a calf strain. *Today*'s Tony Roche recalls Orwin's diplomatic gesture. 'After Orwin had told us he was out of the Test with a calf injury, we asked him which leg it was. He turned to Geoff Cooke, who was some distance away, and shouted: "Which leg was it, again, Geoff?" Draw your own conclusions.'

At the end of the tour, Orwin said he felt 'humiliated. But I fully expect England to beat Australia in November when they tour. And I intend training through June, July and August to stay as fit as I have been on this tour. I want to see the backs and forwards training more as a unit. It doesn't happen in England, and I don't know why. We had the Five Nations forwards, but not a lot of the backs. I think they were frightened of making mistakes.'

Orwin had broken the first rule of captaincy: 'Don't criticise your own players.' Give them a hard time privately, drop them if necessary. But the public must never hear or see the captain laying the blame in this way. The *Standard*'s Chris Jones cannot remember a worse trip. 'It was certainly the least visible of Cooke's tours. There was a massive split between the forwards and backs. They were like two separate units. As we flew back from Fiji to Sydney, we approached Orwin, who was drinking vodka and orange at the back of the plane, for an end-of-tour verdict. "What do you bastards want?" was followed by a request for a financial contribution from all the pressmen, so he could buy presents for his team. He added that he thought boomerangs might be a suitable gift. That just about summed up his subtlety. No money was forthcoming. Argentina, two years later, was also a disappointing tour, but it never sank to these depths. At least there was leadership. They missed Uttley, there's no doubt about that. Neither Cooke, at that time, nor Orwin had the stature to pull things round or give a clear lead.' Cooke was certainly a wiser man after his first year at the helm.

COOKE

The tour to the southern hemisphere was hard. It always is. You face different attitudes and different referees. That's where I started to identify a core. We were certainly still 'iffy'. It was a bit of a patchwork tour. Will came out late, Halliday went home early, Webbie flew back to get married. All reflect the modern demands of international rugby. The other big shock in my first year was the extent of the media attention. That took me time to get used to. I had only been involved at regional level before, but this was a whole new ball game. Then there were the nuances of dealing with committees. Don Rutherford gave me a lot of support and helped me through that, but committees are so time-consuming. And you can't forget or ignore the powers-that-be. If you're going to change the system, then you have to get involved. You must have the committee on your side. You need support to get things through. It's no good wishing the committee wasn't there. It is. It exists. You have to get on with it. But that side was far more demanding than I envisaged.

Uttley had kept a close eye on proceedings from Harrow School. 'After the early results, I thought England had a good chance of winning the first Test. But Australia were awarded a try when it appeared that the ball wasn't grounded properly. That tipped the balance, and after that the wheels came off. It was disconcerting to read the newspapers. We had thought of Orwin as a Bill Beaumont-type leader. But you have to lead from the front for that. Orwin struggled. I was very concerned because I was going to have to pick up the pieces before Australia arrived here in the autumn.'

Those concerns were not yet Carling's, but he could not fail to have picked up the bad vibes, especially after his welcome.

CARLING

When I arrived, I noticed a tremendous division between the forwards and backs. There was certainly a lack of respect between the two, and that is never healthy. If there is no humour underpinning the traditional hostility between the two, there is trouble. Orwin publicly criticised the backs. I couldn't believe that. It built up resentment both ways. It was not a happy tour.

Orwin didn't set any captaincy standards for me. He didn't influence me a great deal. I must admit that I didn't take a lot in from the other captains in my first year with England. I was struggling to stay afloat. There's nothing I can think of that's stayed with me. Both Nigel [Melville] and Mike [Harrison] were good guys. I always called Mike 'Dad' because he was that old.

Carling had problems of his own, anyway. His exams had not been a great success. That did not concern him but, more important, a major stumbling block had appeared in his way. His clear road ahead had suddenly forked. To the left was the Army; to the right was his international rugby career. The Army had made it painfully obvious to Carling that the two could not join up for at least a year.

Chapter 9

Second Lieutenant to Captain

Because of the Official Secrets Act, I can only reveal that we tramped up and down the German countryside. The instructor bent over me as I was giving it my all with a machine gun. 'I think you'd have a better chance of hitting the target if you took the safety catch off.'

WILL CARLING

The Army had been as much a part of Carling's upbringing as rugby. His father had combined his love of rugby with a professional career in the forces. His brother made his way to Sandhurst. And Sandhurst figured in Carling's future alongside Twickenham. Plans for his Army future were set in motion before he set off on his round-the-world trip after leaving Sedbergh School. On his return, Carling appeared before the Regular Commissions Board and gained his Army scholarship to Durham University.

Carling had always been fascinated by the Army and war. His father's helicopter-flying career provided only half the attraction. The mental battle intrigued him as much as the physical conflict. 'I've always liked books about people, events. I tend not to read fiction now, although *The Hobbit* was my favourite book when I was growing up. I remember reading biographies of Churchill and General Slim. I didn't see them as war heroes, but I was interested in how they reacted to extreme situations. I've never been a hero type. I wanted to know how they made decisions and why. I was fascinated by how much people can take. How they perform when exhausted and under intense stress. That was my thesis at university: how people reacted to stress. It was the one part of my university course I enjoyed, about the only bit of work I did in my three years.'

Carling's consolation for missing out on the 1987 World Cup was an Army exercise in Germany. His actual Army involvement before that had been limited; he was a member of the cadet corps at school, but left when no longer required to attend. Carling went on the exercise as a private. 'I was just one of the lads. Members of my squad had been in the Army for between two and twenty years. Because of the Official Secrets Act, I can only reveal that we tramped up and down the German countryside. I enjoyed the experience. The ranks lead very disciplined lives. I admire them. They have got an idea of what's important in life and what is not. I think I amused them. I was adopted as the squad mascot. It was interesting and useful to see it from both sides. Had I stayed in, I would have been sent to Northern Ireland, but not the Gulf War. The regiment were stationed in Hong Kong at the time.'

Carling remembers one embarrassing incident on the shooting range, as he was proving his prowess with a machine gun. 'The instructor bent over me as I was giving it my all. "I think you'd have a better chance of hitting the target if you took the safety catch off."'

The Services rugby tradition had continued in the 1980s with Rory Underwood and John Orwin, among others. England's flying wing and fighter pilot, Underwood has provided masses of free publicity for the RAF. It looked as if Carling would do the same for the Army and, initially, he was led to believe that the Army thought his rugby was as important to his future as he did.

CARLING
After an Army game at Twickenham, I met the general of the Land Forces. He took me outside the changing-room. 'We are delighted with your rugby. Don't worry about it.' I'd already spoken to my dad about whether he thought there was going to be a problem. I was about to go to Sandhurst. Would they let me play international rugby? Dad thought so. But he made further enquiries and the word that came back, yes, they would give me time off. When the general spoke to me at Twickenham, I took it as official confirmation that everything was okay.

It was while I was on the Australia tour that my father heard on the grapevine that there might in fact be a problem. Sandhurst, it appeared, had changed its mind. They were not going to let me have the time off for representative rugby during the initial training after all. That ran from September through to March – the whole of the rugby season. So I rang Colonel Charles at Victory College, Sandhurst, to fix up an appointment. We talked it through, and he was very honest. He didn't think I was going to get the necessary time or be in a fit state to play top-class rugby. Basically, I asked if there was any room for manoeuvre or if that was that. He said, 'Sorry, that's it.' I replied that I had been given the impression everything would be okay. His answer was that this decision had come from the commandant. I retreated in some shock.

There was no way I was going to risk letting someone else have my England place for a year. There wasn't much of a debate. I couldn't talk to Geoff about it: 'Hey, Cookie, what are my chances this coming season because I've got a major career decision to make?' I felt that it was something I had to decide for myself, although I obviously got my dad's views. So I took the risk that I would be required for national rugby service. Then I told the Army, 'thank you, but no thank you.'

I had decided I wanted to go into the Army towards the end of my school-days. It had always been on my mind. I also wanted something that would allow me to play rugby. I never saw the Army as a career, but the job of platoon commander appealed to me. It's an active role, with immediate responsibility. I liked the role of team leader. I related it to captaining school teams. I like being in control of what I'm doing; I don't like being told what to do. Certainly, I like to influence what's going on. There's the challenge. I wouldn't want to be in charge of 18-year-old raw recruits, though. It's the challenge of leading older, experienced men.

Carling's decision to abandon his Army career left him with two immediate problems. First, the Army had invested more than time in the young recruit. They wanted compensation. 'Buying yourself out is not actually all that complicated. They tell you what it costs. It seemed a lot of money to me at the time: just over £8,000, payable in instalments over five years. But it's the best investment I've made.

I've heard stories that my father bought me out and cleared the debt. That's not true. Again, it just fits the image of the privileged youngster.'

The financial problem was not as serious as the one about his future, however. 'It dawned on me that I wasn't going to be able to do what I'd planned. At that moment my carefully mapped out future for the next four years vanished. I hadn't given a thought to anything beyond the Army.' Had Carling realised that he would be entering a commercial world about to slump into recession, he might have been more attentive to his studies. His treatment of his degree course was most un-Carling-like. The methodical, thorough, attention-to-detail style was noticeable by its absence. Carling was bored with studying. He believed that his rugby/Army future was not going to be affected by his failure as a student, so he got further and further behind in his work.

CARLING
That thesis on stress was my only piece of written work. I used to read a lot of books; unfortunately, few were relevant to my course. I lost interest as the work became more scientific. Statistics was not my favourite subject. People and their behaviour were what I wanted to study. Instead, I was expected to read about 100 rats in cages and come to some sort of conclusion because 75 of them learnt how to work a lever. I just wanted to know why people are different and why they react differently to situations. Why is Brian Moore the way he is?

The basic conclusion is that people tend to make things a lot more complicated than they are. Leadership is the key. Why are some good leaders and others not? The last time I had captained a side was England Schools. I analysed whether I could have done that any better. I wanted to see why I did that wrong. Was it because I didn't confront or face up to the issues? That's why I read psychology. Contrary to public opinion, it wasn't because I had this burning desire to be England's rugby captain when I grew up.

Even today, Carling is rather shamefaced about skipping one of his final exams. The work had not been done, so he saw little point in turning up. England's rugby captain left Durham with a degree in psychology, but only just. He was given a 'recommended pass' – the lowest grade to qualify for a Bachelor of Arts degree. It's below a first, a 2:1, a 2:2 and a third. 'That sort of thing bears no relation to your intelligence. I know I can pass exams. I had simply lost interest in the course. That's not an excuse. It just wasn't what I wanted to do. Certain exams are merely a test of your memory. Nobody has ever failed the psychology course. I think I'm the first person ever to get below a 2:2 on that course. I'm quite proud of that.' Mum was not, though. She felt William had let himself down.

Carling then sat down with Harlequins officials Colin Herridge and Roger Looker to discuss the change of plans. When they asked him what did he want to do, he replied, 'I don't know.' But Carling realised he wanted a career, not just something to fill in the time between travelling the rugby world. The Quins, who have contacts all through the City, suggested the legal profession, marketing or accountancy. Carling was definite on one thing. 'Roger, I don't want to take any more exams.' Carling had decided that he was basically a practical person. Collecting more diplomas was not his game.

Carling eventually headed for a marketing job with Mobil. 'I didn't know if marketing was going to be for me. I was buying time. I needed to get some experience and to see how the big business world worked. I had already suspected that I wasn't a big company man, but I did enjoy my two years with Mobil. It was a good company, and I had a lot of fun. But I learnt that I'm definitely not into routine. The timing was perfect: I had job security, just when I was going to need it. I joined Mobil at the start of October in 1988. By the end of the month, I was captain of England. I don't ever regret the decision I took or missing the Army. I'm sad about it. But there's no way I could have been captain of England and combined it with an Army career.'

Chapter 10

Cardiff Catastrophe – Part I

We didn't have the mental edge to withstand the Welsh pressure. It took us three years to win the championship, a nightmare. We should have done it in the first year in Wales. Wade never came to terms with Norster, and Rory went walkabout again. We had no answer to their tactics.

ROGER UTTLEY

England's victory at Lansdowne Road in February 1989 completed the first stage of Carling's graduation as captain. The progress had not been painless. The concussion he had suffered in the triumph over Australia was the least long-lasting and serious of his troubles. The press battering after the disappointing Calcutta Cup draw left scars that are still visible today. And the realisation after Dublin that the captaincy had put a barrier between him and his team created a situation that would last for as long as he was captain. Yet Carling was not unhappy with those problems. They came with the territory. His desire to do a good job – the best possible – as captain outweighed any personal inconvenience or worries.

France were the next visitors to Twickenham. Pierre Berbizier's side had won their opening two matches, recovering from a 15-point deficit to win 26–21 in Dublin before inflicting a record 31–12 defeat on the Welsh. But France found England in no mood to play ball. The home side ended hopes of a French Grand Slam with the most disciplined performance produced so far under Cooke and Uttley. The England coach was especially delighted with the way his forwards controlled both the match and their tempers. Even the great Serge Blanco, in a foretaste of his 1991 World Cup quarter-final frustration, was reduced to scrapping as France found no answer to the commitment of England's locks Ackford and Dooley, Robinson and Richards. Scrum-half Morris caused the visitors no end of problems with his bustling around the base of the scrum yet, ironically, it was his sluggish service that provided Carling with a moment to savour – his first international try.

CARLING

It was a planned move. The ball is supposed to move quickly along the back-line, then I feed Chris Oti as he comes back inside on the crash. Chris is so hard to stop and always gets over the gain-line. Well, that was the grand plan. But Dewi lobbed his pass to Rob [Andrew] at two miles an hour, and it reached me at about the same speed. However much I might have wanted to give the pass to Chris, I couldn't. Everything was happening in slow motion. I turned and braced myself for the tackles. I couldn't believe it; there was no one there. Lafond, Sella and Mesnel had all converged on Oti, thinking that our laborious passing was all part of the ploy. I didn't hang around. I had a clear run to the line and dived over. Trying to look super-cool, I got up immediately, only to fall over again. Very stylish.

It's a satisfying moment to score your first England try. And quite a relief. It takes the pressure off. If you've been in the team for a while and haven't broken your duck, there's a fair amount of ribbing. Rob Andrew got wound up a fair bit when he didn't score for 30-odd matches. Scoring tries has never bothered me that much, though. I don't see myself as a natural try-scorer. I'd much rather create them. That gives me much more pleasure.

England's two successes had now made them favourites for the championship. Victory in Cardiff, where Romania and Ireland had already won that season, would give Carling the outright Five Nations title. As ever, England had to endure a war of words before the real battle commenced. Former Welsh captain Jeff Squire summed up the general feeling: 'If England don't beat us down in Cardiff this year, I doubt if they ever will.' Neath's supremo Brian Thomas was less accommodating, however. 'The English are mentally inferior, rugby-wise and as a race. They feel inferior. They play inferior. Whenever I played against England, I knew that Wales were mentally the better side. That can still happen – it's all a question of strength and will.'

Thomas was spot-on: England lacked both strength and will in Cardiff that day. The visitors never recovered from the loss of Mike Teague through injury at the kick-off. Gary Rees was the replacement for Teague, but England's line-out was disrupted, a situation which Bob Norster was only too happy to exploit. Carling has always insisted that Cardiff holds no terrors for his generation. Yet they gave a good impersonation of being intimidated as Wales knocked them out of their stride.

Geoff Cooke had made one of his rare selection errors. Throughout his international career, Cooke has been clinical and unsentimental in his choice of players. Quite a few of the RFU 'mafia', who now dislike his high profile and continuing success, chopped and changed the team addictively when they were in charge. But Cooke has always stood by his players, and that is a rare phenomenon in English international rugby. But this time he made a mistake which cost England the championship and Jeff Probyn one, if not two, British Lions tours. Probyn had been ruled out of the France game because of concussion suffered in Dublin. Gareth Chilcott, suspended from the national colours after the violent encounter in Cardiff in 1987, was recalled. And after the French victory, Cooke decided to retain an unchanged side. Now England's scrum, weakened further by the loss of Teague, struggled against a Welsh pack with loose-head prop Mike Griffiths outstanding.

The final margin was only 12–9, but Wales were always in control. Andrew kicked 9 points to give England a 3-point advantage at the interval. Then Underwood, who had been at fault in Scotland's try the previous month, missed Webb with a wayward back-pass, and Welsh threequarter Mike Hall pounced. The cameras suggested that Hall might not have made the touchdown, but England did not complain. That try was scored early in the second half, and England were kept pinned on the defensive in the mud by Robert Jones's accurate narrow-side kicking for the rest of the match. The visitors had nothing to offer. Wales were delighted to extend to 26 years

England's suffering in Cardiff. Welsh captain Paul Thorburn revealed the pressure the home side had been under when he gave the press box a two-finger salute as he left the field. Then, at the post-match dinner, he called the *Sunday Times* rugby correspondent Stephen Jones the 'scum of the earth' and asked him to leave the room. Jones had written that it would do Welsh rugby a power of good if they lost to England, as the shock might provoke the Welsh Union into some much-needed soul-searching. France were equally grateful. That defeat and their 19–3 win over Scotland gave them the title.

COOKE

Our defence had been excellent against France. We went to Wales with high hopes. Quite right: we had been playing well. But we displayed a lack of coolness, of understanding, under pressure. We didn't have the capability to find a way out of their stranglehold. Losing Teague did upset the balance of the side, especially at the line-out. Roger and I still had to work on the mental preparation. We were only just making inroads on the confidence problem. That belief needs to be deep-rooted, and our lads didn't have it. The defeat by Wales was almost predictable. The fact that England had not won in Cardiff since 1963 got on top of them. They didn't believe they could do it. It really felt like a backward step. It was our last game of the season. There was no way for us to redeem the situation.

UTTLEY

We didn't have the mental edge to withstand the Welsh pressure. Geoff and I had short-, medium- and long-term aims. We had achieved the first: stability. The medium-term was next: win the championship. That took us three years, a nightmare. We should have done it in that first year in Wales. Very frustrating. Teague was taken out. Wales were so wound up, got among us and caused mayhem from the kick-off, although it wasn't as premeditated as between England and Australia in 1975, one of the most violent games in recent years. That was the end of Plan A. That left us with Plan B – 'Winters' and Rees on the flank. They have never been effective together. You put one loose forward on the bench. And sod's law, it's never the right replacement for the person injured. That left us with a physical disadvantage. Wade [Dooley] never came to terms with Norster, and Rory went walkabout again.

We had no answer to their tactics. Our only alternative was to kick the ball off the park. So there would be another line-out on our 10-metre line, and the whole process started again. Norster jumped, passed to Jones who kicked back down to our line. The England players couldn't work it out. They got locked into that game.

Although Carling's first campaign in charge ended with a defeat, Cooke was pleased with his progress. 'I certainly wouldn't say he took to the job all that quickly. He wasn't someone of whom you instantly thought, "Here's a very special captain." But he was prepared to listen. And prepared to learn. And learn from his mistakes. He took a few batterings in his first season. But, as far as I'm concerned, it was the next defeat that was the making of the man.'

Carling's first shot at the captaincy had gone well. He was the first to admit his mistakes. But, after the disastrous tour of Australia, England had made genuine progress. To have avenged that defeat, to be challenging for the championship, and not to be satisfied with second place was a big step forward in six months for the national rugby side.

The new skipper's performance was all the more creditable because his injury problem had dogged him all championship. His shin splints had progressively worsened. Carling had been a spectator for nearly all the squad sessions, but not even Cooke was aware how much the injury was bothering him. By his maintaining his form, observers thought it merely an irritant rather than a serious problem.

The British Lions had no hesitation in selecting Carling for the summer tour to Australia, although he had been ordered to rest for a month. He knew it was a race against time that he was losing. He was picked to captain England in Romania in May, but public doubts about his tour fitness surfaced towards the end of April when he visited a bone marrow specialist at Stoke Mandeville Hospital. 'I can get through a game on it. But I've been doing that since January. It's not right, and it can't go on.' Carling finally bowed to the inevitable and withdrew from both the England and British Lions trips. Exhaustive medical tests had discovered a stress fracture of the lower left fibia, and England's captain was advised to rest for a further three months. Carling was philosophical. 'I'm bitterly disappointed that my

81

injury has turned out to need such a lengthy period out of the game. But, at 23, I suppose I'm young enough to start with a new future ahead of me next season in the knowledge that I am fully fit.'

Carling's cloud did have a silver lining: his absence allowed Jerry Guscott the chance he grabbed so dramatically. The Bath centre scored three tries on his England debut in Romania, with Andrew captain and Carling watching from the sidelines. Then he kicked and gathered for the Lions' match-clinching try in the second Test Down Under. The 1988–89 season had ended with Guscott almost unknown. The 1989–90 campaign began with him established as rugby's latest superstar.

Chapter 11

The Ecstasy

The most outstanding performance that any of us have witnessed from an England side of any era.

ROGER UTTLEY

England's Lions forwards came back the heroes of the hour. The British pack had been the force that turned the tables on Australia in the three-match series, and the five Englishmen in the scrum that won the last two Tests were now battle-hardened veterans.

Australia's coach Bob Dwyer condemned the Lions as 'at times the dirtiest team I have ever seen in international rugby. I say this because their use of foul tactics was not occasional, but a common and constant theme of their play. Significantly, the officials accompanying the team insisted we had nothing much to complain about. Sure, there had been a few isolated acts by players out of control, they said, but nothing more than this. One player, a Welsh prop [David Young], was certainly out of control. On one occasion I saw him stomp on the side of Steve Cutler's head. I would find it hard to believe that either Ian McGeechan or Roger Uttley [the Lions coaches] would have stooped to devising tactics of this kind. But dirty play was a persistent, deliberate, all-embracing tactic. The Lions' dirty play took many forms. When the front rows of the scrum collapsed, the Lions' second-rowers kicked their opponents in the

83

head. This did not happen occasionally, but every time the scrum folded.'

Had the Lions lost the series and voiced such thoughts, they would certainly have been labelled 'whingeing Poms'. Paul Ackford for one described that final allegation as 'complete garbage'. The Lions tour had been Ackford's final graduation. After less than a year of international rugby, he had emerged as the outstanding front jumper in the world.

Others have risen to the top as rapidly, become overnight sensations. But Ackford's achievement was unique because his promise had been spotted by the national selectors a decade earlier. It was not a case of his having been discarded prematurely, however. The 1989 Ackford resembled the 1979 version physically, and both had ability. There the similarities ended. The early model, a Cambridge Blue, wandered the London club scene, talented but with no direction, no fire, no fight, and no desire to make any impact on the game. Listening to and reading his thoughts now as one of the game's most astute commentators, you wonder how Ackford could have coped with all those years as a less-than-honest club journeyman.

Ackford had needed a spark, something or someone to kick-start his real rugby career. Dick Best and the Harlequins provided that environment. Best was then still three years away from the national coaching job, but getting Ackford into gear is the best day's work he has ever done for England. Fortunately, Ackford wasted no time in analysing those years in limbo. Just as George Best is plagued with enquiries about why he gave up soccer so early, Ackford is asked: 'Why so late?' But it was not late, merely that Ackford eventually found himself in the right place at the right time to fulfil his rugby destiny. There is more than a good chance that, had Ackford been capped in the early 1980s, he would have vanished long before Carling's glory days. But, once he was picked for England, there was never any doubt that he would stay. After a stopping-all-stations journey, Paul Ackford was up where he belonged.

Ackford played in all three Lions Tests, along with Brian Moore and Dean Richards. Wade Dooley and Mike Teague, who was named as Man of the Series, played in the two victories. Cooke and Carling received another boost with Rob Andrew's assured displays in those two wins, while Guscott's moment of genius and Rory Underwood's solid form were further pluses for the England camp.

Like any other sport or business, rugby is a selfish game. The success of the Lions tour had given England a march over the other home countries. The 1983 tour to New Zealand had been a disaster, and all four Tests were lost. Yet it provided the grounding for Scotland's Grand Slam in 1984, when coach Jim Telfer and his eight Lions used that bitter experience better than the other home countries. Now England had developed the best forwards in the land, with just three places to fill. Andy Robinson and Gareth Chilcott had also been in Australia, while Jeff Probyn, Paul Rendall, Peter Winterbottom, David Egerton and Mickey Skinner were anxiously waiting at home to prove the Lions selectors wrong. Cooke and Uttley were licking their lips in anticipation.

Carling, too, had some ground to make up after his operation. No player likes turning down an invitation to a rugby party. And that sense of dismay was not improved when it turned out to be the most triumphant that British rugby had held for 15 years. Two tries in the final of the Monte Carlo Sevens in August made Carling feel a lot better. The following month, Cooke's Carling prediction came into focus when the draw for the 1991 World Cup was made. The hosts, England, would meet the holders, New Zealand, in the first game on Thursday, 3 October. Defeat in that opening game would have clear implications for England: a quarter-final in Paris and a semi-final in Edinburgh, both against home opposition.

Opening up the tournament in midweek added to what was now mounting criticism of the World Cup organisation. After the inaugural event in New Zealand and Australia, two firm recommendations had come from those who had experienced the problems of 1987. The first was: 'Start organising straight away. There is never enough time.' Second: 'No matter how many host countries are involved, let one organise the event.' That advice could not have been ignored better if the authorities had tried. Very little was in place two years before the event. That was not surprising. Five countries – the Five Nations – were putting the tournament together.

Carling saw the draw as typical, a missed opportunity to promote the World Cup. But England's captain was careful not to get too far ahead of himself. Along with Rob Andrew, he gave up his allegiance to the North at the start of the season. It was inevitable. Neither was turning his back on his rugby roots, but living and working in London made it almost impossible to continue the travelling. 'The North set out a training schedule that would have meant six days off work for those of us living in the south,' said Carling. 'Both Rob and I have England commitments. Harlequins train three nights a week before league matches. Rob is captain of Wasps this season, and it's a lot of time when you are also keeping a career going.'

Carling soon had more time to himself than he anticipated. He was concussed in Harlequins' game against London Irish. Another three weeks off meant that Carling could not take an active part in the squad session before the Test against Fiji in November 1989. His growing influence and the Lions' success had brought about a change, though: Carling and Brian Moore now took over the Friday practice. For Uttley, the step was a natural progression, although stepping back was painful. 'When the players go on the field, they have to be accountable for their own actions. By that stage, the coaches have spent three days working with them, not to mention the last two years. They don't need any more spoon-feeding. We can only be advisers, anyway. They play the game.'

Rory Underwood was the hero of England's win at Twickenham. He shared the limelight with Fijian threequarters Tevita Vonolagi and Noa Nadruku after England's 58–23 victory. Underwood's five tries equalled Daniel Lambert's England record in a match and Cyril Lowe's career record of 18. The Fijians also had the statisticians looking up the record books. Both were sent off for reckless tackles by Irish referee Brian Stirling.

Carling's problems with niggling injuries continued when, the following week, he limped off against Bristol. Not that England's captain got a lot of sympathy from his Harlequins team-mates: Quins had just been drawn to travel to holders Bath in the next round of the Pilkington Cup, and Carling had been the person responsible for that. He was relieved when the RFU reverted to the practice of allowing the president, rather than England's captain, to make the draw. Otherwise, Carling's championship build-up went well. London took the Divisional title, and then Carling led the Barbarians to victory in the annual Boxing Day fixture at Leicester.

Carling was also becoming busy on the commercial front. The Lions in Australia had become increasingly aware of the growing gap between their circumstances and those of players from foreign unions. Rugby was attracting more sponsorship money than ever before, and the players in the southern hemisphere were cashing in. The 1987 World Cup had shown the extent to which the amateur regulations had been relaxed in New Zealand. Several England players, although not Carling, now met with a management group, Prisma, and figures of £100,000 per man were bandied about. Carling was not happy. 'I am a bit saddened by all this. I believe the players should be thinking about the forthcoming championship, not how to make money out of the game. I don't agree with the figures, anyway. How is anyone going to earn £100,000 a year when they have a full-time job? Most players do not have enough spare time now. The only way to make big money would be to give up your job. But what happens then when you get dropped from the England team? Your value would fall dramatically. These reports are no more than sensational. I can't see what the fuss is all about.'

But Carling realised the problem would not go away and considered that the players would be better off controlling their own destinies. He met with RFU secretary Dudley Wood to arrange another meeting with a players' committee consisting of himself, Brian Moore, Rob Andrew and Paul Ackford. It was not just about money, however; it was an attempt to give the players a format by which to consult with the game's administration. Again, it was a system that had been in operation in New Zealand for a number of years. Unfortunately, England are still lagging behind the southern hemisphere.

The team to play Ireland in the Five Nations opener at Twickenham was announced during the squad's Lanzarote trip in January. Props Paul Rendall and Jeff Probyn were brought back after Mark Linnett and Andy Mullins had been given an outing against Fiji. Richard Hill was selected at scrum-half for his first championship game for three years. With Dean Richards injured, Mike Teague not match-sharp and Andy Robinson out of favour, England selected a non-Lions 1989 back row: Peter Winterbottom, Mickey Skinner and David Egerton. Carling's place had also been in doubt, according to press speculation, and Cooke admitted that the back row and centre had provoked most thought. But it was not Carling's centre spot which was ever under threat. The argument was over whether Simon Halliday or Jerry Guscott should be his partner. Guscott's Lions brilliance and undoubted promise won the day.

Carling felt much more relaxed and confident entering his second championship season as captain, and his players noticed the more authoritative manner. The captain felt able to take a more long-term view as he approached the Ireland match. 'We are slightly more sure about our style of play and better acquainted with each other than at this time last year. We have tried to work out the situations we are likely to be faced with and impose our own style upon them. Last year we slipped up against Scotland and Wales, who probably read the situation on the day better than we did. There were times when we wanted to play an expansive game, but it was too wet to do so all the time. I am confident that we are only a handful of games away from producing the 15-man game we want.'

England were actually 72 minutes away from that breakthrough. Until that point, the home side had given no hint of anything unusual brewing. The Irish scrum had been given a pasting, yet England had only gained a 7–0 advantage over a side so obviously their inferiors. Late tries from David Egerton, Rory Underwood (now breaking Lowe's record) and Jerry Guscott transformed the game and the scoreline, and erased the pedantic impression England had created all afternoon. Guscott split the Irish defence for Underwood's try, then Carling sped away to create Guscott's score. Ireland's skipper Phil Matthews declared, 'England have the best pack in the championship.' Everyone knew that. But the backs and their willingness to expand their game were the key to England's revolution. Hill's recall was a success, while Andrew displayed the composure so evident on the Lions tour.

England had set their standards, and Carling was determined that this was not to prove another false dawn. He was right. Within a month, this England side was being hailed as the greatest of all time after two staggering performances against, traditionally, their toughest opponents.

Paris was the next stop. Carling nearly missed it. Quins lost their Cup-tie in the Bath mud, and Carling came off with a badly cut eye after colliding with John Hall. But he made a speedy recovery after the eye was cleaned out, and so he returned to the city where he had made his international debut two years earlier. Paris is a graveyard for British teams: England suffered three horrendous hammerings there in the 1970s; Scotland last won there in 1969, Ireland in 1972 and Wales in 1975. Those first two dates mean that Scotland and Ireland have never won at the Parc des Princes. For England, Bill Beaumont's Grand Slam side broke the mould in 1980, and they won again two years later. A great chance had been thrown away on Carling's debut.

The 1990 success was different from any previous foreign victory at the Parc des Princes. England led 13–0 at half-time – never, on its

Will Carling with the British Lions mascot. A few months earlier, most had expected England's skipper to lead the 1993 side to New Zealand. But, as England failed in their bid for a unique hat-trick of Grand Slams, Carling was not alone in believing that a spell out of the limelight was essential to his long-term well-being and future in the game. The captaincy went to Scotland's Gavin Hastings. Carling was dropped for Welshman Scott Gibbs in the second Test, which the Lions won. He was left with nothing to play for in the closing fortnight, except pride. Carling eventually captained the Lions in their final midweek match, a heavy defeat to Waikato. But Carling came up smiling, displaying his best form and true grit in adversity, and, crucially for England, having dismissed all thoughts of giving up rugby. (*Colorsport*)

Success for Carling, 13, in the Young Boys' dash in the local fair at Carlton Miniott, near Thirsk in Yorkshire, where his father was stationed at the time.

Carling, 14, up to his neck in it during a holiday in Pipione, Italy.

A moody Carling, 15, at the family's chalet in Gruyere, Switzerland.

Carling in the famous 'brown' jersey of the Sedbergh 1st XV.

Carling, outside Winder House, enjoying life in the sixth form at Sedbergh.

Carling (left) with elder brother Marcus. At two years old, he looked more likely to end up as a front-row colleague of Brian Moore's.

The Carling boys at a Sergeants' Mess function, Gravesend, 1968.

William the Conqueror, Christmas 1970, with Marcus less than happy.

Marcus takes the higher ground to emphasise Will's failure to reach six foot.

Carling (right) on his way to open the innings for Terra Nova.

The Terra Nova rifle team were into big trophies. Will is at the left end of the back row, with Marcus at the front on the left.

Will Carling was captain and fly-half of the Terra Nova 1st XV in 1978. The side lost one match, scoring 229 points against 30.

Carling ready for his round-the-world trip, September 1984.

A typical Pom, sticking up for the Old Country in Moomba.

Carling's poker face fooled nobody. It was the face of a loser at cards.

Carling had a few years to go before he could properly fill his dad's Army uniform.

Carling receives the *Rugby World* School Team of the Month pennant for November 1983 from former England captain John Spencer, himself a Sedbergh old boy.

Carling came to national attention with an outstanding Divisional Championship for the North in December 1986. Behind him is Kevin Simms, whom he partnered on his England debut in Paris the following season.

Carling's England debut against France in 1988. Despite being given little chance, England were unlucky to lose 10–9 to a late try against the run of play. (*Colorsport*)

Carling, concussed, being led from the field by RFU doctor Ben Gilfeather a few seconds before England marked Carling's captaincy debut with a 28–19 victory over Australia at Twickenham. (*Colorsport*)

Carling's first England try. A planned move went so badly that the confused French defence allowed Carling a clear run to the line in 1989. (*Colorsport*)

Carling dives over the French line again, this time at the Parc des Princes, to seal England's conclusive victory the following year. (*Colorsport*)

Carling weaves his way through a transfixed Welsh defence at the start of England's record victory at Twickenham in 1990. (*Colorsport*)

Carling touches down, despite Mark Titley's despairing tackle and Andy Allen's late arrival, for the first of England's four tries. (*Colorsport*)

ABOVE: Carling is held by the Scots during 'That Match' at Murrayfield in 1990. England's captain looks for support from Wade Dooley, Brian Moore and Mickey Skinner, but David Sole's (No. 1) Tartan Army are there in force. (*Colorsport*)

RIGHT: New Zealand referee David Bishop signals the try that stunned England at the start of the second half. Scorer Tony Stanger (facing camera) celebrates with Chris Gray while Rory Underwood, outjumped for the try, is grounded in resignation. (*Colorsport*)

The 1990 tour of Argentina was not an easy time for Carling. Relations with Roger Uttley were strained and England lost the second Test. (*Colorsport*)

Dudley Wood, the RFU secretary and self-styled King Canute against rugby's growing professionalism, has stood firm during Carling's reign. (*Colorsport*)

Rory Underwood's Grand Slam try for England v. France, 1991. (*Colorsport*)

ABOVE: Carling and Jerry Guscott offer Underwood their congratulations. (*Colorsport*)

RIGHT: Simon Hodgkinson's goal-kicking was a key part of England's first Grand Slam success for 11 years. (*Colorsport*)

Carling tells his team that they just have to keep their heads against France for another 40 minutes to become winners at last. (*Allsport/Dan Smith*)

Carling, minus boots, finally leaves the pitch celebrations after England's 1991 Grand Slam. (*Colorsport*)

England's rugby captain patiently points the way to the Twickenham dressing-room after the 1991 Grand Slam success over France. (*Allsport/Dan Smith*)

own, a match-winning advantage in Paris, but by that stage France
were reeling. The visitors had played into the wind, and Teague,
reinstated at the expense of Egerton, and the rest of the England
forwards had the French scrum under control. It was the ruthless
manner with which England used their power and control that
destroyed France, though. Andrew's precise kick through created
Underwood's first-half try, and Simon Hodgkinson kicked three
inspiring penalties before the break in atrocious wind conditions.
France had to bounce back. But when a Denis Charvet kick bounced
off Carling, Guscott hacked away before gathering for the decisive
try at the start of the second half. England's captain then had the
satisfaction of leaving Blanco for dead in the closing minutes to
complete the rout by 26–7. Winterbottom, the only English survivor
from the last Paris victory, said, 'This is a much better team than the
one eight years ago.'

Stephen Jones, in the *Sunday Times*, summed up the extent of the
damage: 'England were so good they even robbed the occasion of
some of its drama.' French coach Jacques Fouroux gave a
schizophrenic view of England's achievement: 'If you had put black
shirts on them, they could have passed for All Blacks,' was his post-
match verdict. A day later, however, the assessment was not as
wholehearted. 'England have adopted a style of play which is realistic
and rigorous, but certainly not imaginative. They prop this up with a
kind of fury and ferocity in defence. These are words we are not
allowed to use in France. We talk about fluidity, enjoyment and
spectacle.' That came as rather a shock to those who felt that, for all
France's recent achievements, Fouroux had ruined French flair in his
decade as national coach. As for the 'fury and ferocity in defence',
that was to give France, not England, a bad name in the next two
Anglo-French encounters.

Geoff Cooke grasped the importance of England's display. 'We are
really in a position to be able to look New Zealand in the eye in 20
months' time when we start the World Cup.' Carling, having led
England to their biggest winning margin over France since the
outbreak of the Great War, insisted, 'There really is much more. We
are getting there. This is what we have worked so hard for, and we
have not even reached our potential. The sequence of wins has
generated new confidence. We are prepared to take risks and now
have so many options.'

England were now attempting to win more than two games in the championship for the first time since 1980. That was Carling's main concern. 'Suddenly, we were billed as world-beaters. It seemed as if the Grand Slam was a formality, even taking two Grand Slams in a row before we took the World Cup. I believe in being positive, whatever the situation, but that was ridiculous. Strangely, only a few days after reading that we were the greatest team in the world, England were being told that we would succumb again to the psychological hold Wales had over us. That was another load of rubbish. I didn't believe that either.'

Carling and his team proved they were not frightened by Welsh ghosts in the most emphatic manner. To say that England gave the Twickenham crowd a day to remember does not do it justice. It was a day to savour after all those humiliations by the Welsh over the previous 20 years. Indeed, this revenge probably meant more to the Twickenham faithful than it did to the players on the park. The team was full of relative newcomers, fresh to the fray, while the crowd had enjoyed only odd moments of triumph, which the Welsh tried to take away. In 1974, it was the fault of the 'blind Irish referee', according to Max Boyce. In 1980, Wales, who had Paul Ringer sent off after a quarter of an hour, turned a 9–8 defeat into a moral victory because of scoring two tries to nil.

This time, though, there could be no arguments about England's supremacy in a record 34–6 victory. Carling weaved his way through five Welsh tackles after a quarter of an hour for a brilliant solo try, and Wales never recovered. That had been England's first try against Wales since 1985, the first for 478 minutes. England then added three more for good measure. Uttley, who had suffered at the hands of the Welsh himself, rated this display even better than Paris. 'That was the most outstanding performance that any of us have witnessed from an England side of any era. It had the stamp of greatness and there is still more to come. Even the 1980 side would have had great difficulty living with England today.'

The rugby writers struggled to find more superlatives only two weeks after Paris. The *Sunday Times* man Jones dived in. 'It strains credibility when you see two once-in-a-lifetime performances produced within a fortnight. But there were aspects of England's seethingly glorious victory which rendered the demolition of France a fortnight ago a failure.'

David Hands, of *The Times*, disagreed, though. 'England's overwhelming success was not, in my view, such a complete victory as over France in Paris. Apart from the fact that that was achieved away from home, they took nearly every scoring chance on offer. Against the Welsh, they made openings, but could not complete them, largely because of mishandling and misjudgement in midfield, where Guscott's decision-making was awry.'

It was not a day for holding back, however. The emotional background to this fixture made the victory over Wales so extraordinary. It probably has the most special place in the hearts of the Twickenham faithful of all the successes under Will Carling. So far, England had followed the exact pattern of the 1980 Grand Slam team. Now, as 10 years earlier, they had a month off before travelling north for the Murrayfield finale.

Chapter 12

And the Agony!

When you're captain on the field, you have to take responsibility for what happens out there. There were definite signs of a lack of decision-making. You can't lead by committee in the middle of a Grand Slam game at Murrayfield.

ROGER UTTLEY

Scotland v. England, Murrayfield, 17 March 1990. To more than one generation of rugby followers, this Calcutta Cup contest has become 'The Match'. It gathered together, for the first time ever in one huge melting pot of rugby passion, the Five Nations championship, the home championship, the Triple Crown, the Grand Slam, as well as the trophy donated by the Calcutta Cricket and Rugby Club. The Red Rose versus the Thistle. Bannockburn against Culloden. Passion over power. Forget about winning: this was one rugby match you could not afford to lose.

The initial build-up was understandably tentative. Scotland had to win in Cardiff first. The Scots had enjoyed more success there than England in recent times, while Wales were in disarray. The Welsh coach John Ryan had resigned after the Twickenham defeat, having been in charge for 19 months. The Welsh Rugby Union then turned to Ron Waldron, coach of the Principality's in-form side, Neath. He drafted in seven of his own club players, although their wholehearted club commitment counted for less on the international field, and Scotland won 13–9.

The game was on. Even Scotsmen were paying ridiculous prices for tickets to the rugby match of the century. The SRU, with traditional fervour, investigated the resale of tickets, and secretary Bill Hogg admitted to being 'horrified' by some prices (£1,000 a pair) being obtained on the black market. 'It is entirely out of proportion for a game of rugby.' Trust a Scot to get it wrong: that was dirt-cheap. A week later, a pair of £14 tickets were going for £3,000. No rugby match in history, even including England's 1991 World Cup final against Australia, has ever caught the public's imagination like this one.

This was no mere rugby match. It was the final battle in a war. To the victors would belong the spoils of the enemy. England's form had made them firm favourites: 1/4 on, with the Scots 11/4. Why not? Uttley had gone to Edinburgh in 1980 and collected a Grand Slam.

Carling now felt the full force of the media machine. These were to be his final days as a rugby innocent, the last when the captaincy was not a burden. He was one of four England players to rest from club commitments the week before the match, along with Paul Ackford, Brian Moore and full-back Simon Hodgkinson. England's captain was never out of the papers, on feature pages as well as sport; 'Captain Carling's a darling' was fairly typical, and England's skipper was photographed wrapped in St George's flag. Too much was being made of his contribution to this Grand Slam finale. But nothing could stop the rollercoaster, and Carling was to suffer afterwards. But, rugby-wise, he was happy with England's preparations.

CARLING

We had a good session on the Friday, probably too good. We didn't drop a ball in 45 minutes of work. The Scots were determined that our side should be seen as firm favourites. That worried me greatly. No scenario suits the Scots better than that – outsiders in their own back yard against England. How were we going to counter the Scots' passion? I told the players they had to be strong enough to shut the Scottish noise and antagonism out of their system. Three weeks before the match, I didn't think the Scots would be able to withstand our overflowing confidence. But the night before, I sensed they would be harder to dominate than the teams we had already beaten. I told the players that this was their chance to establish themselves as a great side.

But, as Carling feared, it was the Scots who took their chance to establish themselves as a great side. From the moment David Sole walked out slowly and defiantly at the head of his Scottish team, England were on the defensive. It was a masterstroke from the only Scotsman England feared, coach Ian McGeechan. Paul Ackford saw it coming. 'Ian is such a brilliant coach, as many of the English players discovered on last year's Lions tour, that he is certain to have thought up something original to make our task more difficult,' predicted England's lock forward the day before the match. Scotland had also arranged for two verses, not one, of *Flower of Scotland* to be sung before the kick-off.

Remarkably, the match lived up to all its publicity; the hype had been justified for once. It will be remembered for its intensity and defence. England, playing into the wind, countered Craig Chalmers's two early penalties when Carling rounded Scott Hastings and Guscott dummied his brother, Gavin, to score a spectacular try. Another Chalmers penalty then left England trailing 9–4 when they turned to feel the wind at their backs.

In the first half, England had ignored penalty points in attempting to push the Scottish scrum over their own line. The scrum collapsed, but no penalty try was awarded. Those missed scores proved critical. Shortly after the break, Gavin Hastings kicked ahead and Tony Stanger leapt to gather and touch down ahead of Rory Underwood. Suddenly, the impossible was about to happen. England had plenty of time to recover, but the writing was on the wall. The underdog was about to rewrite history. There had been recent precedents: in boxing, Buster Douglas had toppled the invincible Mike Tyson a few days before Graham Gooch's England cricketers had wiped out the mighty West Indies in Jamaica. Hodgkinson's penalty brought England back to within a score, but a 13–13 draw would have shattered everyone's dream. Instead, only England were left devastated at the finish as Scotland withstood a fierce, late flurry to hold on 13–7.

England were failures. The magnificence of those victories over France and Wales made their comedown even worse. England teams have a problem that the other rugby nations do not: they have to find a unifying cause. The Scots, like the Irish and Welsh, know what they are fighting for. It is perfectly clear when England provide the opposition: a history of English oppression. Let's even the score a bit. Under those circumstances, the Scots are prepared to die for their country. Yet Carling's team, in its darkest hour, now found its own motivation, its *raison d'être*. Murrayfield has inspired generations of Scottish jerseys. But, on the very day it provided its country's greatest triumph, Murrayfield '90 entered the soul of Carling's side. It was to remain at the heart of everything they achieved in the next two years.

The inquests had begun even before the final whistle. They rage today. Carling can be relaxing anywhere in the world, and he is still asked the burning question: 'Why did you run those penalties?' or 'Why did you let Brian Moore run those penalties?' No questions were asked in the dressing-room afterwards, however. Even a wily old campaigner like Uttley had never witnessed such a scene of desolation. Strange: the World Cup had been England's aim, and this Grand Slam was just a by-product. Now that it was gone, though, it had become the most important thing in the world. It appeared as if every member of the England side had just lost their nearest and dearest. Certainly, the pain was comparable. No matter what they achieved from that day on, they could never bring back the 1990 Grand Slam. It was gone for ever; England were going to have to live with that. And the Scots were going to make sure they lived with that. Even now, after two Grand Slams and a World Cup final, Carling's team are the side who lost the biggest game in rugby history. In that respect, David Sole got it wrong when he said: 'People will remember 1990 for Scotland's Grand Slam, not for the team that came second.'

CARLING

Murrayfield was the big turning point for me as captain. I asked a number of players during the game if they thought we were capable of beating the Scots in a certain style. They said yes. It just didn't work. I will never blame anyone for that. But, at the end of the day, I'm the captain. And I'm the one who's going to live or die by those decisions. Although I would still ask and listen, I have to decide the way it is going to be. At Murrayfield, I didn't assert myself enough.

It wasn't really what happened on the field that changed me. It was afterwards when I sat down and thought, 'What more could I have done?' I realised we had to be more ruthless and professional in our approach to these games. I don't believe we lost that game. The Scots won it. Sole's team got it right on the day. They had this plan to beat us and they managed to see it through. I would not – nor ever will – say we lost to the better side. But they beat us. And that's different to saying we just lost it.

I don't suppose we had considered losing hard enough when it came to the crunch. We had been playing so well. It came out of the blue. Now we do consider losing in far more depth. Therefore we are far more prepared for it and how to cope. I just don't think we had considered it enough. When it came, it was one hell of a shock. Once you've been through it, it's far easier to prepare people. It's three years ago now, but the memory is still there, and it will never go. Having been through it once, no one wanted to experience it again.

What really got to me was the faces in the dressing-room. Guys who were my friends. I know England's supporters were disappointed, too. But my responsibility lies with the squad. They were the ones who had put in all that effort. They were the ones who had lost the game. I know it was sad for our supporters, too. But I took that in afterwards. They were looking forward to a Grand Slam. It's great to achieve things and see the fans enjoy them. It wasn't good in 1990. It meant a lot to them, and we got it wrong.

The public verdict was that England had blown it, and Carling's leadership came under intense scrutiny for the first time. Geoff Cooke was angry that Carling was singled out as responsible for the failure. 'Murrayfield was the day we really let ourselves down, and Will took a lot of flak for that. Certainly, it is the lowest point of our time together. It hit us hard. We were the better side, but we didn't come to terms with what the Scots were doing. In the end, we made a nonsense of it. Will took a lot of hammer. I felt fairly protective towards him; he was just one guy. There were many more experienced players around in England shirts that afternoon. The failure was a collective one. No one person was responsible for our defeat.'

UTTLEY
For a second year running, we had blown the championship because of ineptitude on the field. Will was part of that. When

you're captain on the field, you have to take responsibility for what happens out there. There were definite signs of a lack of decision-making. You can't lead by committee in the middle of a Grand Slam game at Murrayfield. It was a nightmare being in Edinburgh that night. We were devastated. I can honestly say that I never experienced anything like it as a player. Rob [Andrew] and Brian [Moore] were distraught. It was taking it all in. We had never considered the possibility. We knew we were demonstrably better.

I turned to Geoff after a quarter of an hour and said, 'We've got huge problems here.' Still, when Jerry ran in that try from half-way, I thought we might establish a pattern. You have to establish some order, continuity, especially against the Irish and the Scots. It's the last thing they want. It's death to them. They want mayhem, chaos. The first inkling I had was that slow march out. It made the hair on the back of my neck rise. It was Sole's greatest moment – brilliant. We could say Stanger's try was fortuitous because of the bounce, or moan that the southern hemisphere referee [David Bishop] awarded scrums and penalties when it should have been penalty tries. But we only had ourselves to blame. The defeat was physically painful. We had a hard time up there. It was as if Edinburgh had taken over from Cardiff as the seat of English loathing. We caught the flak for the Thatcher years, the English control of Scotland. They redressed some of the balance that night.

Carling always puts a brave public face to defeat. His mum Pam, though, was in tears. It wasn't her day either: Carling's parents' house in South London was burgled. There was some consolation, though. The culprits had taken the video that had been programmed to record the afternoon's events at Murrayfield. Unfortunately, there were five million Scots who were prepared to lend or – just once in these very special circumstances – give them theirs.

Carling's captaincy honeymoon was well and truly over. And England's captain had such a traumatic time over the next year that he very nearly filed for divorce!

Chapter 13

Argy Bargy – Roger and Out!

I lost it badly at the end of the match. I was disgusted with the attitude of the players. I really ripped into them on the field. I was fuming. But that was no excuse. It was far too much of an emotional outburst. I made a conscious decision that it would never happen again.

WILL CARLING

The first real crisis in Carling's captaincy career was nearly his last. The stigma of that Murrayfield defeat proved difficult to shake off. The Golden Boy who could do no wrong was now trapped in a downward spiral. The rugby press and officialdom, who had saluted his rise to the top, now turned their attentions to his destruction. And there is no doubt that Carling helped their cause. His confidence dented, his judgement awry, England's captain entered a period of doubt, suspicion and frustration. Eventually, Carling even questioned the value of his leading the national rugby side. Murrayfield was certainly the starting line for that process. But it was his subsequent behaviour over the next year which had long-lasting effects on his relationships both inside and outside the squad.

Carling had a busy end to the 1989–90 season. His Hong Kong Sevens quest with the Barbarians ended in the semi-final against New Zealand. Then he played under his Grand Slam conqueror, David Sole, when the four Home Unions beat the Rest of Europe 43–18 at

Twickenham in a match to raise money for Romania and its rugby. The 1991 World Cup was then brought into focus once more with the announcement of England's preliminary squad for interim training. Mark Bailey, Nigel Redman and Simon Halliday, who was to play in the final, were notable by their absence. Those who were included were guaranteed nothing. Don Rutherford, the RFU's technical administrator, said there were predetermined standards of fitness; players who were not up to the mark would be 'eliminated quite ruthlessly'. Meanwhile, Dudley Wood had some reassuring comments for those who were worried about the growing commitment required to achieve those standards. 'The RFU has examined the time required for preparation at the highest level by players and believe that it is compatible with individuals who hold down a full-time job.' But Wood added, 'The breaking point is not too far away.'

Yet rugby's unions continue to commit their players to more matches, more tours. Raman Subba Row, former chairman of the Test and County Cricket Board, once asked Richie Benaud, the respected Australian commentator, what the cricket authorities could do about the excessive amount of international cricket being played. Benaud replied: 'Play less.'

As Carling and England flew off to Italy for an international at the end of April, there was another reminder of their failure in Scotland. The *Sunday Times* recorded the occasion: 'A forlorn group of wives and girlfriends will see the England party off at Heathrow tonight. Had things turned out differently at Murrayfield, they would have been joining the players on the two-day trip to Italy. It was planned to thank the group for their support of the men who won the Grand Slam. Evidently, supporting the men who came second wasn't quite enough.'

Brian Moore did not come second. The Nottingham hooker was named *Rugby World* Player of the Year. The body of opinion which thought of England's hooker as a lightweight, a show-off, was dwindling. Moore was proof of the power of positive thinking. Everyone had had Ireland's Steve Smith penned in for the Lions Test place in Australia in 1989; Moore had him psyched out in a matter of days. Moore was technically a Nottingham player when he received his award, but had just announced his intention to join Harlequins from the start of the following season. That brought this response from his club coach, Alan Davies: 'He's achieved everything in the game with us, from a teenager to a mature player. It is sad when someone like him falls prey to those who have a job to offer. The whole thing smacks of clubs like Harlequins and Northampton, with a lot of money and connections, organising themselves to get the players they want.'

Jason Leonard's move from Saracens to Quins later the same year similarly caused resentment. The Saracens president-elect John Heggadon was dismayed. 'What it amounts to is harassment and intimidation. I have to say that I don't like the way English rugby is going. It's about time the RFU said openly whether it wants an élite of about six clubs in the country for its England players. That appears to be happening in London, for Quins and Wasps seem to enjoy a privileged position.' Saracens claimed that Leonard had been 'poached' during England's summer tour to Argentina.

England had been due a summer off, and those involved with the squad would have preferred it. But someone – over a pink gin, no doubt – had decided otherwise. Wasn't it about time we flew the flag and forgot about that little mix-up over the Falklands? That someone was, in fact, the late John Kendall-Carpenter. He had taken up jet-setting late in life as chairman of the World Cup organising committee, and England's tour was part of a bigger pay-off.

Geoff Cooke's careful build-up to 1991 was thus disrupted by a tour he knew nothing about. It meant that the team would have continuous rugby right through to the World Cup in 18 months' time. Several key players decided that was too tough a schedule and made themselves unavailable: Carling had with him in Argentina no Jonathan Webb, Rory Underwood, Jeremy Guscott, Rob Andrew, Paul Rendall, Paul Ackford, Dean Richards or Mike Teague. Carling realised this tour was about more than just results. 'I don't see the main objective as to remain unbeaten. My main priorities are that we adapt the lessons we have learnt into our patterns of play, and that the youngsters learn about what is involved in the whole England set-up. It would be bad for us to be so negative and conservative that, at the end of the tour, we came away with played seven, won seven, but the youngsters had not been introduced into the hard games and not given a fair go.' Before leaving, the players spent time with Len Heppell, the movement consultant who has worked with the national soccer side and Frank Bruno, and whose aim is to 'improve the reflexes, movement and balance of sportsmen'.

England nearly won the Test series in Argentina, only a missed penalty by Hodgkinson costing them the second match. But, apart

101

from the emergence of loose-head prop Leonard, Cooke and Carling learnt more about those who were not going to make the grade than about those who were. England lost their first two Saturday matches and, after the second defeat, to Buenos Aires, Cooke was far from happy. 'I couldn't believe what I was seeing. We seem to have left our rugby brains back in England. We made a series of schoolboy howlers and put ourselves under pressure.'

The first Test team contained four new caps: Leonard, Nigel Heslop, David Pears and Dean Ryan. Carling read the riot act beforehand. 'It's a bit sad that we gave away 26 points in the Five Nations, yet it's nearly 100 already on this trip. I don't think we have sufficient pride in our defence. There has not been sufficient pride and dedication for an England tour.'

England responded by giving their best display so far in winning the first Test 25–12. The tourists kept their tempers and nerves under severe provocation; Australian referee Brian Kinsey, who was to upset the British Lions in the first Test in New Zealand in 1993, offered them little protection. At least, with him, the England players had a better understanding of the decisions; they had suffered some bizarre local rulings in earlier matches, and were to do so again. Still, Cooke was relieved with the victory. 'It was important for us to win today. To an extent, style went out of the window, and it was a question of pride and commitment.'

But the final week brought more problems. England beat Cordoba 15–12 in midweek, and stand-in captain John Olver nearly took his team off the field because of the refereeing of Miguel Peyrone from Rosario. Cooke backed his players with words that did not find favour at Twickenham: 'The referee was just incompetent. I don't normally comment on referees, but I feel I can because we got the right result. He had no concept of offside, how to set a scrum or throwing in to the line-out. He would not be allowed to referee a third-team game at home.'

England's attempt to be the first team to win both Tests in Argentina since France in 1974 ended in failure when Hernan Vidou kicked a late penalty for the home side, shortly after Hodgkinson had missed a simple opportunity to make the game safe. The disappointment of the 15–13 defeat accentuated the tour failure. 'We have not made any progress towards the World Cup,' admitted Cooke. 'We had hoped for more. We have to look now at how we prepare a side. We are missing somewhere. I don't know if we are failing to recognise what the problems are. Are we giving the players the right things?

'The frustrating thing as a national coach is that we lose control of the players when they go back to their clubs and we can't decide what they do or even where they play. We have to get coaches back home on to the same wavelength. They have to stop being so introverted and parochial. We need to agree a formula within which they can operate. We can't have three different ways of rucking and mauling. We call meetings of the top 36 club coaches each season, but the problem is getting them to attend. England is the product of what is happening in the clubs, counties, divisions or whatever. The pace of international rugby is greater, but the techniques don't change. Our coaching is poor in England.' More comments which were not likely to win Cooke any friends back home.

Roger Uttley was not a happy man, either. And the problem was Carling.

UTTLEY

There had been a lot of indications that Will wasn't happy with me. It came to a head after the third tour game. We played in a football stadium with a moat. There was a tunnel under it for the players to get to the dressing-room. I waited there at the end of the game. Will was there, obviously highly charged. When I asked him what the trouble was, he told me to '**** off'. That was what ended it for me. I began to feel like a spare part, and that lasted right through until I quit after the World Cup.

With an inexperienced squad, it took time to sort things out in Argentina. After 10 days, I was approached by Will and Geoff and told that they wanted to use Bestie [Dick Best] for a couple of sessions. The impetus for that came from Will. He was obviously unhappy with the way things were going. Bestie was out there as part of his Rugby Travel job. I felt it was out of order. I think Will genuinely felt he was not getting enough support. He felt vulnerable for the first time as captain. Questions were being asked of him, and he was finding them difficult to answer. I don't know why he didn't turn to me. I remember being in a lift with him in Buenos Aires and at breakfast; there was barely a word between us. I found it very difficult to deal with him.

Carling had felt the need to assert himself on the trip. After all, the biggest criticism of his captaincy at Murrayfield had been his failure to take control. But that had gone wrong for him in the tour opener against Banco Nacion.

CARLING

I lost it badly at the end of the match. I was disgusted with the attitude of the players. It didn't seem to bother them as much as it did me that they were losing while wearing the England jersey. I called them together at the end of the match and really ripped into them. 'You've got to have more pride. Otherwise, we'll find someone else to fill your jersey.' I was fuming. Hillie [Richard Hill] came up to me and said, 'Calm down.' I quickly realised that what I did was wrong. Well, the way I did it was wrong. It was far too much of an emotional outburst. I made a conscious decision that it would never happen again.

The trip came too soon for a few of the younger players. And some of the senior players played beneath themselves. I know Brian Moore and Wade Dooley were disappointed with their performances. I think we lacked the necessary desire to win the second Test. We'd won one. We were maybe relieved that the tour was coming to a close. On the other hand, the Argentinians saw this as their last chance, and came out with all guns blazing. Still, we should have won.

The tour finished with the traditional dinner, at which Carling arrived painted as a clown after attending the players' court. The England captain's gesture to raise a laugh was reported back in Britain by a journalist. The tone was critical: Carling did not know how to behave and had insulted his Argentinian hosts. That had never been the intention, however, and nobody was upset. Well, nobody apart from Carling. He was furious. England's captain saw it as another attempt by the media to put the boot in.

Chapter 14

Guilty . . . Until Proved Guilty!

The whole episode really annoyed me. I was guilty until I could prove my innocence. I thought the law of the land took a rather different view of an individual's status. What a strange way to treat your national captain, or any of your players.

WILL CARLING

The Uttley bust-up apart, Carling had done a good job in Argentina. It was his first overseas tour as England captain, and no side can lose eight key players and expect to function efficiently. Carling was disappointed that some of the understudies did not respond to his leadership. But England's captain was being over-critical. The newcomers did not respond because they were not good enough, and that was the fault of the selectors. Their choices had been exposed. But, at this crucial time in his career, Carling felt that his leadership had been found wanting for the second time in a few months.

Murrayfield had sparked his search for the best way of handling the job. Carling, who had never enjoyed the prominent profile, resented more and more being public property. Life had become rather more painful: the back-slapping had become back-stabbing. Carling felt on trial. The *London Evening Standard*'s Chris Jones remembers his anguish. 'He got a good grilling in Argentina. He was asked about

105

those penalties at Murrayfield. Why didn't he grab the ball in both hands and take control? Will replied: "From now on I am going to grab the ball in both hands." It was obvious he was not going to stand for that again. Unfortunately, Argentina was not the right time or place with a newish squad. There was no old guard to protect him. Then a few things happened when he got home and he read the situation wrong. The pressures built up. For the first time, he wasn't in control. It started with the bad press he got over Scotland and Argentina. That was something new, and he didn't handle it well. He felt it was a personal attack on Will Carling. He could see the momentum building up. There were areas he couldn't control, and he didn't like that.'

Carling needed help. But the very body that should have protected him, the Rugby Football Union, had decided that he needed cutting down to size. The more Carling asserted himself as captain, the less they liked it. Cooke, too, they felt, was enjoying too high a profile. The manager was in trouble the minute he started siding with his players and openly criticising referees. Carling's only hope was to keep his nose clean. Unfortunately, his and rugby's increasing popularity, coupled with the massive injection of sponsorship money into the game and the players' resentment at being exploited to get it, made that impossible.

Carling could have ended those problems and made his own personal fortune with a stroke of the pen. That autumn, in the week before the International Rugby Football Board took steps towards relaxing the laws regarding amateurism in the game, Carling turned down a £400,000 offer from Warrington Rugby League club. 'I have never been interested in playing professionally. And I never will. The amount of money makes no difference. None of the England internationals is in the game for money. But I do hope that we are not in for another disappointment from the IRFB. We are looking forward to less restrictive amateur regulations so that, if they want to, players can make money outside the game from personal appearances, writing and broadcasting.' Carling's wishes came true, to a degree at least. But still the Rugby League offers kept coming in and the amounts kept increasing.

CARLING
I remember the phone going. The voice at the other end offered me £1 million to play for Leeds. I said, 'Oh yeah.' 'No, I'm being

106

serious,' he replied. A £1 million deal over five years – guaranteed. I didn't say no immediately. An offer like that makes you think. But, deep down, I knew I couldn't go. I was keen to build up my business. It was no saintly act that I didn't go. It really annoys me, though, when I'm accused of being in rugby for the money. They haven't got a clue why I'm in this game.

I talked it through long and hard with Jon [Holmes, Carling's agent]. I enjoy watching Rugby League. I have great admiration for their players. I have no idea how I would have done. I played with Martin Offiah for the Barbarians. Maybe he was a great loss to Union; he's certainly been a phenomenal success in League. But those two extra defenders in Rugby Union might have made all the difference. I have never had a minute's regret about not signing, even in the worst moments. One thing is certain: I would have regretted going. League is not my game. I've been in love with Rugby Union since the age of 6. I would have gone for the money, nothing else. That would have been wrong. And I would have missed out on the World Cup. That would have been too big a price to pay.

Another rugby body was interested in Carling and money: the RFU. The whispering campaign against him was getting louder. Surely, Carling could not be appearing in all these papers and magazines for love. For England's captain was featuring on front covers normally reserved for the likes of Princess Di, George Michael and Rik Mayall. Mr Macho Rugby Player, good-looking, successful, pretty girlfriends, talking success, money and winning. How they hated him. If this was the rugby player of the future, you could keep him. They got to work and, like the policeman who is determined to find something wrong with your car, they kept probing.

The self-professed guardians of rugby's amateur creed have plenty of disciples. Few of them live in the real world. Many believe that the sterling work they do at club level is directly related to England's two Grand Slams and World Cup final appearance. Yet the only real connection is that these clubs are now as greedily geared to making money and attracting sponsorship as they believe the players are. Their committees consist mainly of players from the 1950s, 1960s and 1970s, whose idea of dedication was to drink a dozen pints after every match and not hit anything on the way home. They bask in the reflected glory of the national side, yet they have little conception of a current England rugby player's life.

Carling was finding the resentment hard to take. His life revolved around rugby. If he was not playing, or training to play, or travelling to play, Carling was thinking about playing. How he could be a better captain, and find that little extra to give England the edge. On top of that, Carling was trying to establish a new business.

The first skirmish with Twickenham concerned a modelling feature in *You* magazine. With their traditional sense of justice, the RFU asked Carling to prove that he had not been paid. Carling told secretary Dudley Wood that money had not been discussed, and the magazine confirmed his story. Twickenham decided to let the matter drop for now. But the word was out, and the following month the RFU were again investigating allegations that Carling had received payment, this time for opening a sports complex in London. A copy of a fee invoice sent by the Prisma company on Carling's behalf had found its way to HQ. What upset him most was the implication that he was guilty, as expressed in the fact that the RFU asked him to prove his innocence.

Carling was ultimately exonerated and left their court without a stain on his character. Not quite; his public ordeal had had the desired effect. As Dudley Wood commented: 'There is a large body of people who are very jealous and protective of the amateur traditions. As a high-profile figure, Will is going to be a target of such people.' That large body of people is also known as the RFU executive committee.

CARLING
I've had three letters from RFU presidents. I had opened a leisure facility near Croydon, and somebody thought it was their responsibility to send a letter to Dudley [Wood]. Just for good measure, a copy was also forwarded to the *Daily Telegraph*. I was hauled in front of the RFU to explain what had happened to the money. I said the money had been given to charity. They said I had to bring documentation to that effect and a letter from the charity. Then I had to sign a letter explaining what had happened to the money – a solemn oath. The whole episode really annoyed me. I was guilty until I could prove my innocence. I thought the law of the land took a rather different view of an individual's

status. What a strange way to treat your national captain, or any of your players.

I have a regular charity that I give money to, a cancer hospital. But that's my business. No one has a right to know to whom and how much I donate. I was accused without proof. The payment, about £250, went to a third party. A lot of people actually resent the fact that there is a fee in the first place. They think the England rugby captain should turn up for nothing. But my time is limited and valuable. I am not a charity. Money was deducted for my expenses, and the rest went to the charity. Dudley very generously pointed out that, if the cheque had been paid directly to the charity and not to the individual, then I wouldn't have had to pay tax on it. I felt my personal world was being invaded. The charity was, and is, my business. There seemed to be very little in my life that was private at the time.

Chapter 15

Guilty Again . . .

It was a farce. I had already been dropped. But Graham Smith didn't have the guts to tell me. I'm sure there were a lot of smiling faces among the rugby establishment when that was announced.

WILL CARLING

Carling was finding that the rugby field was about his only place of refuge. Playing had never ceased to be a pleasure, but soon even that haven was to be denied him. Once again, Carling felt betrayed by those whom he expected to offer some semblance of protection and understanding.

England were popular favourites for the 1991 Five Nations championship. The team demanded more: Cooke, Carling and the senior players knew that only a Grand Slam would suffice. The World Cup was less than a year away; England, for all their promise and performances, had so far won nothing. If spring 1991 was another failure or 'nearly' season, Cooke would have no option but to experiment with new blood on the forthcoming Australian tour. That was the last thing he wanted. His players were not over the hill. But they needed some silverware to show off, imaginary or not.

The Barbarians' centenary celebrations had given England an early-season run-out at Twickenham the previous September. England won, but the appearance of blond Nottingham flanker Neil

Back as a replacement for Frenchman Janik on the Barbarians side was the highlight of the afternoon. Back had also been impressive as a late call-up when England beat Italy 33–15 in May 1990. Here he again confirmed his potential at the highest level. Cooke agreed: 'We are glad he's one of ours.'

England's next outing was against Argentina at the start of November. John Hall was recalled on the flank after three years, while John Olver's long wait on the replacements' bench was finally rewarded with the No. 2 shirt. Carling injured his ankle the week before, but was passed fit, and England won 51–0. As against Fiji the previous year, Hodgkinson and Underwood were among the points, tries and records. Like Fiji, too, the tourists were over-exuberant, and the referee again had to remove someone from the action. Ackford was knocked out by a belting right hook by Frederico Mendez, the tourists' 18-year-old prop. Touch judge Ken McCartney saw it perfectly, which is more than Ackford did: 'I did not see the punch until it was shown on TV,' said the England lock. Sendings-off always excite newspapers and Mendez's dismissal certainly put the *Observer* in a flap. There, lying unconscious on the Twickenham turf, was their star rugby columnist. The sports staff assumed that they would not be getting much sense out of Ackford after the match, and they made rapid contingency plans.

The recent relaxing of rugby's laws regarding rewards for communication had had Fleet Street clamouring for the views of Carling's men. Ackford, Andrew, Moore and Guscott, along with their captain, had all been quickly signed up. Ackford's incapacitation merely highlighted one of the dangers inherent in this for Sunday newspapers.

Mendez was suspended for four weeks, but the matter rumbled on. The Argentinian claimed provocation, and Jeff Probyn was subjected to trial by both video and a three-man RFU panel composed of Denis Easby, Peter Brook and Peter Johnson. There was an outcry that Probyn was being hounded. But Dudley Wood stressed: 'We feel we have an absolute right to take action over incidents which the referee does not see.' Unfortunately, despite this stance, the final verdict smacked of politics and compromise: 'Probyn has not committed an offence which merited further action. The slow-motion picture clearly shows that Probyn endeavoured to avoid the fallen Argentinian player by stepping over him. As it has demonstrated before, the RFU will not hesitate to take disciplinary action when the circumstances demand it. But it must register its concern about the risk of the wrong conclusions being drawn from televised pictures.'

Ever since Welshman Paul Ringer's trial by television before his Twickenham dismissal in 1980 and the referees having been granted the assistance of touch judges in spotting foul play, rugby players have had no excuse for not being on their best behaviour. England, traditionally, is the one country to have had the courage of its convictions over dirty play. Players sent off in club rugby have been ruled out of the national squad for the season, no matter how important they were; John Orwin and Steve Bainbridge both suffered in that way in the 1980s. Other countries paid mere lip-service to cleaning up the game, and England eventually got fed up of standing alone. Still, England's disciplinary record under Carling has been good. They are not saints. But often, especially against France, England's ability to keep their cool has contributed to victory.

Carling, though, was feeling uptight. The festive season brought little cheer. He even managed to get in hot water over football's own *enfant terrible*, Gazza. Carling had been answering questions during a debate on fair play in sport, with Prince Philip alongside him on the top table at a Central Council for Physical Recreation gathering in Bournemouth. Prince Philip is a past master at putting his foot in it, but he bowed to Carling's expertise this time.

The topic was Gascoigne's recent display in a match against Liverpool. 'I have not seen so petulant a performance as that from Gascoigne for a long time. There was obvious abuse of the referee. If that had happened in my sport, there would have been a lot of soul-searching and possibly disciplinary action. If Gascoigne is allowed to behave in such a manner, it is no wonder there is trouble on the terraces. The Football Association has got a lot to answer for.' Carling also described Ben Johnson's return to international athletics after a drugs ban as 'a disgrace'. But Gazza was the flavour of the month. Carling never expected national coverage for his comments but, in the middle of a bad press trot, he should have been more diplomatic. He would not make the same mistake today. The Gascoigne affair was a storm in a teacup, and the pair made it up a few weeks later. But it underlined the fact that England's captain had lost his magic touch for the time being.

After Carling was given the all-clear by Twickenham for the second time, he assumed his problems were now behind him. That was another error. December 1990 turned out to be a terrible month for

Carling, and it ended with press and TV stories that he was about to quit as England captain. Cooke and Uttley were worried: the loss of their World Cup captain would have been a serious blow at this stage. They offered Carling support. The pair were angry that Twickenham had played its part in undermining the captain's confidence and position.

The *Sunday Times*'s Stephen Jones summed up Carling's dilemma: 'What do you get the man who has everything at Christmas? I'll tell you. Carling needs help. He needs parcels of understanding. He is feeling increasingly frayed, and the last few weeks have accelerated the process. There is another side to the coin of success, and Carling has seen it all too clearly. Carling is perceived as the kind of man to whom things come effortlessly. Too true. He is currently drawing heavy criticism without moving a muscle. As England captain he has controversially banded the squad together under an agency. The die-hards on the RFU committee blame Carling for the whole business.'

The rot continued with a bad car crash. Then the ultimate humiliation: England's captain was dropped by the London Division after failing to attend a training session. Individually, perhaps, all these incidents were relatively minor and unconnected. Collectively, Carling was struggling to cope with a run of bad luck and bad judgement. The captaincy appeared to him to be at the heart of the problem. And, if so many people objected to the way he was behaving as England's rugby captain, perhaps he would be better off without it. His parents noticed that he was more thoughtful than usual, but they did not probe. If and when Carling wanted advice, he would ask.

Carling missed London's Divisional opener because of ankle trouble. The following week, when he was supposed to be returning to the capital for training, he was delayed in Glasgow by business matters. Carling did not feel like a lecture on his responsibilities as England captain, so he rang Rob Andrew to ask him to pass on his apologies to the London officials. Carling does not argue that that was an error.

CARLING
I heard very quickly that informing Rob was not the correct procedure. I was in trouble. Everyone involved in the London set-up was aware that I was going through a bad time. Graham Smith [the London chairman] rang. 'We can't make exceptions,'

he told me. He understood my position, but said it was going to be difficult to pick me after what had happened. It was a farce, really; I had already been dropped. Victory for the team over the individual. But Graham didn't have the guts to tell me. I was out, and I'm sure there were a lot of smiling faces among the rugby establishment when the news was announced.

I went down to Gloucester to watch London's match. Graham's wife, Anna, came over to me. 'Please come and speak to Graham. He feels awful about it.' I don't know what he had to feel bad about. I was trying to do the right thing, but I was making mistakes. No excuses. It seems that when you are England captain, you can't make mistakes. And I certainly made too many mistakes at this time.

I had written my car off the week before, coming back from Divisional training at about 10 o'clock. I just lost it. I wasn't used to the power of the car, and I went shooting off down the road backwards. It was terrifying. I wrote off two other cars as well. I wasn't so much frightened for myself, but it dawned on me that I could have killed somebody. One of the other cars had the passenger door caved in, and at the time I didn't know if there had been anyone sitting there. Fortunately, there wasn't. It frightened me to think I might have killed someone through no fault of theirs. It was the first time I had had an accident. I hope it's the last.

The police arrived. Just my luck: he was Welsh. 'Who's going to win at the Arms Park, then?' I couldn't believe it. I told him, 'At the present time, I don't give a damn.' I received nine penalty points and a maximum £400 fine. I should have answered his enquiry with, 'Wales – do you want two tickets?'

Chapter 16

In the Family Way

I was very disappointed. He's got a good brain. I felt he owed it for his own satisfaction to have done better at Durham. It was important. He was wasting a place for someone else. You try to achieve your potential. He does on the rugby field; why not in the classroom? Basically, William has a lazy streak.

PAM CARLING

Will Carling's problems were being played out in public. For such a private person, that increased his ordeal to unacceptable levels. His family and friends were ready to rally round although, as ever with Carling, they waited to be asked. Home has always been a safe haven for Carling since his England career began. Whenever he needs to get a grip on life, his family comes to the rescue.

That has been the case from the day he first crawled. As a child, Carling was oblivious to danger. He loved the sea and several times was pulled out gasping. Even when he was launched with a rubber ring, his mother was horrified to see a little pair of legs sticking out of the water. Carling was 4 when he toppled off the garage roof. A pile of leaves broke his fall. That luck, many contend, has stayed with him. Those accidents were not always his own work, however. His mother, Pam: 'I'll never forget closing his chubby hand in the car door. I was so shocked I couldn't open it. Someone else had to. We

held his hand under cold water, and he demanded his usual biscuit.'
The biscuit was the cure for all ills.

Brother Marcus had arrived 19 months earlier, and Pam was
relieved that the placid William did not arrive first. She was prepared
for the worst after Marcus's tantrums. The sporting gifts fell the right
way, too.

BILL CARLING

Marcus is Willie's No. 1 fan. I can't think he could cope any
better with younger brother's success. It would not have worked
the other way around. William was always the more natural with
a ball. He had a different outlook on life. Marcus was easy-
going, not so confident, not so determined. They were fairly
competitive as kids. Willie hated to lose. Even in family races,
he'd be desperate to beat his brother. At prep school, they
weren't enemies – or friends. Even at public school, they weren't
that close initially. But when they were no longer in the same
environment, they became great mates. Marcus used to visit
Willie at Sedbergh from Lancaster.

They're chalk and cheese in many ways. Marcus is a very
amusing guy, but doesn't see the future as clearly as William.
When Marcus got married to Katy at the end of 1991, William
was best man. In his speech, he mentioned that he was not only
losing a brother, but his best mate. I don't think that has
happened: they still speak a lot on the phone. Marcus is a
property manager in Bangkok, and Willie usually visits him
before Christmas.

MARCUS CARLING

I was two years above him at school. That was quite a difference.
Although I was fairly protective towards him as regards
outsiders, I suppose I gave him quite a tough time. I didn't set
him much of an example at school, either. I was the school rebel,
anti the system. Basically, I mucked about from 14 to 18, much
to my parents' disgust. It's something I regret very much. Since
Sedbergh, I've been pro the system. Joined the Army. There's
no middle line. I'm 100 per cent either way. My attitude, sadly,
meant I didn't get involved in sport at school.

The Carlings are openly affectionate towards each other: Will kisses his father in public shows of emotion without embarrassment. Although his parents' friendliness extends beyond the close confines of the Carling home, their famous son struggles outside of family and friends. That is strange because he has Pam's nature, yet she is very extrovert. *Today*'s Tony Roche: 'His mum is very outgoing; Bill is more sombre. Will has Pam's character, but he feels it doesn't go with the job of captain. Even when I first met him, I thought he was too guarded for a young man, too worried about rugby's new high profile. He didn't have a boyhood. Will was too serious, too young. Strong character, talented bloke – too sensitive.

'His folks have been very supportive, and that's been important. Bill is the strong, silent type; Pam is a bubbling character. She throws her head back and really laughs. I get the impression that Will would like to, but can't. Pam is warm and witty. Will looks like her, but doesn't reveal her traits. She talks, Bill gets on with things. It's a very close family. If there's anyone that Will listens to, it's his dad. And I think he's offered sensible advice at crucial times.'

Indeed, if Will Carling has a real hero, it's his dad. That's not difficult to understand. Everyone else's father drove cars; his dad flew helicopters. The glamour may have attracted him early on, but it is his father's steadying influence which makes him such a trusted adviser.

BILL CARLING
I suppose I was a pretty strict father. I had standards, and they got their bottoms smacked if they didn't stick to them. That lasted until early prep school. He's never caused us any great worries. If there was anything nasty, Willie would tell Pam, and she would tell me – but pick her moment. And when she calls him William, watch out, it's not good news. It's strange. We never call him Will. Will Carling means nothing to us. It's Willie.

He's a different guy when he's at home and relaxes. Willie is certainly a more complicated character now. He wasn't as a kid. There's lot of things he says and does that I don't agree with. If I feel strongly enough, then I have to have it out with him. Sometimes he should appreciate other people's feelings better. The two most important words around are 'thank you'. But that is me speaking as a father; I've never been in his position. I know how little time he has, I have some idea of the pressures. It's an alien world to the normal person – like sitting down with the

Queen. He doesn't sulk, but he can be moody. He's sensitive. It's easy to tell when he's having a bad day. He takes personal attacks to heart. Julie Burchill described him as 'the most mixed-up child'. I wrote her a letter, but got no reply.

I always had a deep-seated ambition for him. Since prep school, I've hoped he'd play for England and captain them. I would have liked him to captain the British Lions, but that's just a father's wishes for his son. I don't regard it as any sort of failure that he didn't, and I wouldn't have if he had not played for England. I've always called him a lucky boy. The ball has bounced his way. He was born with some talents, but similar players have not achieved half of what Willie has. He made his England debut because the two first-choice centres were injured. Those are the breaks you need.

The Carling family competitiveness is now good-natured, but it remains. Will – 'The Little Shit' – has failed on two counts. The first is serious: despite all efforts to grow, he is the only male in the Carling family under six foot. The others tell him there is still time. And then there is the Army. 'That is something he will always regret,' muses Marcus. 'He was particularly fascinated by the SAS. They were the tops, the best, the élite, the real professionals. Willie approved of that.' And every time the Carling family get round to military talk, Will is told to be quiet: 'You've not done this.' His dad does not believe the Army blundered, however. 'It would have been impossible for him to combine the Army with being captain of England. I thought the Army would have been more flexible. I didn't influence Willie one way or the other. He had to take his own decision. I didn't want him to lose his England place because of it. I think he would have been successful in the Army, but I always knew rugby would win if he had to choose. He was disappointed. He still regrets it. It was part of his life that he wanted to do. He hasn't. I've done it. So has Marcus. We talk about it and give him a hard time.'

Carling's parents have been close at hand throughout his reign as captain, and their Clapham Common home has offered frequent refuge. Bill retired from the Army in 1985; the Brewers' Guild in London has been his base since then. Pam has returned to work as an interior designer. She had a second problem with breast cancer three years ago, and Carling lunched with his mum every day in hospital. 'It was very serious at the time. I'm just very glad she's still around.'

Carling has continued to support that charity ever since.

The Carlings are familiar faces on the rugby circuit these days. Pam is careful to offer support without overstaying her welcome. 'We're not groupies. We don't hang around. We let Willie know we are there, and that's it. You can't just appear when the team wins, either.' Her worst moment came after that 1990 Grand Slam defeat. Ironically, the Carlings had lunched with David Sole's parents before the match, and they have kept in touch. Afterwards, with Pam choked, they offered commiserations to their son before departing.

While Bill had rugby ambitions for his son, Pam was angry that Will did not do himself justice academically. Bill concedes: 'It's a rare point of family disagreement. I was happy he got a degree at Durham. I'm sure he could have done better if he had concentrated on his work, but it was not a conflict for me.' Pam had other ideas. 'I was very disappointed. He's got a good brain. I felt he owed it for his own satisfaction to have done better at Durham. It was important. He was wasting a place for someone else. You try to achieve your potential. He does on the rugby field; why not in the classroom? Basically, William has a lazy streak. He only had three lectures a week. If William had been sensible, then he would have achieved more. To be fair, though, he was like a ghost in the last two years. He was absolutely wiped out travelling back and forward between Durham and London.'

Bill was closest to his son during his problems in the second half of 1990. 'He certainly reached a crisis point with the England captaincy during this period. All along I believed he was prepared to weather the storm, but the problems showed no signs of abating. Still, he never said to me that he was going to give up the captaincy. Willie was finding himself. After losing that big game at Murrayfield, he was appreciating how cruel the media could be. Every move he made for a spell was a bad one, though he was slightly naïve. Willie was quite depressed about it, and his game suffered. He just cuts himself off; that's his way of protecting himself. Then he's accused of being arrogant. Willie learnt a lot in that period. He's not the type who asks directly for advice. He takes what he wants. I know that all he wants is somewhere to come back to and relax, and he's not going to relax if we keep asking him, "What's the problem?"'

His friends know, too, that when he wants advice, Will Carling will ask for it. Carling shares his Clapham Junction house with Alex Hambly, who also went to Sedbergh and Durham. Will Fawcett and

Andrew Harle are his other close friends. Carling has helped set up a dining club, Flounders, consisting of 20 school and university mates. 'It's a chance to wear silly clothes and behave badly,' explains Fawcett. 'The whole humour of Durham is sarcasm, piss-take. That certainly appeals to Will. When he first left Durham, I didn't see much of him. Then he caught up with the people he wanted to know. He knows his friends from Sedbergh and Durham are loyal and will stand by him. Nobody's going to fawn over him – just take the mick. Will's quite reserved. He enjoys a wild night out, although he will never be the first to do something outrageous. Will is not one to share his problems. Those are kept to himself. If he wants help, Will knows he will get it. There's a very strong bond between us.'

Carling has needed that solid support. There have been times when even family and friends have not been able to help. But without the family, especially, it is very doubtful whether Carling would have lasted the captaincy course.

Chapter 17

Cardiff Catastrophe – Part II

I wasn't thinking rationally. It was a very emotional time. England had just won in Cardiff for the first time in 28 years. It was an obvious blunder. The hotheads saw it as a chance to do a hatchet job on me.

GEOFF COOKE

England's visits to Cardiff have the merit of concentrating the rugby mind. Defeat there in January 1991 would have ended England's Five Nations season before it had begun – and signalled the break-up of the side. Geoff Cooke decided some change was needed. Instead of preparing in the relaxed atmosphere of Chepstow, as was customary, England were moved into the centre of Cardiff to get the real flavour of Welsh rugby.

It worked. After 28 years of frustration and Welsh supremacy in the Principality, England laid the bogey. Mike Teague, whose injury in the opening seconds of the 1989 match had so badly disrupted England's plan, scored the try, and Hodgkinson kicked seven goals with persistent precision. Carling kept the pressure on throughout, and the 25–6 scoreline reflected England's domination. It was a no-nonsense, no-frills, few-thrills performance. But, as the long-suffering England supporters left the ground to take over Cardiff for the first time in over a quarter of a century, Carling and Cooke were about to make the biggest blunder of their sporting careers. Had the

World Cup not been around the corner, one – if not both – would certainly have lost his job.

How England managed to turn a day of triumph into a chaotic disaster and the worst public relations exercise in rugby history is still bewildering and remarkable. Even more remarkable is that Carling and Cooke, two men steeped in the business of communication, did not appreciate the furore that would follow them turning their backs on the media on this most memorable of rugby days. Carling could perhaps be excused for not thinking straight after the experiences of the previous months; but Cooke knew better. Handling the public face of the England rugby team was one of Cooke's attributes, one of the reasons why he had been given the job in the first place. England could not have come away from Wales with a worse press if they had lost by 50 points, had five players sent off and blown up the Severn Bridge. Even now, though, Carling wonders what all the fuss was about. To the players, it was no big deal.

In one fell swoop, the England players and management provided the Twickenham die-hards with all the ammunition they ever needed to spread poison about players' motives and the evils of money in the amateur game. A company, Player Vision – such an ironic name – had been set up by the squad, and had then signed with the Willises, former England cricket captain Bob and his brother David, to promote the England rugby team. 'They came to me,' admits Carling. 'I liked what I heard, so I got them to meet Brian Moore. There was no doubt that we needed some help, someone who knew their way around the commercial world. Then the RFU's marketing man Michael Coley got involved. I sat in on that meeting, and it went well. What they were planning seemed feasible. But, apparently, when Coley reported back to Dudley [Wood], he went up the wall. We were doing our best to co-operate with the union and keep within the regulations, but to no avail.'

Bob Willis, like everyone else who has worked on the players' behalf, had a major problem: what were the players allowed to do and not do under the International Rugby Football Board's relaxed, but nonetheless confused, amateur regulations? While that remained unclear, selling England was almost impossible. There was another problem, in that Bob Willis's world had been the professional one of cricket. Rugby Union may not look a lot different in its structure, other than the absence of payment. But it moves slowly – too slowly for Willis. Even the cricket world had tried his patience: he quit

Warwickshire in frustration after a short spell on the committee there. He was not to last long in rugby, either.

'No way did we tell the squad not to talk to the media. I regard it as unfortunate that they didn't attend the press conference after the Wales match. It was not a positive thing for the players to get the press offside.' Willis had made a request for a £5,000 fee for exclusive, non-match press interviews during the season. 'I took this idea to the RFU's Peter Yarranton at the end of the previous week. His response was that, apart from the post-match press conference and any live reaction to games, he felt the other interviews were certainly fair game for the squad. That was related to the RFU, but Dudley Wood said that, until he was told differently, the situation would remain the same as in the past. We thought that after 4 December, when we had a meeting with the RFU, things would be sorted out quickly. Unfortunately, the guidelines we all needed had not been forthcoming. That proved very frustrating. The players undoubtedly lost much business because those guidelines had not been set.'

The BBC said at the time: 'We were approached at the beginning of last week and asked to make payments for interviews with England players. The approach was made by the Willis brothers. We sought clarification from the RFU and were advised that, once the players had assembled as an England squad, they would not receive money for interviews.' The BBC's normal policy was to send a small fee for interviews to a player's club or charity.

COOKE
The players had decided not to give interviews to the BBC. That was their choice. But I can assure you that had nothing to do with our decision not to go to the after-match press conference. It was not a dramatic gesture. If I had thought about it rationally, it wouldn't have happened. But I wasn't thinking rationally. It was a very emotional time. England had just won in Cardiff for the first time in 28 years. Jonathan Pryce, the Welsh Rugby Union's marketing executive, came into the dressing-room and said the press were ready. I replied: 'Give us a little more time.' The feeling was that we weren't being allowed any time. The players felt that the media were making increasingly unreasonable demands, and it was becoming unbearable. Then it just happened. We decided not to go.

It was an obvious blunder, and I could understand the press being upset. But it was the RFU's attitude which really discouraged me. I got no pleasure from the whole incident, but it was a small matter. But some of those at Twickenham took it into their heads that it was a slight against amateurism – a personal affront against them. I had no doubt that my position was under threat. The hotheads saw it as a chance to do a hatchet job. Fortunately, there are a lot of good people at the RFU, and the moderate thinkers won the day rather than the hotheads who wanted me out.

It was a close-run thing. England's World Cup ambitions were saved from an unlikely source: RFU president Michael Pearey. 'Albert Agar, Peter Yarranton, John Burgess and Dudley Wood, the inner circle of Twickenham, got together,' explains the *London Evening Standard*'s Chris Jones. 'They wanted Cooke's head. And if they couldn't get him out, then they would make life so uncomfortable that he would resign. That nearly happened, too: I understand Cooke's wife had to persuade him to attend the Scotland dinner following the next match after all the back-stabbing. Pearey, like most presidents, had been perceived as Dudley Wood's glove puppet, but he stood firm. It was World Cup year. Cooke gave assurances that it would never happen again, so the matter was closed. Actually, the file is still open at Twickenham, and they will action it at the first chance they get.'

Wood's words at the time confirmed much of that. 'I simply do not know what is behind it all. It's part of our responsibility to give interviews and answer questions after the game. What they did was discourteous. Geoff [Cooke] is very deeply involved with the players and their aspirations. That is his style. Whether it is good or bad, I wouldn't care to say. But if you look at his results, you might think it was reasonably successful.' Another official source claimed: 'We can easily find another 15 players to play Scotland if it proves necessary.'

Twickenham's influence spreads wide: Cardiff cost Cooke an OBE in the next New Year's Honours List, after the 1991 World Cup. England's captain received one, but Cooke had to wait until the following year. The team manager remained philosophical. He has learnt not to get upset or distracted by such pettiness.

Cooke and Uttley were called to Twickenham to explain their

actions in front of Dudley Wood and Sandy Sanders. Cooke denied that the idea to avoid the press conference had been pre-planned. For his part, Uttley had been aware of the players' stance over the BBC interviews.

UTTLEY
I remember ringing home and telling my wife Christine that I was unhappy with what was going on. In simple language, it was player-power. And it was Will-led. I know the players were unhappy, and I had a lot of sympathy for them. But it really brassed me off. All the extra-curricular activities distracted us from what we should be doing. I have to admit to feeling slightly blinkered; I was still suffering the after-effects of my experiences with Will in Argentina. But I wasn't brave enough in Cardiff. Not turning up at the press conference seemed like a good idea at the time, although I'd been around long enough to know better. When we left the hotel by the back door to get to the dinner, I thought we were taking a short cut. I didn't realise the press were hunting us down.

It showed the management's lack of experience in dealing with a difficult decision. The RFU wanted some straight answers: I don't know that they got them. Being hauled up like that told us how serious it was. Cookie was warned in no uncertain terms that any repeat would mark the end of his England career. Our participation in the events took the heat off the players and Will. We were the guilty culprits.

To be fair to Will, he'd been through a lot since Murrayfield in 1990. He needed help. While it was obvious that he didn't want it from me, it was also obvious that he wasn't going to get it from sources within rugby. I found that sad.

Cardiff apart, Cookie and I were happy that things were moving in the right direction. Yet our efforts were being undermined by Twickenham's suspicions about the captain and the players. They were disturbing and distracting. My time with the team is very limited: I need the players to be concentrating solely on their rugby, not worrying about whether they can cash in on playing for England. If they were honest, they'd probably admit that one of the reasons we had lost in Scotland was that their minds were not completely tuned in. The squad was being asked to commit themselves to England's cause in a way no others had been. But all Twickenham could see were pound-signs and the players destroying Rugby Union. Unfortunately, Cardiff was grist to their mill. The management and the players had got it wrong, and we were going to have to pay.

Colin Herridge, chairman of Harlequins, is not only a close friend of Carling's, but a member of the RFU committee. Herridge has earned a reputation as one of the game's best officials, not only because he enjoys a good relationship with the players; he was once taken aside by one of the Twickenham 'mafia' and told, 'If you want to get on in the RFU, you had better stop being so friendly with the players.' Herridge was a popular choice as England's liaison officer during the World Cup, and is about the only committeeman whom Carling trusts. 'Cardiff was handled badly by everyone – Will, Cookie and the RFU. Will became very defensive during that period. The RFU had been supplied with information that Will had breached the amateur regulations and felt the need to investigate it. It gave the hawks a chance to spread their wings. Nobody benefited, and it left a sour taste. Will felt that the England rugby captain deserved better. I have to agree. It swayed his attitude towards officialdom, and it's remained an unofficial cold war ever since.

'Looking back, Will's captaincy went through a crisis period from March 1990 to January 1991. His captaincy on and off the field was questioned, he was interrogated over his presence in advertisements and articles, the players wanted to set up their own organisation, he had the car crash, then was dropped by London, and finally there was that deafening silence at Cardiff. It's a miracle he survived. Those months certainly shaped his future attitude towards officials and the press.'

CARLING
It was a tough time. I felt picked upon. I don't care how strong you are, everybody needs help. The family were very supportive, but others I thought would help in rugby were not, and I've not forgotten that. The outside pressures can be very wearying. I really got fed up with the business concerning amateur regulations. I didn't know where the next accusation was coming from. I felt under pressure as well at the start of 1993, but for other reasons. That was because my expectations were so high that they were impossible to live up to – the strain came from

within. But late 1990, early 1991 was different. My every action was under the microscope in all areas of the captaincy. The stress came from outside.

If I have a weakness, it's insecurity. It's true. At school, I was concerned about doing the right thing, the right way. My friends know. They see the doubt. I'm not going to show it to anyone else, though. I love being England captain, but there are times when you are on your own. Have I done the right thing? It was plainly clear that I hadn't at this time. I can't even share those doubts with the team. They must be kept private. It wouldn't do the team any good if I was continually asking, 'Am I doing the right thing?' 'Sure, yes, Will, you carry on.' That's not what I'm there for. I can't seek that security from the team. I've got to make my own decisions and stand by the team, but that doesn't mean I don't worry about them. I don't think I ever seriously considered giving up the captaincy. It meant too much to me. It still does. But looking at all the pressures that were building up then, it wouldn't have taken much to push me over the edge.

Cooke was impressed with the way his choice pulled himself back. 'I tried to give him support, but I wouldn't be arrogant enough to say that I was a close confidant. I think what was crucial was the private support Will got at the time. People have always made more of our relationship than there is. It is not possible to get that close – or healthy. We spend so much time apart, although we talk a lot on the phone. I don't know how close he was to chucking it in. He certainly didn't confide in me, and I think you would have to go closer to home to find that out. It was after this that Will really started to blossom as a leader.'

Carling also spent a lot of time on the phone to Rob Andrew.

ANDREW
After Murrayfield, the heat was really turned on. Everyone was analysing Will, and he didn't like it. His play, his captaincy, his lifestyle – an enormous amount of press coverage, lots of it bad. No other British rugby player has had to cope with that. I feel deep down that he is the same bloke as the young student I met in 1986. But he has had to shape his behaviour around being England captain. As the seasons pass, those who knew him in those early days are fewer and fewer in the squad. He's always

been a quiet bloke, but Will's definitely more suspicious and wary now. That's inevitable after all he's been through. When things aren't going well, Will tends to go into his shell, go quiet on people.

His worst period was Murrayfield '90 to Cardiff '91. I spoke to him a lot then. I felt he needed to talk. It really got him down, and that's when you need people close to you saying, 'Chin up. Get on with it. Basically, stuff the rest of the world.' That might sound trite, but when you feel the world is conspiring against you, that's what is required. After losing the Grand Slam, the wheel of fortune – which, to be fair, had been rolling his way for a long time – turned with a vengeance. For the first time, the press had Will Carling's head on the block.

You can't ignore it. I don't care how confident you are. It gets to you. And you take it personally. I should know. You can't hide, especially with Will's profile. I don't think Will got a lot of support during his bad time. Although we are the England team, we are not together much – really only on tour, and for the few days before an international. The phone was often our only point of contact.

I also think Will had had enough of being the front man in the players' fight over the amateur regulations. He wasn't the one leading the charge; neither was I or Brian Moore. It's an issue every player in the squad is committed to and involved in. But Will took the flak from the RFU and the press, because he was the spokesman. And he was the spokesman because he was the captain. Then Brian came forward and others have been involved. I don't believe Will has taken a back seat over the issue.

Chapter 18

Media Attention

I have never given the press what they want, and I'm not sure that I want to. I can't trust them. I know at some point they will criticise me, probably quite rightly, and that will hurt me. And I will have to push them away again.

WILL CARLING

Carling's relations with the media have never really recovered from the Cardiff débâcle. It remains his biggest weakness as captain. He is the first England rugby captain not to be readily available outside press conferences. Carling's exclusive contract with a Sunday newspaper is a convenient excuse for not talking. That has caused resentment, not all based on professional jealousy, either. Carling's comments in the *Daily Express* and, currently, the *Mail on Sunday* have rarely been earth-shattering. But the *Mail on Sunday* see Carling's exclusive tag as a status symbol and enjoy watching their competitors scrabbling round for scraps. The rugby press, though, are a very powerful bunch and, like the cricket writers, they have a reasonable understanding of what happens both in front of them and behind closed doors. Those writing for the broadsheets – *Times*, *Telegraph*, *Independent*, *Guardian*, *Observer* – are ignored at your peril.

Rob Andrew's relationship with the media has been exceptional.

Known as 'Golden Bollocks' to one and all, Andrew has taken some terrible stick: even when performing well, England's most-capped fly-half cannot escape reading that Stuart Barnes would have done it better. Andrew was always a favourite of Cooke's. Peter Williams was England's fly-half when Cooke was appointed; thereafter, he never played for his country again and soon made his way to Rugby League. Williams was often described as a well-balanced player: a chip on either shoulder. He believed he was the best fly-half in England. Nothing wrong with that, and he was probably right when Cooke took over. But Williams predicted, correctly, that Andrew was Cooke's preferred choice in the No. 10 shirt. That left Barnes in the cold, too. All throughout Andrew's 50-plus caps, some influential parts of the press have continued to batter him over the head with the Bath fly-half.

Yet Rob Andrew is the same pleasant, unaffected lad who made such an impression at Cambridge University in the early 1980s. If anyone has a reason to feel bitter at the press, it's Andrew. But he has continued to smile through most of the abuse and kept his cool with rare distinction. Former British Lions fly-half David Watkins claimed that Andrew doesn't have the charisma, confidence or ability to be a top-class fly-half. Former England captain John Scott was more brutal when he described Andrew as the worst fly-half to play for England. Andrew admits the personal attacks have been painful. He has realised that he will never convince those who believe Barnes to be the better player, and he's got his own back by remaining charming, co-operative and accommodating.

Carling has none of those qualities when dealing with the press. He has neither the patience nor the tolerance. Strangely, the bad notices are the only ones he reads; the 'Darling Carling' stuff is dismissed as hype. But when the same section put the boot in, Carling feels the pain and wants to lash back. Stephen Jones, of the *Sunday Times*, has often been critical of Carling the leader, but he maintains a healthy respect for the England captain which is reciprocated.

STEPHEN JONES

When I took 13 guesses to get Will as the new captain, it showed what a bold choice he was. It could have gone wrong. To many, Guscott and Halliday would have been the best pairing if you were picking a team to play for your life. Halliday has always been a great hero of mine. I don't believe Will was a great player until his third season as captain. For me, the gamble over Will was in the balance for a long time. He's certainly not the mystical leader that mythology promotes. I class him as a good captain and a great player. But he has not turned a good team into a great one. His contribution as a player has been high, but no higher than Dooley, Ackford or Winterbottom. They have been the influential ones.

I believe he missed out on his rugby adolescence. He went from the infant to the grandfather of the side, and that comes through in slightly childish ways. Nobody wished ill on him, but there was a strong feeling during the 1993 championship particularly that it would do him the power of good not to be captain of the British Lions. I feel he's slightly removed from the team. He wants to be alone. That's the way he comes across. That affects him, the team, the press and the RFU. You've got to be careful when you cut yourself off in a team sport.

I'm a great Roger Uttley fan. There was a time when Carling and Cooke needed his credibility. A coach doesn't have to be the new Carwyn James. Motivation and bringing a side together – that is as much a part of coaching. You need someone in an amateur game whom you have to face in the dressing-room. Someone you don't want to let down. A Brian Thomas at Neath, or Jack Rowell at Bath, or Roger. Roger was treated badly all round. Finlay Calder didn't even mention him in his Lions report after the 1989 tour. Finlay went vertically down in my estimation after that; he was, after all, not one of the great Lions captains. Maybe England thought they had gone as far as they could with Roger. For me, Roger was the bridge by which Carling and Cooke crossed from inexperience to experience.

Cardiff 1991 is still a mystery to me. As a journalist who has learnt absolutely nothing from 17 years of press conferences, I've never been worried whether they take place or not. I'm not sure the players knew why they did it. It didn't become Cooke or Carling, but it was a storm in a teacup. But the RFU made such a fuss. Cooke should just have been told, 'Don't be silly.' It was obvious it wasn't going to happen again: Cooke has been wonderful for the press, while Will has discharged his obligations. It was a total fiasco. No one emerged with credit. The players made a big demonstration, but the reasons were never clear. You don't march up Whitehall without people knowing what you're saying.

I'm totally on the side of the players. The RFU keep asking the players to do more, and they drove the players into that corner. Fitness standards are set and, if they're not reached, players are ruthlessly chopped. Their amateurism is held against them. The RFU take great pleasure in denying the players. That's why they've lost the squad's respect.

The increasing demands on the players have not been the sole preserve of the RFU, however. Media requirements have grown, some for reward, but generally for nothing other than the good name of rugby and the player's image. That has always been the rugby way, and even today's international player gives freely of his time. But England had arrived in Cardiff complaining of excessive and intrusive media attention, and one name cropped up regularly: Peter Jackson of the *Daily Mail*.

Jackson is a crackerjack reporter. After spending most of his working life in Wales, he had recently taken over the rugby correspondent's job from Terry O'Connor. Jackson does not let a story go and the players were not used to such persistence. If they really felt enough was enough, though, the players should have had it out with Jackson, instead of moaning among themselves. But they attempted to get other journalists to interfere, although Rule 3 of the Rugby Union Writers' Club constitution states: 'The Club will in no way endeavour to dictate policy or influence opinion of rugby writing nor shall it have any concern with the policy of newspapers or their relations with employees.'

If the players were honest, however, Jackson was not the real problem. The squad had not been happy with the media coverage since Murrayfield, and the new amateur regulations meant that the players were now less willing to give it away for nothing. The Prisma meeting 18 months earlier had filled their heads with nonsense about what they were worth. Figures between £500 and £1,000 for everyday feature articles were promoted. That was rubbish: those entrusted with selling the players had no idea of the media world and the going rates. Anyway, the recession was digging deep, and cash in hand had long disappeared. The Inland Revenue was on to the earning potential of sports stars, and they were not interested in amateur status – just in tax evasion.

The rugby press have always been fairly generous in sharing their expenses with the players. Taking a player for dinner or buying him some drinks was fair exchange for his time and trouble. But notebooks had begun to be brought out of pockets more regularly than drinking vouchers in club environments. Journalists were seen to be working all the time, even at the bar in the wee small hours and that was an unwelcome change. Players, press, referees and administrators have always enjoyed a frank exchange of views late at night. It is the traditional way of ending disputes, of making amends, of rebuilding bridges or taking your punishment like a man. Now the style was more 'hit-and-run', and the players didn't like it. They were being treated like professional sportsmen. Still, several were taking pieces of silver from the media moguls, and that irony was not lost on the journalists.

Chris Jones, who had warned Carling about attacking the press in Ireland in 1989, met up with the England players the day after Cardiff, as they were watching the B international at Gloucester. 'Will, Paul Rendall and Mike Teague were there. "Let's buy you a drink," they said. "There's nothing to worry about." The players seemed genuinely mystified by the storm. Will told me the reason was because of the tremendous demands being put upon them by the press.

'The Saturday night had been like something out of the Keystone Cops. We got hold of [Peter] Yarranton and asked where were the team manager and coach. Players were slipping away back to the hotel out of a back door. It did Carling countless damage, far worse than Murrayfield. It almost cost him the captaincy. Cardiff was the first sign of something that has appeared regularly since: "The press don't deserve us." Carling's voice was the loudest. Cooke argued with him. I regard it as Will's first serious mistake.'

Today's Tony Roche had been Carling's first regular contact in the media. Carling had got in touch with him during the summer of 1990; *Today* was the paper his mum read, and Roche had always been friendly. There is no side to Roche. In the wake of the Murrayfield disaster of that year, Carling had wanted a newspaper platform; that way he could put across his views without sensational headlines. It was a feather in Roche's cap, and the two worked together up until the 1991 World Cup final. By then, Carling had become involved with Jon Holmes of Park Associates, the best in the business, the man who has taken Gary Lineker from Leicester to

135

Everton, Barcelona, Spurs and Japan with a minimum of fuss and a maximum of reward. Holmes had acquainted his new client with the facts of life about how lucrative a Will Carling column would be.

ROCHE

We only had a gentleman's agreement, and nobody could have complained if he had gone off. *Today* didn't have the dough to compete. But Will told Jon that he'd made a promise and was going to stick by it. I found him very reliable, very straight. We did first-person pieces before internationals, and he would never criticise other players. I rang him when he first got picked for England, and he didn't know how to talk about himself. Very little was known about Will then, and I think that's still the case. He's a bit like an iceberg, with most of him hidden below the surface. After a few months, he realised that I was someone he could talk to in the press who didn't always have a pen and notebook out. He was trying to find out how the press viewed him.

I thought he handled Murrayfield brilliantly. His folks were close to tears. The stiff upper lip stood him in good stead that day. Cardiff was a different matter altogether. It had been brewing for ages; you could feel the tension, and not just because England hadn't won there since 1963. I was in the office 48 hours after their pre-planned block on the press when Will rang – 'You're speaking to me again.' Then I told him what a cock-up the whole affair had been. He asked me if I would go down to the Harlequins that night as he, Rob [Andrew] and Brian [Moore] wanted to meet some journalists to discuss the matter. I told him not to be selective, as that would only make matters worse. But he was adamant that that was the way it had to be. I said I wasn't going and I would not ring anyone.

They were going to invite Terry Cooper of the Press Association, John Mason of the *Daily Telegraph*, and David Hands of *The Times*. There would be no *Mirror*, *Sun* or *Mail*. That told me what they thought of certain journalists, especially 'Make-them, sell-them, retire-them' Jackson. Moore described him as a Rottweiler because he was so difficult to shake off – which is ironic because Brian himself is known as 'Pit Bull'. The players felt he was obsessed with players turning professional. John Olver once asked him, 'If you like Rugby League so much, why don't you go and cover it?' But how Jackson does his job is his own business. I told Will it's the ones you're having trouble with that you should be talking to, and certainly not planning meetings behind their backs. They got it desperately wrong in Cardiff and never got their message across. It was a stance against the press, the RFU, arguments about money. I rate it the biggest blunder of his career.

CARLING
I've never given the press what they want, and I'm not sure that I want to. It's my weakest area. There are certain rules with the press which nobody tells you. You have to learn them the hard way. I like to believe I'm honest with them. I'm not a manipulator. David Campese plays games with them and fools around, but I can't do that. I find press conferences very hard work. I'm not natural. If I was, the press might think they were getting close to me. I wouldn't want that because implicit in that relationship would be trust, and I can't trust them. I know at some point they will criticise me, probably quite rightly, and that will hurt me. And I will have to push them away again. I accept criticism, but it still hurts. I know when I've played badly. I'm quite sensitive in that respect.

I should work harder at playing their game – maybe that's the next stage. England are usually in a no-win situation, but it's our style not to complain. If we had a go at another country or player, it would cause chaos. So we play it straight down the middle, and that's precisely what the media don't want. They want some reaction, some emotion, something to get their teeth into. They don't like me being flippant, either. They don't understand that I don't take myself too seriously. You have to treat the press differently.

I don't mark people for the paper they write for. Some are very knowledgeable, others are good at giving the reader a visual image though, occasionally, I think that the guy must have been at a different game. I do have more time for certain journalists. But, as with players, I've got to be careful about showing it. That wouldn't go down well.

I got it wrong in Cardiff, but I still believe our cause was just. All we managed to do was alienate people, though no national squad has been as co-operative as us. The lads just wanted to put

137

that awful Cardiff record to the sword, but we feared the after-match circus. Many of us were aware that whatever we said could be interpreted in any number of ways. I accept that things did get on top of us. We certainly did not intend our decision to lead to such a backlash. It had nothing to do with finance: all we wanted was for guidelines to be established. Nearly three years on, I'm not sure we are much further up that path.

Chapter 19

Winners at Last

I seriously wonder how long I will continue to play because of the pressures. I realise that, at the age of 25, it is an amazing thing to say, but it may be I have only another year left in me. Everything that is happening around the sport is burning people out.

WILL CARLING

After Cardiff, the Grand Slam became even more of a necessity for Carling. It was not only the media who were upset by England's behaviour. The Gulf War had begun the day before the Wales international; however justifiable the players believed their stance to be, this was not the time to be seen squabbling about money, press harassment or whatever. Rory Underwood knew that better than most: a few days later, the country was shocked by video pictures of Lt John Peters and the treatment he had received at the hands of his Iraqi captors. Underwood and Peters had trained together in the RAF, and Underwood was later to dedicate his Triple Crown try in Dublin to his colleague.

As in 1990, England had a month's break before encountering the Scots. Carling thought it wisest not to try to hide from the memory of Murrayfield. Better to remind his team of the pain and humiliation. He rounded up press cuttings from the previous March, and the players were made to read and inwardly digest. 'It wasn't pleasant

139

reading, but it reminded us how much it meant,' was Carling's view. Meanwhile, the skirmishes with the RFU continued. The union signed a second £1 million agreement with Save & Prosper. Then the company organised buses to take supporters from Richmond Station to the ground for the Calcutta Cup. They found the team less than willing to participate in the publicity arrangements, however. Save & Prosper had been caught in the crossfire again. At their pre-championship dinner the absence of the England players was due to the sponsors' refusal to pay a fee. Again, the players had been badly advised: major sponsors cannot be treated like that. Fortunately, Save & Prosper took a long-term view, sensibly assessing that this was not their war; the players' behaviour, however outrageous, was not really directed at them.

The weather, too, was conspiring against England. Frozen conditions curtailed both preparations and match practice, and the squad trained on an artificial surface in the days before the match. Comic Relief's plan to put red noses on the red faces of the England squad nearly backfired. Cooke originally wanted no photographs, but eventually relented. The strain from Cardiff was showing. 'We want to help the charity, but we don't want to look like a bunch of clowns before a big match. It will make us look like idiots if we lose the game, and we'll be crucified.' The players helped persuade Cooke that the adverse publicity of not doing the pictures might provoke a repeat of Cardiff.

The bad weather and lack of match practice could have been a recipe for disaster, but Cooke and Uttley kept their team's attention focused on the Grand Slam and the World Cup. For, without the former, the players could forget about conquering the world in nine months' time. England made no mistakes against Scotland this time. The pack squeezed the life out of the visitors, and Andrew's tactical and Hodgkinson's goal-kicking boots did the rest in England's 21–12 victory. The game's one try came from Heslop after full-back Hodgkinson had come into the line. Carling's victory verdict – 'I think we demonstrated today what it is we most want to do' – was designed to answer the growing criticism.

For Carling and his team were now under fire for winning. For winning efficiently. But this time the press had got it wrong. England were being castigated for throwing away the glorious adventure of their play in the previous championship, while the team were merely ensuring that there were no slip-ups this time. The measure of their determination was obvious and necessary a fortnight later in Dublin as the wind, the rain and the Irish conspired in an attempt to deny them the Triple Crown. England were a point behind with seven minutes remaining, when late tries from Underwood and Teague won the day 16–7. The pack, with Dean Richards again outstanding, finished strongly. It was a mature performance, the sort of tight game England have often lost in the chaos of Lansdowne Road, despite their forward supremacy.

The display certainly impressed Scotland's coach Ian McGeechan. 'England can play any game they want. That's as good an England team as I've seen. They have decided on a no-frills game because they don't want to let any other side into the game.' But the sniping continued: England were not being true to themselves. Carling was perplexed and annoyed.

CARLING

The press adopted a negative attitude towards England's style. It's still around today. Once they got the idea in their heads that we weren't playing expansive rugby, that was it. It is difficult to shake off those labels. Take the Aussies: people have the romantic view that they run the ball all the time. They don't. The 1971 British Lions are regarded as having one of the greatest back-lines of all time – Gareth Edwards, Barry John, John Dawes, Mike Gibson, Gerald Davies, David Duckham and J. P. R. Williams – and so they did. But watch the Test matches. The ball hardly went past Barry John. The myth with England is that we don't play 15-man rugby, but I think we have played as much as anyone. The Aussies kick for position, then they run. That's the reality. It is not the romantic notion of running the ball from anywhere – there's an awful lot of kicking. The Aussies play very disciplined rugby. And quite rightly. But the image has grown up that they are the great entertainers.

France had demolished Wales 36–3 in Paris on the same day that England won their first Triple Crown since 1980. Another Grand Slam finale beckoned. And this time England had the home advantage, although France had only lost once at Twickenham since 1979. England selected an unchanged side, the first time the same XV had gone through the championship for 31 years, and only the second time ever. Rory Underwood lined up for his 43rd cap, equalling Tony Neary's England record.

141

England should have won by a mile. Yet France outscored them by three tries to one, and the home crowd has rarely endured such a nerve-racking final quarter. If England needed reminding of what French flair and imagination could conjure up, Serge Blanco's backs gave them a magical practical demonstration early on. When Berbizier gathered Hodgkinson's failed penalty attempt behind his own line in the first half, a try at the other end seems as likely as when the Barbarians' Phil Bennett began to side-step his way out of trouble against the 1972–73 All Blacks. Blanco saw the possibilities; Lafond, Cambérabero, Sella, and Cambérabero again all caught the mood. The French fly-half chipped ahead up the right touchline, regathered and cross-kicked towards the posts where Saint-André, if anything, let the ball bounce once too often. But the French fortune held, and the winger was through to score under the posts. England were scattered all over the pitch in disbelief. There were elements of luck in the try, but it was not a lucky score – it was breath-taking. Some rate it the finest try ever seen in international rugby.

The England team of a year earlier might have cracked, panicked or recklessly caught the French mood. Not this bunch. They went on their way relentlessly, as they had done all championship, although Underwood's try did not suffer in comparison with the three French scores. France were always too close for comfort. Blanco's team refused to concede defeat, and England's nerves prevented them from finishing off the job. A late penalty miss by Hodgkinson while leading 21–19 ensured a captive audience to the very finish, when Welsh referee Les Peard, who had kept a tight and considered grip on proceedings, signalled England's first Grand Slam for 11 years. Carling's team were winners at last, and how Twickenham celebrated. A year to the day since the worst rugby experience of his life, Carling was carried shoulder-high from the field. Two fans slipped away with his boots, souvenirs of a memorable day.

UTTLEY

That French try could have been our death-knell. But after that we gave Blanco no room to operate. There was a great sense of relief after all the frustration of doing so much and coming so near. We were all under a lot of pressure. We were into our fourth season and hadn't won anything of merit. I hadn't expected us to take so long.

* * *

CARLING

I remember going up to Durham after the Grand Slam to see a
mate. I wandered down to the university ground. It didn't seem
so long ago that I was just a young student trying to make my way
in the rugby world. I thought about what had happened over the
past year: all my problems, good times and bad. There just
seemed so much pressure. For a few minutes, I thought I'd love
to go back to being unknown and just playing rugby purely for
the fun of it, without all the off-the-field demands. Was I still
playing the game for the right reasons? That was to worry me for
the next two years, until the 1993 defeat in Cardiff. But then, for
me to be just another player, someone would have to take the
captaincy away from me, and I would go absolutely berserk.
That's what you have to keep reminding yourself. You can't go
back. And you can't have it both ways. There's a lot about the
job I could do without. But I love the captaincy. I would be
telling a lie if I didn't enjoy many of the trappings. I'm lucky to
have the job.

The pressure was off England; winners at last. Or was the pressure on
England; winners at last, and the northern hemisphere's big hope for
the World Cup? Blanco did not think so. 'We will face England in the
quarter-final – and the home side will win again,' insisted France's
captain, believing that their Paris advantage would tip the balance.
England had scored only five tries to four in the 1991 championship,
compared to 12–3 in the previous year. So what? The 1991 team had
got the job done. Only the most pedantic were pedalling those
statistics at Twickenham that night. Carling's side were in the record
books, there for all time, the latest of the 25 Grand Slam sides in the
competition's history.

It was enough for Uttley, the only man to have played in and
coached a Grand Slam side. He had decided before the championship
to bow out after the World Cup, come what may. His deteriorating
relationship with Carling was not the main reason, however. Uttley
felt that the time was right, although it was becoming increasingly
difficult to disguise his isolation.

Carling, too, was more and more going his own way. The England
players, wives and girlfriends enjoyed the fruits of their labour late
into the Grand Slam night. It is a shame that MTV's 'Unplugged'

programme did not record their jam sessions at the Hilton when they took over the band. Guscott and Richards were on drums, Heslop on tambourine and Dewi Morris on guitar, while singers included Ackford, Dooley, Hodgkinson, Probyn and Uttley. The chorus line on the dance floor consisted of Halliday, Underwood and most of the wives. The repertoire was varied, including *Rawhide* and an even longer version of *Hey Jude* than the Beatles classic. Carling, along with Teague, Skinner and Rendall, was elsewhere in London, drinking with Ian Botham. England's captain was mixing in fairly exclusive circles these days.

At the time, Carling admitted his season had not been without strain. 'I seriously wonder how long I will continue to play because of the pressures. I realise that, at the age of 25, it is an amazing thing to say, but it may be I have only another year left in me. Everything that is happening around the sport is burning people out. It hasn't been made easy for us, but the most satisfying aspect has been the way the people around me have risen above it. I have been part of an England team who have had the character to ignore distractions. But people don't understand the strain it puts on you psychologically, the difficulty of relaxing and forgetting about the championship in between games. The sad thing is, it has been made clear to me that certain members of the RFU committee want me ousted from the captaincy.'

If he sounded rather thoughtful in March, England's captain was back to top form when he accepted an invitation from the Oxford Union debating society to join Sir Arthur Gold, chairman of the British Olympic Association, in proposing the motion in April, 'This House believes that there is too much money in sport'. Opposing the motion were soccer star Garth Crooks and Graham Kelly, the chief executive of the Football Association. The motion was carried by 147–95.

It was Carling's manner that showed he was over the worst. 'First, I wish it to be known that I am receiving no fee for this speech. No fee has been sought ... nor indeed offered. I have, however, received superb hospitality. Potato soup served in its own skin, and something that looked remarkably like Bill Beaumont's ear, served in gravy. I say this in case there are members of the press present and, more important, any members of the Rugby Football Union. It might surprise you that I, as an amateur sportsman who lives under such constant financial monitoring, should support the belief that there is too much money in sport. Surely you must expect me to claim that, in fact, there is not enough. I know some of you saw me arrive in a brand new Mercedes sports car, but I can honestly claim that it is not mine – it's my agent's. And some of you will point the finger and accuse me of motivating the England team into one of the most money-grabbing outfits in rugby history. This is not the case. They need absolutely no motivating.' Carling continued by describing the joys of being steam-rollered by '300lb of French livestock' and of 'voluntary acupuncture delivered by aluminium studs'.

Carling had regained his sense of humour after a tough year. Lesser men would have crumbled under the pressure. But England's captain had finally come up smiling. Now for the World Cup.

Chapter 20

Final Rehearsal

It was a good tour for us. It showed that we were not at Australia's level. So we had no false illusions about what we were up against. We were well shafted in the Test.

ROGER UTTLEY

The 1991 summer tour to Australia was very important to Cooke and Carling's World Cup build-up. They worried that a four-month lay-off was by far the greater of two evils. The forwards suffer when laid up, as Bob Dwyer discovered when Australia came to England at the end of 1988, and Cooke was sure that it was better to keep England's pack ticking over. Others, however, many in the media, felt that the rest would have been more beneficial. They believed the tour could cost England the World Cup, with the players worn out by the time October came.

The trip was a factor in England failing, but not for the reasons expected. Instead, it affected their strategy and selection. The manner of England's Sydney defeat swayed their tactical thinking in the World Cup final.

Just as crucially, it marked the end of Simon Hodgkinson. His goal-kicking from full-back had been an integral part of England's successes over the previous two seasons; his personal tally in the Grand Slam triumph alone was 60 points. As the World Cup

147

approached, it seemed inconceivable that England would enter the competition without one of the great international goal-kickers as their No. 1 choice. But they did, and it probably cost them the final. It certainly almost lost them the semi-final at Murrayfield.

Unfortunately, those pressing his claims had memories of the earlier Hodgkinson, the kicker who calmed the French storm in Paris, who silenced Cardiff with a calculated swing of his right boot. But the Australia tour became a nightmare for the Nottingham full-back. A bang on the nose affected his confidence early on. The doubt spread, and Jonathan Webb subsequently regained his place for the Fiji international. Webb liked the southern hemisphere. The Bristol surgeon made his first England breakthrough there when Marcus Rose was injured during the 1987 World Cup, and he had been a regular until Hodgkinson was brought in for the Romania game two years later. 'Simon doesn't seem to be on his game,' explained Cooke when Webb returned. 'Whether the bang on the nose affected him more than we thought, I don't know. But he's not even striking the ball well, and we felt a change had to be made.'

By the time they faced Fiji, England had already lost three tour matches, against New South Wales, Queensland and Fiji B. But those setbacks were overlooked by the rest of the rugby world. For Wales were also touring Australia, and that most devout of rugby nations was suffering as never before. On the day when Carling's tourists lost by 6 points to Queensland, Wales were crushed 71–8 by New South Wales; the state side's total of 13 tries included five from David Campese. A week later, in the Test, Australia could not match the baker's dozen – only the 12 – as Wales lost 63–6. What had become a sordid affair continued with scuffles and bad language between the players at the post-match reception at Ballymore. The Neath contingent had closed ranks behind coach Waldron and captain Thorburn and felt the whole squad should do the same, but players such as Cardiff's Mike Hall were not going to be dictated to. Even Gerald Davies, one of rugby's legendary threequarters, himself came under attack for telling the painful truth, in explaining why one of the great rugby nations had become a laughing stock. Davies suggested radical changes. Many in Wales felt that his duty was to support the nation in its time of trouble, but Davies knew that the bitter in-fighting was a major factor behind the current disastrous state of the international team.

Within 24 hours of returning home, Ron Waldron was admitted to

Swansea Hospital with chest pains. He resigned his position and Alan Davies, the Nottingham and former England B coach, took over for the World Cup only. Even that appointment was clouded by controversy. The Welsh Rugby Union executive committee had recommended Tony Gray, who had been Wales's coach during the 1987 World Cup, but his nomination was rejected. For the first time ever, one of the home unions had gone outside its own structure for a coach. Two days later, Wales captain Paul Thorburn retired from international rugby. 'I know I will be called a quitter,' said Thorburn after 37 caps and 304 points. 'That's nothing new, because I have become accustomed to abuse rather than support. I just don't think I can face another three months of intensive pressure.' So Wales went preparing for the World Cup with a new coach, a new manager in Bob Norster, and a new captain, Ieuan Evans.

England's tour problems were certainly not as serious. Wade Dooley was to miss his first international for four years, although the policeman had only himself to blame when he broke a bone in his left hand, retaliating against Queensland's Sam Scott-Young. Cooke was not impressed with the defeat against Fiji B. 'The classic case of how not to play against Fijians,' was his view. John Olver was England's captain in that game and, as in Argentina the previous year, the tourists had problems with a local official, Laiakini Colati. 'I told the players they had to be whiter than white,' was Olver's diplomatic approach. 'He was letting the Fijians do things for which we were penalised. He became very aggressive towards me when I asked him what he wanted. But if we had known what we were doing wrong, we might not have lost our discipline.' Again, a Fijian departed before the scheduled end when Savencia Aria was sent off for a short-arm tackle on Ian Hunter.

Chris Oti returned for the Test as well as Webb. Yet the Fiji game will be remembered chiefly for the introduction of Martin Bayfield because of Dooley's injury. Ackford came off with an ankle injury, so Bayfield was paired with Nigel Redman in the second row. Fiji drew level early in the second half, while England were looking anything but potential world champions with a series of basic errors. But Bayfield did his future a lot of good by rising above the mire and keeping his side afloat with quality line-out possession. England scored 16 points in the final quarter of an hour, including Andrew's first try in his 37th international. The scoreline, 28–12, at least was respectable.

149

England then moved back to Australia to face the national side five days after the humbling of Wales. There was more controversy when Emerging Wallabies prop Geoff Didier stamped on Simon Halliday's face in the warm-up game before the Test. Didier had already been sent off while representing the Emerging Wallabies on their tour of England at Stratford the previous November. Touch judge Phil Thomas saw the offence on Halliday, but Didier escaped with a lecture. Halliday, who had been trapped on the ground after a tackle, was angry. 'I can't believe I could be trampled on like that without someone being sent off.'

Australia's 40–15 win over England was a triumph for their coach Bob Dwyer. When England set out on tour, Dwyer was still coming to terms with the loss of 13 players in just over a year. Rugby Union is not the first- or even second-choice winter sport in Australia. Every time the Wallabies find a great side, the Rugby League cheque books appear like wands to destroy the spell. Dwyer had respect for England. He had picked a World XV before the tourists arrived, and his side included Carling, Ackford, Dooley, Moore and Richards. Obviously, Dwyer was still feeling the effects of that 1989 Lions tour.

Australia's victory over England gave Dwyer hope for the World Cup. Beating Wales by such a margin had told him little, but this was a performance of pace and potential. Campese's two tries gave him a career total in Tests of 40; Mike Lynagh passed 600 points in international rugby. But it was a brace of tries from young flanker Willie Ofahengaue that was more satisfying for the coach, while Tim Gavin and John Eales's displays meant that Dwyer had a pack to take on the rest of the world. England had not played that badly, but Australia made the most of their chances for their five tries. The tourists were beaten by a side quicker in thought and quicker in deed.

Cooke and Carling responded positively to the lessons, rejecting the insinuations that their World Cup hopes were now in the dustbin. Cooke insisted, 'I like to think we have made some progress. But, as a country, we have a long way to go. We have had to recognise differences of style in Australia which have forced us to adapt. I still don't think we are as good as we need to be, but I think we're getting there. The players are much more analytical and have a better understanding of what is going on than I recall from the first tour here in 1988, when I was still wet behind the ears and discovering what international rugby was all about.'

Uttley similarly rejects accusations that the Australian tour was a mistake. 'It was a good tour for us. It showed that we were not at Australia's level. So we had no false illusions about what we were up against. We were well shafted in the Test. Their back row was exceptional. It was a relief when we heard that Tim Gavin would miss the World Cup because of injury.' Dick Best, the London Division coach, had been added to the official party and was now the firm favourite to take over from Uttley at national level. Uttley's relationship with Carling was not helped by the captain's obvious preference for Best. But personal differences were put aside as England prepared for the greatest rugby show of all time. The World Cup was just round the corner. Cooke and Uttley had spent three years planning: the next three months would decide whether they had been on the right track. Cooke could allow himself a small celebration already. The man he had chosen to lead England into the tournament was still around and ready to conquer the world.

Chapter 21

The Great Divide

The governing bodies have to be careful. On the one hand, they preach about tradition, ethics, loyalty; on the other hand, they drop the BBC for the World Cup. Why? Money, pure and simple. To the rugby authorities I suggest, be careful, you must practise what you preach.

FINLAY CALDER

Will Carling had been in the England side for three years, during which time the game had changed rapidly. But, to the relief of the RFU, certain things had stayed the same, despite frantic activity. As England prepared for the World Cup, distractions continued to mount up for Carling and his squad.

One of the first hints of the World Cup's imminence was the unveiling of England's World Cup jersey in March 1991. A jersey is a jersey – unless it's not all white, and the World Cup one wasn't. The RFU had signed a four-year deal with Cotton Traders, with a similar option for renewal. Yet the RFU committee subsequently voted to revert to the traditional strip after the World Cup. Tony Neary, a former England captain and director of Cotton Traders warned that the union could be in breach of their contract, although his company was blocked by the High Court from bringing an injunction in December. But, at the same time, the judge also questioned the 'legal identity' of the RFU; in the event of enforcement and damages, each

153

committeeman could be personally liable, rather like the open-ended responsibility of Lloyd's syndicates. That put the wind up the committee. They had always assumed themselves to be above the law, answerable to nobody. Now they were learning a few harsh facts of life.

Dudley Wood said, 'No matter what Cotton Traders say, the committee of the RFU has the right to decide what jersey the England team will wear. The committee had never agreed anything apart from the fact that they would accept the design of a shirt produced by Cotton Traders for the World Cup. Last July, the committee said that, after the World Cup, England would revert.' That sounded a good deal: a company negotiates a four-year deal, with a four-year extension, to cover an event lasting a month! Neary gave it to the RFU straight: 'There is no mention of the World Cup in the agreement negotiated by Cotton Traders and the RFU. If England play in white, we would regard this as a breach of contract.' England did wear white for the 1992 championship, but a new strip appeared the following season.

The RFU had more cause for complaint over the World Cup itself. The inaugural tournament in 1987 actually ended up costing England money. The event made profits of only £1.5 million, a tiny pecentage of what had been projected, and England found themselves over £75,000 out of pocket after receiving just £46,000 from the proceeds. After recommendations from the organising committee, the RFU offered to take charge of everything, including sponsorship and marketing, for 1991. Twickenham's marketing department, set up in 1985, had been a thundering success, and the RFU already had provisional agreements worth £20 million in the bag – three years before the event. But the International Rugby Football Board flatly refused England's offer of help, and rugby was to pay heavily for their stupidity. The Scots were primarily to blame: they were still in a huff over the 1988 Calcutta Cup affair, and so they campaigned against England's proposal to such an extent that it was never properly discussed. The unions moan about players taking money out of the game, but that one afternoon's business cost British rugby millions because of Scotland's pettiness. And, on the same day, the IRFB told all countries involved in preliminary qualifying for the World Cup to finance those matches themselves.

Carling watched the developing problems of the World Cup's commercial operation with interest. After all, it was the players who were going to be putting on the show. In November 1988, John Kendall-Carpenter, chairman of the IRFB, said, 'We hope to have our marketing operation in place by the end of the year.' A year later, it still wasn't, but the World Cup was nonetheless expected to make a £35 million bonus. Despite England's offer of free help, the IRFB had appointed Alan Callan, managing director of the Keith Prowse Agency, as its commercial adviser. Through him, companies would be asked to tender for broadcasting, tickets, press and public relations, hospitality, travel, publishing, merchandising, and licensing and sponsorship rights. The commercial adviser would receive a fee and performance-related bonus not restricted to the 1991 World Cup, while the overall marketing of the tournament was handed over to CPMA, an offshoot of the Prowse organisation, of which Callan was also a director.

Callan said, 'I am absolutely convinced and charmed by the integrity of the people on the World Cup committee and their intention to use commercial resources that will be developed for the benefit of the game. In business terms, they are as Corinthian as you can get, and it is wonderful to be part of it.' Carling had no arguments with that last statement. Three days later, the World Cup broadcasting rights went to ITV to end the BBC's traditional monopoly of the sport.

On the same day, Callan claimed that six of the eight hoped-for major sponsors had been identified. It was planned that each would contribute £2 million. Kendall-Carpenter in turn claimed that the World Cup was already assured of £23 million, two years before the event. 'It is not the intention to pass sums of money down the line. It's more a question of ensuring coaching facilities, publications, and the chance to improve the game world-wide in countries which are not so well off.' That was a clear indication to Carling that the organisers would ensure that the money was diverted anywhere, so long as it was not to the players.

The World Cup suffered two setbacks at the start of the summer of 1990. First, Kendall-Carpenter died. Second, by 29 June, no major sponsor had been named. Rugby World Cup Limited said that they had had offers in all categories, while Callan said that some sponsors had requested no publicity until announcements could be linked with the 1991 Five Nations championship. 'In my view, probably no more than one will be a British company. Rugby World Cup is still not recognised by commerce as a four-year occasion.'

In October 1990, Marcel Martin, a director of RWC, insisted, 'Our role is not to announce figures we do not know we can achieve.' The first sponsor was named on 23 October. Heinz, with former British Lion Tony O'Reilly at its head, snapped up a World Cup bargain for £800,000, and had the stage to themselves for nearly six months before Ricoh UK also came in for the same amount. It was another masterstroke by O'Reilly; Heinz got the deal of a lifetime. A higher figure was actually put on the Ricoh sponsorship – to include copying machines and the like which they were going to supply, but which were never part of the deal and which certainly weren't money into the rugby coffers. Famous Grouse then climbed aboard in April. The RWC commercial advisers 'remained confident of reaching a target of £10 million from sponsorships,' said *The Times*. Callan added, 'Despite the Gulf War, despite the recession, despite all the difficulties, we will make what we expected to achieve. We have held together what has been the most complex marketing exercise on the planet.'

Three months before the World Cup, O'Reilly predicted, 'When the game produces another figure with the charisma of Serge Blanco, it will simply be too tempting to sponsors to avoid him. That player will then become a million-pound rugby player. Already, I believe a six-figure sum is possible for the best players in the world, given proper marketing. But it is one of my fears that this march towards professionalism will threaten the Corinthian fabric of the sport. However, it need not necessarily destroy that, as long as we try to make rugby an exemplary sport. Professional golf is a sport in which people behave themselves and play by the rules; professional tennis is the reverse. It is possible for rugby to continue to exemplify grace under pressure.' O'Reilly added that he was disappointed at the lack of publicity surrounding the build-up to the World Cup. 'People cannot say there is no rugby around at the moment. England are playing a game in Sydney on Saturday which could be a foretaste of the World Cup semi-final. Ireland have just lost to Namibia, and there is great debate concerning rugby in Wales. We would certainly like the build-up to start now, for there may not have been a sufficient dynamism in the projection of the event so far.' Carling agreed; he had been gearing up to the World Cup since 1988, as had the England squad. But outside that grouping it was very hard to spot the first symptoms of World Cup fever.

Less than a month before the tournament started, that part of the

Keith Prowse operation which had won the contract to supply corporate hospitality collapsed. To anyone in that business, it was no surprise, although Nigel Rushman of CPMA had believed that the hospitality arm was sound. Yet when Keith Prowse were awarded the rights, a report on them had said: 'The company [KP Holdings, the parent company] is in a very difficult financial position. The company is heavily borrowed and has insufficient capital base.' A rescue deal, put together by receivers Grant Thornton, CPMA and Wembley plc, saved the 20,000 hospitality packages already sold, at a cost to RWC of £400,000 in tickets and £1 million in food. It was the least they could do: the organisers were legally bound to provide the tickets, while failure to provide hospitality for those already booked was hardly likely to inspire confidence and attract business in an area where numbers were below expectation. Even without that setback targets for income and profits from the World Cup had already dropped substantially: as the tournament began, it was expected to make £20 million.

The England players watched all this with limited interest. Over the same period, Carling's team had been involved in their own battle.

In January 1989, it was hinted that the IRFB would introduce a system of trust funds for players that April. A few days later, however, an official word came back that, for their part, the RFU would frown on such a system. So John Simpson, the president, met with the England players before the Calcutta Cup match – just to ensure that they had their minds on the job in hand. The RFU claimed that the players may not have properly appreciated the full implications of trust funds – though, of course, they did. Dudley Wood fired the first shot: 'Our greatest asset in obtaining the sponsors we do is our amateurism.' By April, the IRFB had agreed with him; they reinforced their amateur regulations and set up a special meeting on amateurism to take place that August.

After that meeting had taken place, but before its results were made public, the RFU became afraid that the IRFB might now allow players to earn money from fringe activities. Get your retaliation in first, is Wood's style. 'People do not understand the implications of what they are saying. They are talking about professionalism. The fact that players would not be paid for actually going on the field has nothing to do with it. They would still be professionals, making money out of an amateur game. There is no pressure coming from

157

inside the game at all.' Wood realised that would raise a chuckle, and added: 'I like being modelled on King Canute. He is one of my favourite characters. I have a simple feeling about players, though. They will take what they can get.' Carling knew that that comment encapsulated Wood's current attitude to the England team.

In December, the IRFB proposals were made public. They were: 1. Compensation for loss of earnings incurred during home internationals will be permitted following confirmation of that loss from a player's employer; 2. Coaches and referees to be similarly compensated; 3. Players can accept payments for writing books, media work and personal appearances; 4. Players will not be allowed to engage in advertising and promotional work related to the game.

Wood lost no time. 'Paying players for time lost when they are on international duty looks pretty innocuous, but the implications behind it are worrying. If this is the sort of game everyone wants, then fine. If you join a club, you have to abide by the rules, and we would have to make the best of the new situation.'

The then Scotland and British Lions captain Finlay Calder gave a player's view. 'The governing bodies have to be careful. On the one hand, they preach about tradition, ethics, loyalty; on the other hand, they drop the BBC for the World Cup. Why? Money, pure and simple. To the rugby authorities I suggest, be careful, you must practise what you preach. I hope the authorities will try harder to be one step ahead of the players' needs, and not continually one step behind. Without the players, after all, there is no revenue. Why can the IRFB condone allowing 90 officials and their wives to travel to South Africa on an all-expenses trip and, at the same time, refuse to allow the partners of the Lions to accompany the players to Paris for two days, when the French authorities were happy to meet any expense?'

Some of the England players met with management group Prisma in December, although Carling did not attend. Prisma representative Tony Carter projected an annual income of £2,125,000 for Rugby Limited, a company that would organise events and distribute income earned from 350 speeches at £500 a time, 200 public appearances at £1,000, 60 kit sponsorships at £5,000, 500 newspaper articles at £1,500, 100 TV appearances at £1,000, and 20 advertising/ modelling campaigns at £30,000. All this was, of course, dependent on the IRFB's relaxation of the laws relating to 'communication for reward' in the spring. Carling was not convinced by these figures.

The RFU met to discuss the proposed changes in January 1990. The IRFB wanted a reaction by 5 February. For once, Wood took off his RFU hat: 'A personal view is that they would not be put into practice in their present form.' Thereafter, the IRFB's meeting in April produced what was described by England's Simon Halliday as 'the fudge we always knew it would be.' The IRFB extended compensation payments to cover home internationals, but a working party was set up to look at 'communication for reward'.

RFU president Mike Pearey made his views clear in August 1990. 'We in the RFU have been dead scared of players and officials getting paid for their involvement in the game. But, if their fame produces money outside the game, we have got to accept that. If we stand in isolation, we shall be passed by. We have to bend a little. It will not affect 95 per cent of the players in the game anyway – they will carry on the same as always.'

Finally, in October, the IRFB recommended allowing 'communication for reward'. Rugby players were now free to ply their wares in the market-place; they could take fees for opening supermarkets and product endorsement – as long as it was not rugby-related. But there was a get-out clause for the RFU, in that the application of the new rules was left to the discretion of each individual union. And Geoff Cooke identified it as such. 'A good chance has been missed. I don't think the Board has given a strong enough lead, and by allowing individual unions discretionary powers they are causing enormous problems. It's a tragic error on their part. They should set down procedures and rules by which everyone abides, on and off the field.' The following month, the RFU called for a rethink on the new amateur regulations. Their committee had met and expressed 'grave concern and disappointment at the IRFB decision, which it felt completely undermined the essential amateurism of the game.' So much for abiding by the rules of the club.

The Prisma deal having faded, the company formed by the England squad, Player Vision, signed a promotional agreement with the Willis brothers that same November. The Cardiff silence followed two months later. A code of conduct was then sent to the England players and, the next day, their agreement with the Willis brothers was ended. Carling, who made the statement to that effect, added: 'The decision has been made bearing in mind the point at which the players find themselves in the Five Nations championship. The players will continue to devote their energies to continuing success on the field. There are no plans to appoint another agency in the foreseeable future. All commercial activity will be dealt with internally until further notice. The RFU will act as a clearing house for any deals proposed by the players.'

A Timberland advert, featuring England players, was then banned from the programme for the Scotland match. The irony was, the players had not been paid, while Timberland had received enormous exposure and publicity for an advert that never was. And further irony: contributory to the Cardiff incident had been the fact that Carling's men had seen the Welsh players appearing in an Umbro advertisement before the match. Wood explained the ban: 'The whole point of the new amateur laws is that what the players do should not be rugby-related. If you have them appearing in a rugby programme, this is clearly rugby-related. We decide what advertisements go into our programme, and we have decided this time. The players' code of conduct clearly excludes anything with a rugby connotation.' The RFU had extended the rule from merely the product to cover the place where the product shall appear. Yet the RFU still used the players in their own advertisements. In February, Michael Coley, the RFU's marketing executive, was made the England team's agent. Coley was serving two masters, but only one was paying his wages.

At the IRFB's annual meeting on 16 March, it was confirmed that the individual union's discretion applied. Albert Agar, one of England's two representatives, said, 'If England are consistent with their earlier decision, they will not implement law 4:3:2.' Sir Ewart Bell, retiring chairman of the committee on amateurism and now in charge of the World Cup, insisted, 'We have tried to find the middle ground. The next stage is to clear up the grey areas.' No wonder England's players were angry. But, throughout all these discussions, Carling's team played some fine rugby and clinched the 1991 Grand Slam.

On 3 May, England announced their forthcoming 'Run with the Ball' campaign, in conjunction with Parallel Media. Again, figures of £2 million were bandied about. There would be eight élite sponsorship packages, and the players would share £300,000 in the first year. It was proclaimed by Carling to a select, hand-picked bunch of journalists. 'The World Cup is a unique window of opportunity. This offers the chance of a huge promotional exercise designed to benefit the whole game – not individual players. The players have taken the initiative, but we have kept entirely within the guidelines set out for us in writing by the RFU. I do not anticipate opposition from the committee. How could anyone turn down £1 million?'

Mike Reynolds, chairman of the Institute of Sports Sponsorship and executive director of brewers Courage, responded. 'It may be that they have spoken to other sponsors, but I am not aware of soundings having been taken, and when you are trying to put together a package in a short space of time, it's sensible to test the water. I think existing sponsors will find additional expenditure hard to justify at this particular time, though whether there are new sponsors available is a matter for conjecture. The players are coming on to the market asking for sums of money per sponsorship which are quite high, at a time when they may find it is not there. They really don't have a long time in which to get it sorted out. They have to balance their needs and the needs of the game against the realities of the market-place.'

The RFU hesitated and decided to hold an extraordinary committee meeting on 8 June. Although they had agreed in principle to the players' 'Run with the Ball' scheme, the executive felt that the decision had been railroaded through. On 8 June, the RFU agreed to a number of safeguards. Then Ireland, with help from Scotland and Wales, got into the act and expressed their concern about the RFU's liberal stance. So much for individual discretion of the unions!

On 9 September 1991, 'Run with the Ball' was launched by Richard Hill, Rob Andrew and Brian Moore, 40 days after the RFU had given their blessing. Virgin, Hutchinson Telecom, Wilkinson Sword, Sony and Capital Radio were involved, while Courage and the *Daily Mail* would be holding 'Run with the Ball' clinics at Richmond during the World Cup. And England's World Cup recording of *Swing Low, Sweet Chariot* would be available later that month. There was a sting in the tail, however: the players would not receive anything until the IRFB had approved the scheme. In the event, the World Cup season, including the 1992 Grand Slam, earned the players just £5,000 a man. The squad began 1993 still waiting for 80 per cent of that money.

The England squad's distractions were not restricted to money. In August 1990, shortly after Moore and Leonard had announced they were joining Harlequins, Wood insisted there were no plans to introduce regulations to inhibit player movement 'because they do so for all sorts of reasons. We appreciate that some of those reasons could come within the orbit of the amateur regulations, which would be a major concern.'

Just before the World Cup season, Leicester's paid coaching administrator, Tony Russ, complained that other Midlands clubs had been trying to poach his players, Dean Richards included. 'I could name 15 players approached and offered inducements to play for other Midlands clubs this summer alone. It is the people behind the scenes at clubs who are responsible. I see nothing wrong in asking a player whether he would like to join another club. That is the right of any club at any time. After all, we do that from time to time. But we do not offer a player any inducement, which is not the case generally today. Another player in our squad was offered £150 a match if he joined another club, and I know of two internationals who were promised a five-figure sum if they switched clubs last season.'

It was then revealed that England's World Cup props, Jeff Probyn and Paul Rendall, had registered with Askeans from the third division. The RFU reacted to the poaching claims, with Wood predicting, 'Let there be no mistake, the truth will out. We are going to have to act, because my first reaction is horror that such things are happening. We must stop these people ruining the game, because it will ruin rugby if it is allowed to continue uninterrupted.' Wood added again that there would be no changes in regulations concerning player movement. A fortnight later, stricter legislation was proposed. Carling was not surprised at all the back-tracking. It was par for the course. The players were supposed to be totally professional in their preparation and performance. Yet, if the RFU had been judged on their performance in the build-up to the 1991 World Cup, England would not have even qualified!

Chapter 22

The Greatest Amateur Show on Earth

*On that evidence, Australia haven't got a World Cup-winning side.
There's no doubt about that.*

ALAN DAVIES

The Rugby World Cup had been coming to Britain for four years.
Rugby players and the rugby media knew it. But the general public
had little inkling. Ultimately, the overwhelming success of the
tournament was down to one team: England. Superficially, it would
not have mattered if England had not reached the final; Twickenham
would still have been a sell-out. But it was Carling's men who ensured
that rugby World Cup fever reached epidemic proportions in the
autumn of 1991.

The tournament had originally been scheduled for the four home
countries. Then France entered the fray, giving the organisers the
problems of having four groups in five countries, another language,
and numerous other broadcasting authorities to deal with. Thanks for
the extra confusion were due to the persistence of the president of the
French Fédération de Rugby, Albert Ferrasse, one of the most
powerful men in the game. He will be enjoying a well-deserved
retirement by the time of the next World Cup in 1995, so he wanted to
make his mark on the event before bowing out. Therefore, in the
time-honoured tradition of sporting politics, some goalposts were

uprooted and taken to another country. There were other repercussions: when, eventually, the authorities met to decide on the venue for the third World Cup, a remarkable seven host countries had already been used up in the first two events.

Carling did not need public awareness to tell him the World Cup was on. The tournament had been on his personal agenda from the minute Cooke had made him captain three years earlier. He felt in a much better frame of mind than the previous year. The Grand Slam had helped, but he had also matured into the job. He no longer felt threatened by the responsibilities and pressures. He no longer felt afraid to ask for help from those who he thought had his best interests at heart. Still, it had taken him a while to find assistance, and at the heart of that problem was Carling's reluctance to lean on anyone inside the team or the England set-up. Cooke understood that, although Uttley felt rejected. But Uttley has never bothered with the world of RFU politics, while Cooke has had to play that game. He was at the sharp end.

Carling had learnt that the best way was his own way, right or wrong. The perceptions of who and what the England captain should be were numerous and growing as his and England's success continued. Now he had found his own way and, if people objected, hard luck. There was not enough of Carling to please everyone. This way, at least, one person was satisfied – Will Carling. Some team members felt he had become too isolated, too aloof, too self-centred. But even they failed to appreciate the strain that Carling had been under. They, like the public, had been dazzled by the public image of English rugby's golden boy.

England put on a united front for the World Cup. It was not a false face: the majority of the squad had been making sacrifices for three years in order to be included in the final selection. Barnes missed out. So did Bayfield. And Back, Hunter, and John Hall. David Pears and Nigel Redman were preferred to the first two.

England's three warm-up games in September included the first visit to Twickenham of the USSR. And the last. Protocol being what it is at HQ, the RFU kept a daily eye on the ongoing break-up of the Soviet Union, wanting to make sure that the side had the right title on the day of the match. Everyone called them Russia, although they were officially the Union of Soviet State by the Saturday. Either way, the Red Army were given short shrift. Carling knew the opposition were not up to scratch, but England had to ignore that. 'We have to play in a manner good enough to beat the All Blacks. We have to be that ruthless, that single-minded. We must come off the pitch having controlled the game, having worked on the areas that will be vital on 3 October and satisfied with the work we have put in. This is a good England side. I have always believed that. But we have to play to the best of our ability. We didn't do that last season, and the Australian tour exposed our weaknesses.' England won 53–0, but Simon Hodgkinson's hopes of finding a way back were dashed when he was stretchered off with an ankle injury early in the second half.

Gloucester provided the next test. England won 34–4, but Richards needed repeated attention for a shoulder injury. The England Students were the last of the warm-up opposition, although Carling sat that one out. The students came out in black shirts to prepare England for their World Cup opener against New Zealand, and the seniors won 35–0. Opinions were divided: some thought England had proved nothing by winning so easily. Had they struggled, however, the critics would have still swung the boot and claimed they were not ready.

Some of the worries about the World Cup organisation were now coming home to roost. The RFU, who had voiced doubts from the start, attacked the organisers for failing to meet targets. 'There are two main areas of criticism. The original claims for, and offers of, sponsorship have not been fulfilled. And we were disappointed by the decision to allocate so many tickets to the commercial side.' English clubs were up in arms after receiving just two tickets each for the final. Each of the host countries got 5,000 tickets, although Twickenham increased England's allocation to 9,000. Dudley Wood made the point that if you belonged to a Welsh or Irish club, you had a 10-times better chance of getting a ticket than an Englishman. Wood knew that, as neither of those two countries were likely to make the final, their tickets were sure to find their way on to the black market.

The TV coverage was in far better shape. TSL had won the contract to sell the broadcasting rights, and they exceeded their targets. The BBC lost one of their traditional sports to ITV, and the familiar voice of Bill McLaren moved to Radio 5. ITV, who had previously been frustrated in several bids to show live international rugby in Britain, made up for lost time. Frank Bough was the linkman in the studio, surrounded by an array of rugby talent: Gordon Brown, Clive Norling, Nigel Carr, David Kirk, Steve Smith and Fran Cotton were among the star names. Even the commentators were former internationals, John Taylor and Alastair Hignell. ITV spent £7 million, showing 75 hours of rugby, including live action from 25 of the 32 matches. They also wired up the referees for sound, although the results were not for public consumption. France coach Daniel Dubroca's hopes of bluffing his way out of trouble after attacking New Zealand referee David Bishop after the quarter-final were substantially reduced as a consequence, as Bishop was still wearing his microphone at the time.

Meanwhile, as rugby geared itself for its biggest test on the world stage, Twickenham gave us a taste of the good old days. RFU president Peter Yarranton made the draw for an early round of the Pilkington Cup live on radio. After the draw, the sponsor tactfully pointed out that not only were Barker's Butts in the wrong half of the draw, but a team beaten in the previous round, Broughton Park, had been given another chance. It is on these occasions that Dudley Wood is at his best: 'As a member of another union said the other day, the RFU will do anything for publicity – and we are proving it. The only thing to do when you are wrong is admit it. We have egg on our faces, but we have to do the draw again.'

Rugby cannot plan anything without a dinner. On 28 September, five days before the tournament proper started, a sumptuous affair was held in London, and France interrupted their preparations to fly back and forward across the Channel. The players realised that rugby had a real fan at that dinner in Home Secretary Kenneth Baker – he wished 'Wayne Dooley and the British team' the best of luck.

Not that the opening ceremony at Twickenham the following Thursday was any better. That had originally been planned for a separate day from the opening match, although common sense eventually prevailed, and it took place before England met New Zealand. The organisers had wasted no money on any lavish, spectacular production: Michael Ball sang the official World Cup song, which was fortunately not heard of again. ITV's theme based on Holst's 'Jupiter' from the Planets Suite, *World In Union*, sung by Kiri te Kanawa, was instead the World Cup song that entered the charts, along with the England squad's version of *Swing Low*. Before Prince Edward officially opened 'Rugby World Cup 1991', schoolboys dressed in the participating countries' colours, and a few old heroes such as Gerald Davies, Bill Beaumont and Colin Meads, made a circuit of the stadium. This was the honest, grassroots face of rugby, the organisers told us; it proved that the game was still pure and could not be tarnished by the events of the next month. It was certainly an amateurish display, and merely confirmed the organisers' reluctance to spend money.

Carling did not care. All his thoughts were focused on New Zealand. The result did not matter in a way, as both teams were bound to qualify for the quarter-final. England's performance, against the World Cup-holders, was important, though. Very few of the England squad had personal experience of the All Blacks: the last contact had been a tour to New Zealand in 1985, when Leicester centre Paul Dodge was captain. Mike Teague had played in both Tests there, while Hill and Dooley came on as replacements in the second match.

The 1991 World Cup got off to a stuttering start, as Scottish referee Jim Fleming kept tight control. Both sides were, not unnaturally, apprehensive, and England led 12–9 at the interval. Flanker Michael Jones scored the game's only try in the second half as New Zealand won 18–12. There was no rousing finish. Both sides appeared to settle for that scoreline and their respective paths to the knock-out stage. All Black coach Alex Wyllie stated, 'It was like the first match of a tour. Winning was more important than style.' Carling was disappointed. 'We have to play a lot better and a lot faster than we did to win the Grand Slam. We also have to make a lot fewer mistakes.' Carling had also experienced the All Black power for the first time.

CARLING
I don't think I've ever been on the field when a team has dramatically changed tactics. If you are winning, then why change. If you're losing, then there is very little you can do about it. You just have to react to the situations around you. Most teams try to persevere with the same game plans. Obviously, you can vary the line-out, go for more scrum positions, or play a looser game. Occasionally, I just ask, 'Has anyone else got an answer to what's happening out there?' But I remember the All Blacks slipping up a few gears in the second half. It was deliberate: they just wanted to show us what they could do and who was boss. It was difficult to cope with. And pretty impressive, too.

Twickenham was not a sell-out. That was not the fault of the

167

Thursday afternoon timing: unsold packages and undersubscribed overseas unions' allocations meant 1,700 tickets had become available, and they were still trickling back to the RFU 24 hours before the kick-off. The authorities felt the tickets could not be advertised because of touts. Most were sold, but Twickenham were still unhappy. 'There was a sense of fury about,' said Dudley Wood. 'We can't have it happening for the final.' It did.

Barring disasters, England could now look forward to a Paris date with France in the quarter-final, while New Zealand would meet Australia in the semi-final. Attention moved away from Group One and centred on Wales, where the home union was battling with Australia, Western Samoa and Argentina. New coach Alan Davies had a bad first weekend. 'On that evidence, they haven't got a World Cup-winning side. There's no doubt about that,' was his verdict on Australia after their 32–19 victory over Argentina at Llanelli. Two days later, Western Samoa achieved the victory that all Wales was fearing; a week later, the hosts were out of the World Cup. And failure at group level meant that Wales are to trek the qualifying rounds in search of a place at the final stages in 1995. Davies said he would stick to his earlier decision to quit after the World Cup: 'I've not changed my mind because I don't think I've got the strength of character to bear the hopes of Welsh rugby on my shoulders. Nor does any Welshman in creation. There are too many ills.' Two years on, Davies still carries that burden.

England's players tried to keep an eye on the other matches from their Basingstoke hotel, although Carling and his squad did travel up to Otley to watch the two other sides in their group. Italy beat the United States 30–9; it was a pointless exercise. Carling was unhappy about the whole trip, especially when the organisers slipped in a dinner the night before, at which Carling was on speaking duty again. It was two days of travelling, being pestered and smiling for the cameras. The players could have done without the hassle.

England beat Italy 36–6 at Twickenham, but Webb's record 24 points were overshadowed by the 37 penalties awarded by Scotland's Brian Anderson, largely against the visitors. The Italians had shown flashes of inspiration against the USA and later surprised the All Blacks. Against England, however, they reverted to the negative tactics favoured by their soccer side. It was a farce, but Anderson and Carling kept their heads. The referee said, 'I did consider sending off an Italian player for persistent infringement. Certainly, I have never awarded so many penalties against one team in the whole of my refereeing career at any level. But when I thought of the ramifications of a sending-off, I decided it would not have helped what was becoming a farcical situation. It could have inflamed the match. I repeatedly spoke to the Italian captain, but it was water off a duck's back. It was literally like talking to a brick wall.' Carling decided not to kick the game to death. 'We wanted to play a fluid game. It would really have done us no good to kick about 20 penalties. At the end of the day, we practised scrums in certain positions.'

The England squad went to Richmond the day after the Italian game to fulfil part of their 'Run with the Ball' commitments. If the RFU had any doubts that the players were serious in their efforts to help with rugby's future, they would have been dispelled here. Carling, Andrew, Underwood, Winterbottom and the whole squad, along with Uttley and Cooke, worked with hundreds of youngsters. The awe in which Carling and company were held by these kids told the authorities who was really stimulating the growth of the game in England. Even New Zealand diva Kiri te Kanawa – now that the All Black game was over – appeared with the England team. The squad then watched the Australia-Western Samoa match in the Richmond clubhouse. The Aussies struggled to a 9–3 win in the Pontypool mud and lost their scrum-half and skipper, Nick Farr-Jones, with a knee injury.

England made eight changes for the final group game against the USA. Gary Pearce came in at prop for the first time since 1988, although Morris and Pears were kept on the bench, where they were to remain all tournament. Carling overtook Bill Beaumont's record of having been 21 times England captain when he ran out for the game. There was little else to celebrate in the 37–9 victory. 'It was hard to concentrate for any length of time. That was because of the mix of some players coming in for their first game and being desperate to impress, while several others were playing their third game in nine days and may have been a bit lacklustre.'

The quarter-final pairings were resolved over that second weekend. Scotland beat Ireland to earn a home tie against Wales's conquerors Western Samoa, while Ireland – who had been unhappy at the way Finlay Calder had crashed into their full-back Jim Staples in that encounter – entertained Australia. Canada also qualified, to meet holders New Zealand at Lille. Those three ties were easy to predict: wins for Scotland, Australia and New Zealand. Not so the other quarter-final. The France-England clash was the tie of the round, and it was too close to call without a large degree of patriotic bias. This was the revenge match Serge Blanco had predicted that France would win after losing the Grand Slam at Twickenham in March.

Chapter 23

The Greatest Game

The quarter-final was the hardest game I've ever been involved in, mentally and physically. Blanco's outburst showed how wound up they were. France were on the edge. When Blanco hit Heslop, I immediately thought, 'I'm glad I'm not the ref!'

WILL CARLING

Saturday 19 October 1991 was the day Will Carling's England came of age. Sadly, it was also the day Rugby Union finally lost its last, lingering innocence. The game's most sacred tradition was violated when France's coach Daniel Dubroca, a former world-class player, attacked the referee after the game. Rugby was now just another international sport with unruly participants. The affair rumbled on for nearly a week as the World Cup organisers somehow misjudged the seriousness of the affair, while the French blamed the rumpus on an orchestrated attack by the British media. It ended only when Dubroca resigned. But Dubroca was not the only Frenchman who let himself down at the Parc des Princes that day.

Serge Blanco, whose international career was to continue for only as long as his country's involvement in the World Cup, lost his cool in the opening exchanges. With a little help from flanker Eric Champ, Blanco floored Nigel Heslop shortly after the kick-off with a flurry of quickfire punches, for which referee Bishop would have been justified in sending him off. To see one of the most flamboyant rugby entertainers of recent times reduced to common thuggery was one of the saddest moments of the World Cup. Blanco and Dubroca's behaviour reflected the pressures of the tournament: it had reached the do-or-die stages.

England's preparations for the match began with a weekend family break in Jersey. Cooke felt that their presence in the build-up would give an emotional edge to England's performance. The squad then moved to Montmorency, just north of Paris where, after the relaxing atmosphere of Jersey, Carling told Cooke and Uttley that the players wanted a rigorous work-out. They certainly got it, not least when Moore and Richards had a momentary dust-up. The following day, Richards was dropped, though it had nothing to do with the incident.

'That was one of the great training sessions. Deano [Richards] would have seen from the training line-up that he was probably out. He wanted to make his point,' remembers Uttley. Cooke made the public announcement: 'If you had suggested a few months ago that Dean would be dropped, I would have said it was inconceivable. He has been the backbone of so much we have done.' Words of tribute, but of little consolation to the Leicester forward. Richards's demotion had been on the cards for a while. He was off his game and, therefore, off the pace; England could not afford the gaps he was leaving. Teague moved to No. 8, with Skinner coming in on the flank. Heslop was also brought in on the wing at the expense of Oti. Tony Roche of *Today* remembers the story going the press rounds – not printed – of Oti wandering the hotel with a baseball bat looking for his former Durham University colleague. 'Where's that ****? He's ruined me. Where's Carling's room?'

Carling's team were reminded that they were three games away from immortality. More imminent, perhaps, they were one game away from ignominious failure. One of the four favourites for the World Cup was about to be eliminated. The seedings had been based on the 1987 tournament, which left England, despite only two defeats in the past three Five Nations championships, the seventh seeds – another example of the organisers' ineptitude. Whoever came second at the Parc des Princes would be a World Cup failure. Carling was determined that it was not going to be him. The World Cup trophy was on show for all the players to see during the match.

* * *

CARLING

I try to make my team talks fresh. That's difficult when you're emphasising the same old things. I focus on different points and new angles, though it's impossible to come up with something new every time. Whatever I do, I try to be positive. I don't discuss things that have gone wrong in the past, or highlight mistakes, or say, 'We must not let this happen again.' I try to create as positive an attitude as possible. That's the environment I want the players to take on the field. It's about do's – not don't's.

There's some emotive stuff. But emotion is not going to carry you all the way through. It's not the English way. My thrust is about England achieving their potential. I have always believed that the England team has great potential. If I gave them the history bit, as the Irish, Welsh and Scots do, the boys would crack up. It's probably valid for the other countries, but not for us. But I'm sure there is a lot more national pride in the England side now. I don't want us to be seen as good losers.

Every player is different. Skinner is so full of confidence that you have to keep him on the straight and narrow. Get him to remember he's a team player, not an individual. I've spent more time bollocking him than anything else. Webbie needs his confidence building up, as does Wade. Winters just wants you to be honest. Making him feel involved is important. You have got to give it to him straight. I never felt I made much of an impression on Mark Bailey or Fran Clough. Paul Rendall, 'The Judge', was hard work, too. He viewed me as the young whippersnapper. I stood for change, the end of his era, his style. He quite rightly has pride in his game, the set piece. I've had good support from Mike Teague, and I have tremendous respect for him. He's very loyal and totally unselfish. He's very quiet, like Winters and Deano. Jeff Probyn, like 'The Judge', has pride in his performance though, to him, I'm just one of the flash boys in the backs.

I don't call for quiet. I wait for silence. I don't shout or pick on someone. The players are fired up anyway. I like eye contact with all the players. You can tell immediately if you've hit the right chord or not. It was never more obvious that everything was spot-on than before this World Cup quarter-final. We always seem to have been in a good frame of mind against the French. But this was perfect. We couldn't have been in better shape as we ran out for the game that would make or break us as a team.

England immediately took the fight to the French. Andrew hoisted a high kick, Blanco was bowled over, then was churned out of the ruck as he had been dozens of times before. Champ squared up to Skinner on the supporting bill. Most international matches start that way. Referee David Bishop could be heard in the commentary box: 'Champ. All right. Come on, get out of it.' Then Heslop gathered a wayward clearance and returned it to Blanco. The French full-back called for the mark and was hit late by Heslop. All full-backs are used to such treatment; it's part of the job. But Blanco decided enough was enough. A sweeping left hook exploded into Heslop's face. Then, in a twinkling of an eye, Blanco skilfully transferred the ball to his left arm to prove that his right-hand punch was just as lethal. Champ, who had had his arm round Blanco as the full-back made the catch, also used the quick left-right combination. The second right hand hit Heslop round the back of the head, and England's wing slumped to the deck, instinctively pulling his gumshield out of his mouth as he hit the ground.

It was almost too quick for the human eye to see; certainly, Champ's significance in the events only became apparent after numerous TV replays. The repeats also showed that Blanco and Champ, who had in fact taken more of Heslop's impact, were ready and waiting for the initial collision. Blanco's part in the affair was clear, and it seemed inconceivable that Bishop would allow him to stay on the field. Yet it was just as inconceivable that the French captain, one of the most respected players in the world, would end his distinguished career by being sent off. Bishop consulted with touch judge Keith Lawrence, a fellow New Zealander, then took the long-term view – the next 77 minutes, in fact. He decided that this showpiece might turn into a nightmare if the popular home captain was dismissed, and Blanco was given a stern lecture instead. 'The referee warned me that I would go for another punch,' said Blanco afterwards. 'But he said that he was a good friend of mine. It was his duty to see that I did not leave the field in that way. This World Cup was meant to be a festival of rugby, but it's turning into a festival of referees.'

* * *

CARLING

The quarter-final was the hardest game I've ever been involved in, mentally and physically. Blanco's outburst showed how wound up they were. France were on the edge. When Blanco hit Heslop, I immediately thought, 'I'm glad I'm not the ref!' There was no denying he was in an unenviable position. Heslop had thumped into Blanco, but not that hard. What Blanco did was so blatant. Whatever action Bishop took could have been dangerous. If Blanco had been sent off in front of his own crowd, the place could have erupted. I don't know how the French crowd would have reacted. Anything could have happened. By not sending him off, however, Bishop could have been giving the green light to an afternoon of violence and mayhem.

I'm never happy when I hear, 'The next punch and off you go.' I've heard it too often. Too often, it doesn't happen, and that's the worst thing a ref can do – give a warning and not follow it through. When Clive Norling said it, he meant it. So did Les Peard. And Jim Fleming.

I wasn't unhappy that Blanco stayed. I was desperate to win, but I didn't want to see such a rugby talent retire in disgrace. I felt the incident had given us the upper hand. It put the French on the back foot. We had kept our cool. It was a black mark against the French, and it put Blanco under even more pressure. If Blanco was that unstable, and the referee had seen that, what state were the rest of the French side in?

England had not only gained the upper hand, but a 3–0 lead. Webb's punishment of Blanco's behaviour was important: the match was less than five minutes old. And Carling was right: Blanco's action had alienated the referee. Webb kicked a second penalty when Cecillon was penalised for a dangerous tackle on Teague that might normally have gone unpunished. England then gave away a penalty under their own posts, but Rory Underwood regained their advantage with a try in the left-hand corner. Dooley's two-handed catch at a short line-out started the move. With the England back row causing diversions, the ball sped from Hill to Andrew to Carling to Guscott, who made the breach and sent Underwood clear. England turned round 10–6 ahead and prepared for the French onslaught that everyone knew was coming.

175

Sella and Andrew were the next pair to be lectured by referee Bishop. Andrew had made the mistake of restraining Sella as he tried to support Blanco, and another swinging French hook was the reply. But it was ultimately a legitimate confrontation that turned this quarter-final. The press box had an excellent view of Skinner's crunching tackle on Marc Cecillon; the French forwards were driven back, and England were awarded the scrum. Skinner's tackle was a statement that the French understood perfectly. This England side were going to keep going. And now they had the confidence to win.

France got back on level terms shortly afterwards with Jean-Baptiste Lafond's sixth try of the tournament, the winger rounding a still-dazed Heslop en route to the line. But England had weathered the storm. French indiscipline was about to cost them points yet again, and prop Pascal Ondarts – not for the first time – was the offender. Bishop tried to restrain Ondarts after awarding England the penalty. The prop was lucky not to hit the referee as he attempted to escape from his grasp, and Blanco rushed up to pull Ondarts back. Carling stood there shaking his head in disbelief before signalling an attempt at goal. Bishop went to Blanco: 'Serge, No. 3 dived in, not even going for the ball. Tell him to cool it. Tell him to cool it. He's on dangerous ground.' France should really have been penalised another 10 metres, but it didn't matter. Webb kicked the goal, the ball just clearing the bar. Blanco in fact jumped up and tipped the ball on to the bar, but the touch judges' flags were already up.

The final word was to lie with England and Carling. Hill chipped up the blind side; Lafond gathered, but was bulldozed over the French line. By the time the mêlée hit the deck, Carling had the ball, and Bishop raised his arm: 'Try to Carling, try to Carling,' for the benefit of the unsighted commentators. Even Peter Winterbottom, normally the most restrained of players, could not hide his delight. Webb kicked the conversion, and Bishop blew the final whistle. England, 19-10 winners, were in the semi-final.

That wasn't the end of the hostilities, although Blanco now regained the composure that had deserted him earlier. After embracing his son, Blanco said his goodbyes in the England dressing-room, and there was genuine sadness among the victors to see him go. Unfortunately, at the same time, another Frenchman was behaving in a less conciliatory fashion outside the dressing-room. Dubroca had confronted the referee: Bishop was grabbed, abused and spat at. Ondarts was also involved, and a punch was swung at Bishop.

Dubroca appeared at the press conference as word spread of the incident. The French coach laughed: 'It was a fraternal gesture to a referee I have known for a long time.'

The whole matter may have remained one of rugby's great open secrets, but for Jeff Herdman. The former Swansea and Barbarians hooker was working in Paris for the BBC. He saw the whole thing, reported it, and refused to keep quiet for 'the good of the game'. Such a credible witness to such an incredible scene meant that the World Cup organisers surely had to take decisive action. No chance, despite RWC chairman Russ Thomas's remark that, 'There's no question of the truth not coming out, this thing being whitewashed, or things being swept under the carpet.'

Later, statements from the powers-that-be included 'No further action against Dubroca,' and, 'There has been no official complaint from the referee.' Then it was deemed an internal French matter, before Rugby World Cup finally bowed to public pressure, took back the responsibility and promised an enquiry. Other tournament referees were upset at the lack of official action. Rugby's most sacred law had been desecrated, and the game would never again be able to hold itself up to the world as different from the rest. It was no longer the one sport where the official's word was respected and always obeyed. Bishop was barred from talking about the incident for a year, but he did not need to: Herdman's recollections were not the only evidence. Bishop's match microphone had still been switched on, and the TV commentary team heard it all. Dubroca was damned out of his own mouth. Still the organisers dithered, though. The next decisive action came from Dubroca himself. He resigned six days after the match, blaming the British media for a concerted campaign to get him out.

Dubroca had certainly stolen some of England's thunder. Not that Carling and his squad wasted any time on the French after leaving Paris on the Sunday. England had new priorities. The French performance had reinforced their ambition. It was a display of character, of resolution, of maturity, probably the finest by an England team since beating New Zealand at Eden Park, Auckland, in 1973. Going to Paris to meet France was the quarter-final which the holders had dreaded. England, as far as the All Blacks were concerned, had drawn the short straw. Now, for the first time, the southern hemisphere's two rugby giants saw England as potential World Cup champions.

* * *

CARLING
I knew we were through the second I touched down for that try.
This win meant we weren't World Cup failures. That was my first
emotion. I remember the stigma the team carried round after
losing to Wales in the 1987 quarter-finals. I don't think many
people expected us to win in Paris. But we did, and in style. We
showed a lot of discipline, determination and character. I was
proud that night. Not just for me, but for the team and for all the
supporters who had made such a noise that afternoon.

Chapter 24

World Cup Knock-out

*We'd win good ball, then look up expecting to see it drilled down
towards the Australian line. Instead, the backs were throwing the ball
around, getting caught, and we would have to trundle back 30 yards for
another scrum. We weren't happy. What had happened to our plan?
Worse than that, it wasn't working.*

JEFF PROBYN

England's World Cup campaign showed Carling at his best. In
triumph and adversity, England's captain presented the outside
world with the acceptable face of international competition. There
were no public tears when the dream was finally dashed, just a smile
in defeat as Australia raised the trophy. The World Cup went to the
team who were the favourites, and England had given it their best
shot. But had they? Several England forwards and their coach believe
that Carling threw it away by abandoning the planned strategy. That
the captain wavered and succumbed to the slur campaign which was
waged against England's style.

Australia's coach Bob Dwyer had been chipping away steadily
since that 1988 Twickenham defeat. After England's quarter-final
victory, Dwyer claimed: 'I am a little disappointed with England's
philosophy. They just restrict their game, but it is up to them. They
have more capability than they show, and it seems a shame not to

179

utilise that potential.' A week later, after England's Murrayfield victory in the semi-final, Dwyer increased the pressure. 'I feel a bit sorry for England. I didn't think that any team, apart from New Zealand, was capable of winning in Paris and Edinburgh. They would be stupid to depart from the game that has won matches for them. If I find it boring, then I find it boring. If England win the World Cup, it would have a terrific positive effect on the game here, which would outweigh any tactical approach they might have. We have considered the possibility that England might change. But I expect them to play a similar game in the final. It would be quite difficult to play a game that was remarkably different from your standard one.' No wonder Dwyer is highly regarded. Here was a psychologist of the first order.

Australia were lucky to be still involved in the World Cup after the quarter-finals. Gordon Hamilton's late try in Dublin was the moment of the tournament. It was pure Irish magic. Australia should never have been allowed near Ireland's line in the remaining few minutes of the match. But the home side made a mess of the kick-off after Hamilton's try, Australia took their last chance, and Lynagh scored in the corner to give the Wallabies a 19–18 win.

Australia then returned to Dublin the following Sunday to face the holders, New Zealand. England travelled once again to Murrayfield to face the Scots. That semi-final never recaptured the passion of 1990, despite the prize at stake. Rob Andrew's late dropped goal settled the outcome after Scotland had led 6–0 after half an hour. Webb succeeded with only two out of six penalty attempts, and England might have paid the ultimate price if Gavin Hastings had not missed a simple penalty with the scores tied at 6–6. Hastings had an outstanding World Cup but, sadly, that miss will linger longest. Hastings has the strength of character to live with that.

England were in the final and, ironically, facing the country that had started Cooke and Carling's quest exactly three years earlier. Even a week in sport, as in politics, can be a very long time. It was a major achievement to be exactly where Cooke had planned so long ago. Yet the sniping continued. 'If England win the World Cup, God help rugby,' was the assessment of New Zealand's assistant coach John Hart. Scotland's Ian McGeechan added, 'They were going to strangle the game and we were trying to keep it alive.' Geoff Cooke was getting fed up with the attacks. 'It's all right for the armchair critics to sit there and pontificate. But I would say that for any side to beat France and Scotland in consecutive weeks is a major achievement.'

The team headed south to find that England had gone World Cup-mad: Carling was receiving hundreds of cards daily. Most of the country seemed to be looking forward to Saturday. And back to 1966. Carling was being compared to Bobby Moore, another who presented a dignified image as England captain, every mother's favourite son. The nostalgic slant was not beneficial, however. The soccer heroes of '66 were assured of their places in history. Carling's men were not.

Two matches were playing on Carling's mind, both against Australia. One win, one defeat. The win was that 1988 victory, when England picked up the torch carried by the Divisional sides. The loss was in the summer of 1991, when the tourists tried to keep it tight and Australia took all their chances. How England were going to play the final was consuming Carling, although publicly he admitted, 'The pressure has gone. In certain games you might need to run the ball to win the match. We have every intention of playing to the style that suits us.' His *Captain's Diary* revealed the internal conflict during the last week of the World Cup, however. 'I didn't feel as emotional or as patriotic at Murrayfield as 18 months previous. The whole affair was low-key, amazing when you consider what was at stake. It's a much more relaxed team now that we've got to the final. All the hurdles and the dread of not getting there are gone. We know that we're going to change tactics with this final, not because of media pressure. We can't afford to take notice of what the media say. We will change tactics because we won't dominate them up front the way we've dominated France and Scotland. If we play solely a kicking game, we will not win, because the likes of Lynagh and Campese can kick the ball an awfully long way. If we get points up, we will win. But, I worry that they're such a good defensive side; if we go points down we will struggle. That's what happened in Sydney in the summer. We started playing catch-up rugby. And they're lethal at exploiting any mistakes. So, it's got to be a very tight game.'

England were not left to their own devices during the week. Even the World Cup organisers got into the act. Ray Williams, former secretary of the Welsh Rugby Union, showed less than the expected neutral view. 'Two years ago, when they just failed to win the Grand Slam, England played great rugby. But since then they have tightened up their game, they have closed it up. I think that's a great pity, because they have the ability to play a more expansive game.'

If Welsh envy was an irritant, then the Scots really got under Carling's skin that weekend. Finlay Calder had earlier handed England the World Cup: 'I think England will win because the Australian pack will not be mature enough to handle them. The England forwards will play as the Lions did in 1989. They will grind the Australians down and they will win.' That was not the Scots' stance on match day, though. They turned up in Australian scarves, voicing support for anyone who was playing England.

CARLING
When I first met the Scots in 1988, they weren't like that at all. The change when we went up in 1990 was unbelievable – so nationalistic. We've been there twice since, and I think we're used to it now. David Sole certainly got tartan fever late in life. When I first came across him, he was playing for Bath, and missing was the thick Scottish brogue of later years. He was very English. When Sole moved to Scotland to work, he went the other way, maybe to prove himself. He became very much a Scot.

I've nothing against fervent nationalism. It helped players like J.J. [John Jeffrey] and Finlay [Calder] play out of their skins, especially against us. Their nationalism was nothing new to us. Nor was their hatred of England when we met them. But it upset the England boys when they turned up in Aussie scarves for the final. Wade [Dooley] confronted Gavin [Hastings] at the dinner that night. 'Why did you do that? I've been on a Lions tour with you against Australia.' Gavin replied that it was just something the Scottish lads had thought would be a laugh. Winters and I had a similar conversation with Craig Chalmers. It was obvious that it was the idea of a couple of the senior players, and the rest thought it best to go along with it, not wishing to be seen siding with the English.

I don't think it went down well with the England supporters at Twickenham. The final wasn't about England against Scotland. It was about the northern hemisphere against the southern hemisphere, which had traditionally ruled the rugby world. This was a chance to switch the balance of power. If Scotland had been in the final against Australia, we would have been supporting them wholeheartedly. England wanted the northern hemisphere to win rugby's World Cup. If it couldn't be England, then we would follow whoever carried that flag.

Saturday, 2 November 1991 was rugby's showpiece day. The World Cup final was beamed live to 40 countries, nearly treble the number in 1987. That game had been a disappointment. France's peak had been their thrilling 30–24 semi-final victory over Australia, and the All Blacks were in control throughout, winning comprehensively by 29–9. This contest was to be different.

The Princess Royal and Prince Edward were in attendance, while Conservative and Labour parties united as John Major and Neil Kinnock lent support to England's challenge. The Queen herself was introduced to the teams beforehand. And a right royal final Her Majesty got. To the impartial observer – and there were many who sided for the day only – it was a cracking contest. Australia got their noses in front, then hung on for dear life; Carling's prophecy about falling behind proved spot-on. England threw everything at the Australians, except the kitchen sink. The kitchen sink might have been more appropriate: England would have squashed the Aussies if they had battered them with a single large object, namely the England pack. But it was an emotional day. And England got carried away. Everybody got into the act, and nobody let the side down. But that emotional wave allowed Australia to survive.

Nick Farr-Jones's golden Wallabies were running on empty. No one envied or decried England their knock-out victories, but the Aussies had suffered a hell of time in Dublin. Ireland's quarter-final display had shaken them to the core. Ignore the brave noises afterwards: the Australians had thought they were out of the World Cup. And the semi-final win over New Zealand was just as tough. Two first-half tries, inspired by Campese's magic, gave Australia just enough breathing space to survive a continual All Black onslaught.

Webb, with the wind, missed penalty chances in the first half, and England turned round 9–0 behind. Michael Lynagh had kicked a penalty, then converted a try scored by prop Tony Daly from a line-out. Australia were that close to the England line after a spectacular break out of defence by centre Tim Horan. Campese missed his chance after a kick-and-chase when the bounce was for once unkind to the Wallaby winger.

Meanwhile, England were flinging the ball around with gay

abandon. Carling had seen that the opposition were tired, and his plan was to run the Aussies off their feet. But it was flawed: it allowed all 15 Australians to die for the cause. All England had to do was wipe out the Australian forwards, and their backs need not have entered the fray. For that's what Uttley had planned, and that's what the England pack expected. Jeff Probyn remembers the shock: 'We'd win good ball, then look up expecting it to be drilled down towards the Australian line. Instead, the backs were throwing the ball around, getting caught, and we would have to trundle back 30 yards for another scrum. We weren't happy. What had happened to our plan? Worse than that, it wasn't working.' The sorry story brought back memories for Uttley. In his playing days, England's forwards would regularly dominate proceedings and still see the scoreboard registering a big nothing for all their efforts.

Webb eventually found the mark for England, but Lynagh restored Australia's advantage immediately. England now became desperate in attack; but Australia were equally desperate in defence. Time and again England made a thrust, only to be denied by last-ditch tackles. The Australians instinctively knew that just one missed effort would mean the end of their World Cup hopes. If they fell behind, they had no resources left with which to fight back. In the end, even Campese, who had been snapping verbally at England and Carling all month, was reduced to committing rugby's version of the professional foul: the deliberate knock-on.

Campese's infringement came at the end of a frantic 33 seconds of play – only half a minute, but a lifetime on the rugby field. Hill took a tap-penalty near half-way. Ackford drove forward, Probyn and Teague drove on. Dooley ripped the ball back, which was knocked out of his hands by Poidevin's tackle on Australia's 10-metre line. Hill gathered again and fed Skinner in space. Skinner was well tackled by Horan, turned and, with support from Winterbottom and Andrew, Hill fed Carling on the blind side. Carling got his pass away as he was up-ended by Little, and Guscott fed Webb, who put Halliday away. He was tackled by Egerton inside the 22 and passed inside blind. The ball went loose, fortunately eluding Moore's dive. Teague snapped it up and drove again at Australia's defence. Probyn was on hand and helped the ball back to Hill. England moved it quickly. A long pass found Andrew, and in one stride it was with Guscott, in another with Carling. Carling straightened and passed to Winterbottom with Underwood outside him. Campese now saw the danger all too clearly: Winterbottom's pass would put Underwood clear. The nearest defenders, Horan and Lynagh, were alongside Carling. So Campese decided he had no option: he deliberately knocked the ball forward. There was no pretence at a catch or one-handed take. Carling took immediate revenge by stepping on Campese's privates as the Australian was bowled over by Skinner – a futile gesture of retribution, but it still made the England captain feel better.

Campese was human after all. Like Blanco in Paris, one of rugby's great entertainers had succumbed to the pressure. Winning the World Cup was the overriding factor. Nobody blamed Campese that afternoon. The England team resented it, of course, for Campese had been spouting all manner of criticism about Carling's side and the way they played their rugby. But, at the death, Campese was more calculating and less emotional about his rugby than they were, and his gamble paid off. Welshman Derek Bevan awarded the penalty, but not the penalty try. Webb put it over, but England were still a converted try or two penalties away from drawing level. It was a penalty kick too far. Australia held on to become the second World Cup champions by 12–6.

Carling led England up to receive their runners-up medals from the Queen. There was no wiping of the hands as Bobby Moore had done 25 years earlier before lifting the Jules Rimet trophy. Carling shook the Queen by the right hand and took the medal in his left. It lies in his house, still not inscribed. Then Carling turned to the crowd, smiled and waved his right arm in salute. He lingered for a second and took a deep breath. England had been a fingertip – Campese's – away from the World Cup. Carling was choked. But, as at Murrayfield in 1990, the public face did not crack. He accepted the defeat with dignity and maturity, and even his critics were impressed with his performance. Adversity is a far tougher test of character. Carling has enjoyed more success than any England rugby captain. He has also endured the two most painful defeats, Grand Slam 1990 and the World Cup final. Yet Carling cannot be accused of not being able to take a beating. In many ways, he copes better than with success.

Nick Farr-Jones managed to raise the World Cup to the crowd, but only just. Within a few minutes Australia's captain was soaking in one of Twickenham's individual baths, and was to remain there for half an hour. The reason was simple: the scrum-half was exhausted and could not summon the energy to get out.

This was Roger Uttley's last official weekend with the England side, and it was not a happy farewell. He still does not understand why England's game plan went so astray.

UTTLEY

We had enough possession to stuff Australia out of sight. The forwards did enough to win the game. There was a misapprehension that Geoff Cooke and I were not happy with England spreading it wide after losing the Grand Slam at Murrayfield – that somehow we stifled the potential of the side. That's not true. As we approached the World Cup final, we agreed to play in the style that had served us well in Paris and Edinburgh. At some point, it was changed. Sitting in the stand, I couldn't believe what I saw when we started running from everywhere. I've never felt so sorry for a pack of forwards in my life. Mike Teague was in tears, and I couldn't blame him. The World Cup was ours for the taking.

CARLING

We played as well as we could. We lost to a great side. I don't have any sense of frustration. We did everything and still lost. The 9 points Australia managed to score in that five-minute spell was the turning point of the game; we never quite came back from that. Still, I think it's probably the best game this side ever played. England had a great tournament. The reaction the players had from the public made it easier to come to terms with losing. We brought a lot of pride to English rugby, and I know that it encouraged lots of youngsters to start playing. That was the measure of our success.

Carling and England, having been visited by John Major in the dressing-room, later joined Australia, New Zealand and Scotland at the special end-of-tournament dinner that night. The speeches rambled on. But Kenneth Clarke, the current Chancellor of the Exchequer, did his political ambitions no harm. Clarke has been in the House of Commons long enough to recognise waffle when he hears it, so, instead of adding to the misery, the then Health Minister cracked a couple of jokes, added a rhetorical 'you don't want to hear any more from me', and sat down to the loudest applause of the night. The England players' wives and girlfriends were excluded from the Royal Lancaster function. Unfortunately, other women were not, as

186

many of the sponsors had mixed tables. Try explaining that away to the other half when she demands to know why there are pictures of you and some Virgin Atlantic air hostess at a 'men only' function. Richard Branson, as ever with an eye on publicity, had offered the players £30,000-worth of free flights if they won the World Cup. That offer remained in defeat.

Carling's girlfriend, Victoria, did make the papers, though: the *Sun*. Their cameras recorded the fact she was wearing stockings and, because she was going out with the captain of England, who had just lost the World Cup final, that had to be front-page news. 'Scrum and get me, Will. Carling's darling dresses to kill,' was the headline. Rugby really had hit the big time now.

Chapter 25

Wine, Women & Song

I've always been amused by the fascination about who Will Carling is going out with. The press seems surprised that the England rugby captain has a girlfriend; I'm sure they would have been a lot more interested if there hadn't been any women on the scene over the past five years.

WILL CARLING

Carling has done his best to keep his sex life under wraps. All Britain's sporting stars have noticed a growing interest in their off-the-field activities over the past decade. Generally, though, it has been England's cricketers who have borne the brunt of front-page, private-life exposés in recent years. Carling's elevation to the captaincy had young girls swooning and mothers plotting: rugby had a sex symbol. Young, dark and handsome, with a Kirk Douglas cleft chin, sparkling eyes and a cheeky smile, Carling was quickly recognised as one of the most eligible men in the country. When the Prince and Princess of Wales announced their separation, Carling's name was published in the list of suitable replacements for Princess Diana. At first, the attention flattered and amused him. However, as England's rugby success increased so Carling's profile grew and it began to embarrass him.

England's captain positively squirmed when 'Good Morning's'

189

Judy Finnegan and Richard Madeley combined with ITV sports presenter Alison Holloway to explore rugby's sex appeal. Carling was hounded until he admitted he was 'fanciable'. England's captain knew he was partly to blame. He had appeared – oiled-up – with his shirt off in a Sunday colour magazine. 'You learn from your mistakes. The photographer said: "Go on! It will be fun." Then it's snap, snap, snap. And then all hell is let loose.' Any such appearances give Carling's team-mates plenty of ammunition. So when national newspapers headlines ask 'Will Carling ever find a girl to make him happy?' and describe England's captain as 'scrumptious', there is no escape. One former Quins team-mate said in the article that followed: 'He's too intelligent and conscious of press interest in him to be caught with some old boiler of a barmaid in his hotel bedroom.' They had always been amused by Carling's repeated 'I'm in love. This is the big one' statements. 'The boys saw through that one,' admitted Rob Andrew. 'We stopped taking any notice.' But dressing-room interest revived when the captain revealed that his fan-mail included begging letters.

CARLING
There were married women, enclosing pictures and saying please call on this number when my husband is out, then come round. I used to open all my mail, even the letters that had been sent care of Harlequins or Twickenham, but I was so shocked at some of the explicit things I read, I ask that the letters are opened before they get to me. Of course, I didn't take any of the inducements the lads offered me to pass a few of the numbers on! I'm not a great flirt. I can't handle women coming on. So many people, not just women, have a preconceived idea of what I'm like. It's an effort to break that down. Often, I don't bother. When I'm introduced to my friends' new ladies, they often say that the girlfriend has been dying to meet me. 'Why? I'm just your mate.' Hero-worship from kids I understand. I was the same way when I was young. I find it hard to handle when adults approach me in the same way. That attitude can make it difficult with new relationships. The people who don't push themselves forwards are probably the types I would get on with best. I don't like it when people come on strong. If a woman does the running and tries to corner me, I'm out of the door. I can't stand being crowded. I'm rather traditional in that way. Basically, I'm an

out-and-out man's man. I'm not uneasy with women, but I'm more comfortable in men's company.

Carling has been at great pains to keep his private life private. He has never denied the existence of girlfriends, but insisted that they had nothing to do with his public profile and rugby career. The press labelled one – Deborah – as 'mysterious' because Carling refused to reveal her surname and occupation. Nikki Turner became 'Mrs Carling' for a day when he was invited to Wimbledon in 1989 and the Royal Box guest list gave him a wife. Generally, Carling has been attracted to blondes, although dark-haired Sky sports presenter Beverley Webb was a brief exception. That relationship did not last long, as business and pleasure do not easily mix in Carling's life. It was too open. Not only did other players know about it, but so did the rugby press and that made Carling feel vulnerable. Discretion has been a hallmark of his friendships, not only with girls. Friends are very loyal as they are only too well aware that Carling is very protective of his privacy. Carling once said in an interview: 'I think this whole idea of me being a heart-throb is a sick joke. They should speak to some of my ex-girlfriends.' Yet Carling was very upset when Victoria went 'public' after he started seeing Julia.

Rugby has always enjoyed a chauvinistic reputation that is well deserved. Rugby tours and rugby teams have always attracted camp followers. Carling's army has been no different. But the new fitness and health disciplines of this current England rugby team leave little scope for the indulgences of yesteryear.

CARLING
I love rugby and have a great respect for playing and the guys who play it. But when it comes to rugby coupled with beer, dirty songs and abusing women, you can leave me out. That's not my scene. Anyway, I'm not big enough to abuse anyone. I know some of the older brigade are sad that this way of rugby life is ceasing to exist. It doesn't matter. I would never have fitted into that mould. I find it mindless. I've always shied away from that type of rugby image. I prefer to go out for a bloody good night with four or five friends. I'm not comfortable in a big public environment among large groups of people. I don't like standing around in the Harlequins clubhouse because I don't get a chance

to talk to the people I want to. That's a problem for me. I'm not being big-headed, that's just the way it is.

The England rugby captain has to worry about more women than most. The wives of RFU committee men have always liked to fraternise with the good-looking skipper. And Carling has to worry about the wives and girlfriends of the other players, too. Here he has to be careful not to show favours. When Victoria declined lunch with the Princess Royal before the World Cup semi-final, Carling passed the invitation on to Cooke's wife, Sue. 'I would have put my life on the line if I'd have asked one of the other wives. Word would have got round. "Why did Will pick her?" Maybe it was a bit cowardly, but I know it was the best option.' Carling often has to face an aggrieved wife as well as a dropped player.

CARLING
The wives and girlfriends are very loyal. I've had a few words said in my direction when they've not been happy. Geoff has certainly involved the families much more. I don't disagree with that. The support from home is vital, especially given all the time the players are away. But you can't include them in everything. The England squad has about the right balance at the moment. Wives can never be involved in team matters, but a few question selection. It's human nature: they want their man to be successful. I understand that, but I won't ever discuss those sorts of decisions with them. It's never become a problem. Susie Ackford, Sara Andrew and Karen Hill like to talk about matches with me. The safest thing is to agree with them, because if a change is made to the side, it gets back that Will has said one thing and done another. I'm pleased that they enjoy rugby, but discussing selection decisions with them is the last thing that I want.

Few of Carling's own girlfriends have been that interested in rugby or sport. Nikki Turner, the PR girl who went out with Carling for over a year before heading for Australia after they split in 1990, was fairly typical. Carling commented: 'She came to the matches, but hadn't the slightest interest in rugby.' That is the way Carling likes it. England's captain enjoys little enough respite from rugby without the other half wanting to discuss rugby matters. Most have been friends

192

of friends or part of a group, though Victoria was an exception. He met her at a sports dinner at London University, where she was an economics student, in March 1991. When she saw his collection of Five Nations shirts, she asked Carling if they were all the teams he had played for. Julia, who is due to marry Carling in the summer of 1994, was a close friend of Nikki Turner's. Julia's previous heroes have been in the pop world, not the sporting arena. Quite a few girlfriends have been home to meet mum. That did not reflect the seriousness of the relationships, more the closeness of the Carling family and his respect for his mother's judgement. Interestingly, former girlfriends of both Carling boys still remain in contact with mum and dad.

Carling was already a personality when he went to Durham. One early tutorial became an ordeal when he jokingly suggested a woman's place was in the home, having children and keeping the bed warm. The two female psychology students missed, or chose to ignore, the wind-up and used the opportunity to lay into Carling for nearly an hour.

CARLING

In one of the early interviews while I was at Durham, I was asked about my girlfriends and 'What's it like being a sex symbol?' My response was 'What are you talking about?' I believe if I wasn't captain of England, it wouldn't happen to me. I can't look in a mirror and say I'm a genuinely good-looking bloke. I tend to get embarrassed. But I can't win; nobody's going to believe it if I claim 'I hate it'. But, honestly, I really can't understand what all the fuss is about. Even my girlfriends call me boring. Women are attracted to sportsmen: they're fit, in better shape than most blokes and rugby players tend to be fun. Other players have given me a lot of stick. There's not much I can do about it. It's a fair point that if I hate the label so much, why do I model clothes and appear in advertisements? I'm not trying to promote myself. I'm just modelling a face that people recognise.

I've always been amused by the fascination about who Will Carling is going out with. The press seems surprised that the England rugby captain has a girlfriend. I'm sure they would be a lot more interested if there hadn't been any women on the scene over the past five years. But they present it as if I'm some kind of man about town. I'm not a disco or wine-bar person. If I was always nightclubbing, fair enough. But they could follow me for months and be bored out of their brains. I've always been careful about the women I get involved with. These days, players are very aware of being set up, especially on tour. I'm lucky: the more I drink, the sleepier I get.

Carling is certainly not one of rugby's legendary drinkers. During his 1992 summer split with Victoria, he would call up Peter Winterbottom and Jason Leonard on a 'Mission to Get Drunk'. Carling was not a regular socialiser with team-mates. They tended to see more of him when he was unattached. That has not been often. More than once that summer, a tired and emotional Carling was sent home about 10 o'clock to allow the serious drinkers to carry on with the business in hand. Carling is not a big drinker or a frequent one. He sees no point wasting hard-earned fitness that way. Sometimes, drink is a release, especially after a tough international. Occasionally, the alcohol allows Carling to get something off his chest. Eddie Butler was one who faced Carling in that mood after his television criticism. But Carling has to be careful, even on international match night. There are too many eavesdropping ears for the indiscreet word or deed, as the press continue to probe or committee men air their thoughts on the day's proceedings. Everyone wants to talk to Will Carling. Often, England's captain does not want to talk to anyone.

Bawdy, i.e. dirty, rugby songs have largely disappeared from the scene. The singing has continued with classic pop songs or nationalistic chants. Carling's rugby team was given *Swing Low, Sweet Chariot* by the Twickenham crowd. It is their anthem. Now it can be heard wherever, whatever England are playing. But whenever it is heard, Twickenham and Carling come to mind. 'Swing Low' has become the ultimate rugby song. Carling believes there has never been a stronger bond between England supporters and their team. 'I am much more aware of the Twickenham crowd than I used to be. We all are. They have come over to our side. It used to be fairly dead. The fans were there to watch rugby, not to support England. Now they have the same pride as us. Twickenham is an intimidating place. Other countries notice it now. Everyone used to go on about how difficult it was to win in the championship at Cardiff. Well, Twickenham is the ultimate challenge now.'

Chapter 26

Ooh, La, La!

The incidents increased after the World Cup. I seemed to be getting stamped on a lot. By and large, referees look after me. One or two don't. The impression is, 'You're a big star. Can't you look after yourself?'

WILL CARLING

No sooner had England licked their World Cup wounds than they were contemplating trips back to Murrayfield and Paris in the 1992 Five Nations championship. Carling was pleased that his 'Dad's Army' squad had remained almost intact. Paul Ackford had retired, but the rest soldiered on, although Teague's neck injury kept him out for the season. Probyn returned to Wasps after one match for Askeans, while Andrew announced that his work was taking him to France and Toulouse. Tim Rodber, not Richards, took Teague's place, while Bayfield came in for Ackford. Dewi Morris returned as scrum-half after three years, and Hill moved back to the bench. Carling realised that this was probably the last throw for this team, and others thought so, too. Halliday and Webb suggested that they would retire at the end of the championship, while Dooley, Winterbottom, Underwood and Skinner had already given similar indications.

The New Year's Honours List brought an OBE for Carling. Roger

Uttley had already been to the Palace to collect his during the World Cup, but Cooke was noticeable by his absence. The RFU tentacles stretch a mighty long way. That Cardiff silence was still loud in the memory.

The World Cup had changed the perception both of rugby and of the leading players in England. The die-hards shook their heads when it was revealed that Jerry Guscott missed a Bath league game because of a modelling assignment in Miami. There had been rumours that Guscott would go to Rugby League immediately after the World Cup. But he stayed, and found himself in much demand. As times were changing, so was the rugby. Bath fought back from 18–0 down to draw with Harlequins in the Courage League. It was a wholehearted tussle in which Quins' Australian World Cup final victor Troy Coker was sent off, while rival hookers Brian Moore and Graham Dawe fought their usual private war. 'The game was harder than when I started playing international rugby,' reflected Stuart Barnes.

Back-to-back Grand Slams had not been achieved since the 1920s, again by England, led by W. J. A. Davies (1923) and a former pupil of Sedbergh, Wavell Wakefield (1924). Murrayfield and Paris held no new terrors for Carling's men, and the parlous state of Irish and Welsh rugby made England firm favourites.

Edinburgh was first up. Carling noticed two missing faces in the opposition, as both Calder and Jeffrey had called it a day after the World Cup. Scrum-half Gary Armstrong was also out of the Scotland side through injury. Yet England struggled in the first half, and their forwards even suffered the shame of a Scottish push-over try. Only Webb's boot kept England ahead. Then new cap Rodber was carried off after an hour with spinal concussion although, fortunately, the paralysis proved only temporary. But his exit allowed Richards to enter and grab the game by the scruff of the neck. The pack's response said everything about Richards's immense influence. They fed off his power like a battery charger. Soon Underwood was sprinting away for his first try at Murrayfield. Morris then added a second, and Guscott's marvellously lazy dropped goal finished proceedings, England winning 25–7. Carling's view was shared by most observers: 'After half-time, I was very pleased with the way we played. But that opening was too lethargic for us to be satisfied.'

Carling had no such reservations after the Ireland game a fortnight later. Rodber had recovered and Richards returned to the bench; influential though Richards had been, Geoff Cooke is always keen to give newcomers a fair run, and the rarity of one-cap wonders in his time is testimony to good and consistent selection. Ireland never recovered from Webb's try after only 23 seconds, as England revived memories of the victory over Wales at Twickenham two years earlier. Ireland were run ragged. 'If anything, it was too good a start,' admitted Carling afterwards. 'The classic opening, 6 points up in the first minute. But, after all the pre-match hype, we just sat back and thought "That's it. The game is over." In the end we were shattered, and it was the most tiring match I have played in since Australia 1988.' Ireland's coach and captain, Ciaran Fitzgerald and Phil Matthews, both described it as the finest England performance they had witnessed, but Brian Moore, England's pack leader, was not satisfied with the 38–9 victory. 'If we had played with more discipline in the second half, the score could have been 60 points. But we were tired and became greedy.' That week, Moore had become involved in a public wrangle with TV personality Henry Kelly, who had attacked the England hooker in print for saying that he needed a bit of hate to play at this level of rugby. 'Kelly said you did not,' responded Moore. 'But I can tell you that playing against a rival international front row is not like appearing in a television game show. I have done both and know what it takes.'

Having made his point, Moore headed for Paris and another showdown with France. Richards was this time restored, and England broke French hearts with a third successive triumph (31–13) in the stadium where the rest of Britain could not win. Again, Carling's men kept their heads, especially in the closing stages, when Irish referee Steve Hilditch sent off two Frenchmen. Stephen Jones, of the *Sunday Times*, commented: 'French rugby crashed in flames in Paris. It burned itself to death. The team lost to an England side who were superior in rugby ability, but far more significantly so in heart and soul. France also lost their sense of shame.'

France again blamed the trouble on an Anglo-Saxon conspiracy, and Blanco, now in retirement, singled out Brian Moore as the instigator of much of the trouble. But the ridiculous point of the sendings-off was that they came when the contest was long over. England were streets ahead and playing out time when police inspector prop Gregoire Lascubé stamped on Bayfield's head, then hooker and café owner Vincent Moscato followed for punching.

197

Jean-François Tordo, who became France's captain in 1993, was lucky not to become No. 3.

CARLING

It's important to keep your discipline against France. It also helps if you can get the French thinking about something other than rugby. Our guys are experienced enough to accept the physical intimidation. There's very little I can do as captain out in the backs if someone gets punched and decides to get his own back. But, for the team's benefit, it's best to treat the macho stuff for what it is.

The referee was brave, but he was left with no choice. Those incidents were more stupid than really dangerous. The prop stamped on Bayfield's head, and everyone accepts that as a sending-off offence. Then a scrum broke up, and Hilditch warned the forwards. The next moment the French hooker was punching. Again, Hilditch had no choice. Off the Frenchman went. He achieved nothing.

People ask what it is like to play in a game like that. It wasn't actually that bad until near the end, when France had already lost the game. There are always flashpoints, though, and England aren't blameless or angelic. We've done things wrong. The current England side won't sit still and be kicked around. But I believe that we've shown we are mature enough to concentrate on the rugby. Jason [Leonard] was stamped on the head against Wales last year. Nothing happened. Our disciplinary record is good.

I remember my *Captain's Diary* created a furore when I wrote, 'I've come across a few players who you know will try and stamp on you if they catch you on the floor. Or gouge your eyes if you're stuck in a maul. A couple of Welsh forwards spring to mind. Some French forwards are tricky, too, but for them it's only an extension of their club rugby, which is the most brutal in the world. You don't feel that their violence is directed against you personally. But those Welsh forwards I mention go in to maim individuals, and everyone knows what they're up to. But you look at these blokes as you leave the pitch and think, "Do I really have to drink with you tonight?" Which is a shame.' I stand by those words. But they were a mistake. I'm not one who abides by rugby's unwritten rule of silence on all matters of violence.

But I should have identified the culprits if I felt that strongly. Or kept quiet.

Of course, I'm a marked man. But there's no use complaining about it. The more you complain, the worse it gets. If players want to make a point or get noticed, they do Will Carling. The best way is to keep moving on the field ... and keep quiet. I know Jerry [Guscott] has the same problem. But the advantage of being a well-known name is that you know the best people to look after you. Opposing centres aren't going to worry about me, but they might if Winters, Jason or Deano comes after them. Skinner has always promised to look after me: 'I'll be there, skipper. Any trouble and let me know.' The trouble with that is, if he does come to my rescue, I hear about it for weeks. 'That's one you owe me, skipper. What about a drink?' The others see it as part and parcel of the game. They protect you without a word.

The incidents increased after the World Cup. I seemed to be getting stamped on a lot. By and large, referees look after me. One or two don't. The impression is, 'You're a big star. Can't you look after yourself?' I've been very lucky with serious injuries, much luckier than Melville, Halliday and Oti. The game has become more competitive at international and club level, though that's been balanced with the greater involvement of touch judges. I believe it's cleaner than it used to be. I'm amazed when I talk to the old players about what used to go on. I hear officials laughing in the bar about the mayhem in the old days – then they pontificate on the modern game and how it needs to be cleaned up. Just another example of the double standards.

I believe referees could do with even more help from touch judges. There's so much to watch. Referees do make mistakes, though not as many as the players. Good referees are hard to find, and that's why I was amazed when Fred Howard was missing from England's panel last season. I've never understood the structure. Fred was one of the best, and recognised and respected by the players as such. Suddenly, he was out. The same happened to Clive Norling. And to Les Peard. I don't see why the countries should share around the refereeing duties. If there are one or two in form, then let them take charge of most of the championship matches.

The biggest problem is, there doesn't seem to be a common

interpretation between the countries. I'm not just talking about the northern and southern hemispheres. Often, players get a sense of frustration in the championship. What's acceptable in one game is not in the next, and who is refereeing the match becomes a key factor.

I try to keep as quiet as possible with refs; accept their decisions. Sometimes, that's hard. But some refs don't want to explain their decisions, even to the captain. Occasionally, I'm told to go away in no uncertain terms. But how can a captain sort out a problem if he doesn't know what it is? What I don't like is when a ref calls the two captains together when things are getting a little fraught, and he issues a general warning that the next offender is going to be sent off. Then another punch is thrown, and nothing happens. That's what causes real problems. Players prefer referees who mean what they say. Players quickly know who the disciplinarians are. I don't mean that they are whistle-happy – most of the best let the game run. But when they issue a warning, that's it. The best are those who have a feel for the game. I like referees who talk a lot. It's useful for players.

The Welsh officials have worked well as a trio in my time. All three – Norling, Peard and Bevan – are top refs in their own right. Again, I don't understand why the World Cup organisers decided to invite only two referees from each country and split up an experienced team. The best referees, like the best players, seem to be resented by the authorities for enjoying too high a profile.

Chapter 27

The Buzz

When I'm up there, I take it all in as if it's the first time, and maybe the last. I try and store away the special feeling. I know that I will miss this most when I finish, more than playing.

WILL CARLING

The 1967 All Black touring party to Britain were labelled 'the unsmiling giants'. New Zealand's rugby stars have traditionally kept themselves to themselves, happy with their own company and wary of outsiders. British rugby teams have no such history. The social nature of the game has always generated friendly contact with all involved and in Wales at least, the players feed off that national support. England's rugby players, however, with rare exceptions, have been able to walk the streets in peace. Even Bill Beaumont was not a national celebrity in his playing days.

The World Cup and rugby's increasing profile changed all that. Carling's players became household faces and names. But the team had already begun to take a more detached stance, drawing its strength from within. The Murrayfield Grand Slam defeat and its aftermath was the cause of that. The playing demands on the modern rugby star had also grown dramatically, while other unsolicited requirements became more tiresome and intrusive. As a result, the England group took on the persona of an All Black squad. They went about their task in a business-like manner; outsiders were made to feel unwelcome; an invisible wall appeared around them. Carling had his own problems with the press and the attention, but he was not alone. Few enjoy the pressures of being public property.

The team offered Carling relief and sanctuary. England's captain felt able to relax in their company, first among equals. And, in common with the rest, the international weekends were Carling's favourite time. 'When I end my England career, those few days together are what I will miss the most,' admits Carling. 'It's not just playing the internationals, but all the time the team is assembled. There's such a special atmosphere, which is the major reason why many of the players have carried on so long. It's an invitation to a party which nobody wants to turn down.' Carling's preparation for that big party begins on Wednesday morning.

CARLING
WEDNESDAY. I pack my kit, along with my Walkman and tapes. Most of them are W.D.C.C. compilations, music that will help my state of mind before the match. When Twickenham is the venue, I arrive at the Petersham Hotel during the afternoon. The rest will appear early evening. Already, I have started thinking about what I'm going to do over the next couple of days. What I'm going to say, who I'm going to speak to, what's going to happen at the practice sessions.

New caps are no longer strangers. All have been involved at B level and in the training weekends. The squad is so experienced that new arrivals slip in effortlessly to this well-oiled machine. If they feel a little lost, it's probably just the running gags and in-jokes. But the senior players always try to break the ice. I hope they find it a friendly squad. It's certainly a lot more relaxed than when I was first capped. No matter how confident a player appears on the field, coming in at international level is an ordeal. Ian Hunter got very nervous, and Martin Johnson was in a state of shock after his late call-up, although he quickly came to terms with it. Tony Underwood always looks so cool, but he was apprehensive. When Stuart Barnes returned, I told him he had my full backing. I didn't want his talent stifled.

The first practice is at the Stoop [Harlequins' ground] about 7:00 on Wednesday night. Dick [Best] runs that session. The squad is split into forwards and backs. The pack is sometimes

202

opposed by the B team, while the backs go through their paces, any new moves. As far as we're concerned, it's just a loosener. The session is really for the forwards, to get them working. Afterwards, the squad eats in our private dining-room at the hotel. Normally, it's early to bed on Wednesday.

THURSDAY. I get up at 8:30 and switch on TV for the 'Big Breakfast' on Channel 4. When I'm at home, it's usually Capital Radio. I'm not big on breakfasts, though – usually, a couple of bananas, toast and cereal. We meet at 9:30 on Thursday morning and again, Bestie takes charge. This time he concentrates on the opposition. Then it's off to the Stoop for a hard session, though there are problems with only two days to go before the match. It's too close for a really heavy session, and you don't want to work the players that hard. Thursday is normally a closed session. We spend 20 minutes warming up, then go through all the variations. That finishes about midday. Lunch, then the press conference. The media are asked not to attend any earlier. That involves Cookie, Bestie and me. It's rarely scintillating.

I head back to try to sleep in the afternoon. That's not a problem. Then there's an hour's signing session before another meeting at 6:30. We study the opposition on special compilation videos showing their work at line-outs, scrums and in the backs. Geoff and Dick start the discussion with their opinions before the players get stuck in. Senior players such as Brian, Rob and Winters obviously have a regular input, but Geoff likes to encourage everyone to feel involved. Normally, there are about 15 rugby tapes around for the lads to watch individually, and a local shop provides a dozen of the latest film releases.

Although we are still fairly relaxed, there's not a lot of mucking about. That is reserved for the weekend squad sessions and the after-match festivities. There are three tables in our dining-room at the hotel: one is for the management, and the players take the others. There is no back/forward, young/old split. They all sit down as they come in. After dinner, I begin to talk to the players, checking out that they are not too tense or too relaxed. I also work out what I want to do and say on Friday. That's when I take over.

FRIDAY. You can begin to feel the tension. Everyone is far more switched on. We have a crisp 45-minute session at the Stoop, watched by the public and the media. Often the forwards and the goal-kickers stay behind. It's the TV and press interviews for me straight afterwards. Then it's on the coach, back to Richmond, lunch and another afternoon nap. Some of the lads wander into Richmond or watch videos. I'll join them after an hour and a half's sleep.

I'm in charge of the 6:30 meeting. It's the only talk I really give. I try to be positive and concentrate on the good things we've done. Like Cookie, I try to involve everyone. We always finish off with a bit of humour. My appearance with Mr Blobby has become a favourite. So is the one with Jerry's out-takes on HTV. A home video of Winters when he is rather the worse for wear is also popular. The plan is to ease the tension at the end of the meeting. The cinema is a popular destination on Friday night, but I don't always go.

Whatever happens, I never miss my Friday evening walk up Richmond Hill with my Walkman. I'm not superstitious, but I can't imagine a Twickenham international without it. The music is usually the inspirational sort, like the theme from *The Mission*. I find my walk keeps everything in perspective. I remember being a kid and wanting to play for England. I remind myself that I'm here because I enjoy it. And I must enjoy it, because you never know when it's going to be your last international. So much can go wrong – I might get injured. It would be nice to think I can bow out gracefully, but there's no guarantee. So when I'm up there, I take it all in as if it's the first time, and maybe the last. I try and store away the special feeling. I know that I will miss this most when I finish, more than playing.

Some of the lads are still up when I get back. I'll sit down and maybe have a hot chocolate with Jason and Webbie. It sounds like I have a set routine, but that's not true. Only the walk up the hill is a must. I chat to the lads who are still up. Are they happy? Then it's off to bed. I never have any trouble sleeping.

SATURDAY. I must admit that there's a huge adrenalin surge when I wake. A cup of tea is delivered at 8:30 and I read most of the papers, although I don't take much in. I'm not one to go rushing to the window to check the weather. I'm not bothered – it's the same for both sides. And I always feel we're better equipped than our opponents to adapt to most conditions. The players wander down for breakfast about 9:00. I will have some pasta at 10 o'clock. An hour later, the backs and forwards have separate meetings before going up to pack for the match. We all meet at 12:30, with coffee, sandwiches and bananas available.

The coach leaves at 1:00. And, after signing the police outriders' programmes, we're off. That 12:30 meeting just before we leave is very quiet. And so is the atmosphere on the bus. I put the headphones on. Sometimes I listen to the music that's playing on the bus – unless Brian has put it on. Everyone, though, has entered their own little world by now, backs and forwards. No one is too chirpy by this stage.

PRE-MATCH. We walk through a packed crowd, but I don't really take any notice. Normally, it's about an hour and a half to kick-off. The first thing is to dump the kit – in the same spot – then go out and inspect the pitch, as well as checking what new stands have been constructed in our absence! It's important to walk around Twickenham to feel how the wind varies. I talk to others such as Brian and Rob about it. Obviously, a strong wind in a definite direction can play a part. We also discuss the toss. Again, there are no set rules. It depends who we're playing, what sort of mood we're in. I don't always make a choice of ends. If there's little wind, I might take the kick-off.

When we get back to the dressing-room, I announce that I want everyone ready with 20 minutes to go. Rory just sits in a corner and reads his programme. Winters and Jerry change quickly, while Brian talks incessantly. Mike Teague and Winters don't say a word. I'll have a quiet word with each of the players. Then I change, but don't put my boots on until later. Smurph [physio Kevin Murphy] is busy strapping. Most players have their ankles done. Players are also getting rubbed down. Cookie comes in and out, but there's not a lot for him to do. Bestie stays in all the time, and so does Slem [Mike Slemen]. Bestie gets very nervous and uptight. As the match approaches, Bestie wants to do more. He gets very keyed up. Roger [Uttley] was similar. He'd been there and done it, and now he was frustrated he couldn't play. Their worst feelings come when they realise that there's nothing more they can do. Cookie is quite clever at hiding his anxiety. The worst thing a coach or manager can do is pass on those anxieties. I don't think Roger ever got used to it, or that Bestie ever will, but Cookie has. And if he gets nervous, he just disappears from the dressing-room.

Don [Rutherford] wanders in, but we're not keen on RFU

hierarchy being present at this time. John Burgess used to come in and give the players a kiss and a hug. Nobody wanted him there, so he was asked not to come in. I don't want to talk to people outside the immediate squad at this stage. It's very quiet.

There is a scrummage machine in the dressing-room and a tackle bag for the players to work up. The referee comes in to check the studs, and I find out from him if there is anything we should concentrate on. We toss up half an hour before kick-off. Then we get together in a circle, arms round each other. There's no shouting, ranting or raving. It's just to get us as one. Brian normally follows me out as I lead the side on to the field. Several times, I've had to take a back seat, allowing Rory, Winters, Rob or Wade to celebrate a 50th cap by running out first. That's no problem for me, and it gives the crowd a chance to acknowledge their achievement. There's always the anthems, and often presentations. I always cross myself before the start. I've no nerves. They were left back in the team room at the hotel. At this stage, all you want to do is play. Then the whistle blows and you start.

POST-MATCH. You're either very happy or very disappointed. Either way, I'm shattered. One of the first duties is a BBC interview, although you're still high and not ready to come to any considered conclusions on what has just happened. I have to work very hard at not saying something stupid, and I don't always succeed. But I am not going to give anything away at that stage.

Even when we win, not many people are allowed in the dressing-room. That's our private area. The forwards tend to sit around for a while and wind down from the physical battle. Of course, there's a lot of talk about the referee. After Rory's mistake in Cardiff [in 1993], nothing was said. There was no inquest. Nobody wanted to intrude on his private grief. Anyway, I don't believe individuals lose matches. Nor do they win them.

Shirt-swapping is the norm these days, but I rarely get involved, although I got Gavin's this year. I usually give my England jersey to charity. I have got a full international set, including those from South Africa's Danie Gerber, All Black Craig Innes and Australia's Tim Horan. I've always worn the England No. 13 shirt. As I've stated, I'm not superstitious, though Jerry doesn't like it, and Bath don't have a No. 13 jersey.

The schedule is hectic after the match. A quick bath and change, then it's off to the press conference with Dick and Geoff. Again, the press want a detailed analysis of what has happened, and that's easier for Dick and Geoff to provide. The press are also looking for any fuel to fire controversy over tries or refereeing decisions. We try not to provide any. You are still in quite an emotional state, especially if an expected victory has ended in defeat.

I work on my *Mail on Sunday* column before heading off to the Rose Room to see my folks. It's like a madhouse in there now. The players have a roped-off area, but I still feel on show. There are so many people after autographs that it's impossible to hold a conversation. I remember my grandad coming to one game and I never got the chance to talk to him. And getting from our area to the bus takes about a quarter of an hour. The bus leaves for the Hilton about 6 o'clock. It's all a bit chaotic. It's such a crazy rush, mainly because there is a 45-minute bus ride into the middle of London. In the end, you get little chance to enjoy any of it. The bus is packed with wives and girlfriends, and often you don't even get a seat.

I don't start relaxing until I get into my room at the Hilton. That's the first place I'm left on my own. There's peace and quiet, and I can start to come down a bit. That's only for a few minutes, and then it's down to the dinner. The captain is stuck on the top table, although I try to spend as much time with the lads as possible. It would be nice if they let the captain sit with his team. I don't give my speech any thought until about five minutes before I stand up – it's hardly the Gettysburg address. I have to thank quite a few people: the team, the referee, the opposition, remember anyone's birthday, and try a funny. But I'm still England captain, and that's the role I have to play all night. Often, I'm still signing autographs after midnight, when I just want to relax and be left alone.

The RFU claim the dinner is there to thank all the people in the game who help, and I can see their point of view. It's obvious where their priorities lie. It's not held for the benefit of the players, and it's certainly not the ideal wind-down after such an intensive build-up. The wives and girlfriends are at a separate dinner. The players tend to spend a lot of time at the bar. If I had my choice, we would have a mixed dinner in Richmond with all the players together. But, as I've said, it's made very clear that the dinner is not for us.

The dinner after the Hong Kong Sevens is the best that I've been to. Every team has to do a little skit, and it's great fun. Paris and Dublin are good nights, too. We haven't been made to feel particularly welcome recently in Edinburgh, though I had a great night out with Scott Hastings and Alan Tait after my first win in 1988. People imagine the result will determine the sort of evening you have. Still, 1993 was fun in Cardiff with Robert Jones and Scott Gibbs. Normally, finishing is early-hours time.

SUNDAY. It's a very flat day. At least it's a chance to really reflect for the first time on the events of the previous afternoon. Strangely, it's usually Tuesday or Wednesday before it sinks in. I remember that after Scotland 1990. Midway through the week, I suddenly realised: 'Christ, we've lost the lot.' That's the worst feeling I've ever had.

Chapter 28

Easy, Easy!

Other international players seem reluctant to approach Will. All they know is what they read. Will is shy. Not an extrovert. He won't push himself forward in a group he doesn't know, so he probably seems aloof and arrogant.

ROB ANDREW

The Grand Slam was on again. As Carling prepared for the 1992 visit of Wales, this verdict was passed on his men: 'I believe this is the most skilful and fittest team England have ever fielded. I take enormous pride in the way the side has conducted itself. This was epitomised by their tremendous discipline in Paris. But the truly great thing has been their total dedication to the things in hand.' The speaker? Cooke? Uttley? Best? Or Carling? Even Don Rutherford? No, it was Peter Yarranton, who was RFU president that season.

Yarranton may have been full of praise for Carling's team, but he was also a prime mover in frustrating the players' commercial aims and keeping things as they were in the '80s – that is, like the 1880s. Yarranton had also skilfully managed to walk the South African tightrope while representing both the Sports Council and the RFU, two bodies about as far apart on their attitude to the Republic as the Afrikaaner and Zulu. Yarranton was about to move to become chairman of the proposed UK Sports Commission, while another RFU stalwart, Ian Beer, became chairman of the Sports Council. The success of Cooke and Carling's England was carrying all sorts of adversaries along for the ride.

A more significant announcement regarding the new rugby world concerned David Sole's imminent retirement. Scotland's captain was to call it a day after his country's summer tour to Australia. Sole was only 29, a mere pup on the front-row time-scale – Jeff Probyn, England's most-capped prop, had not won his first cap until he was 31. Sole had made his international debut alongside Gavin Hastings in 1986, although Norman Mair, Scotland's most respected rugby writer, remembers him from even earlier, in his first Scottish trial. 'It was such a shame. He was marvellous around the field, but he couldn't scrummage. I never thought we would see him again. But he went back to Bath and worked so hard. When he returned, the transformation was remarkable.' Sole never became a formidable scrummager, but he at least learnt to stand his ground at the highest level. And under the influence of Jack Rowell at Bath and Scotland's Ian McGeechan, Sole became an international player and captain of stature. Murrayfield 1990 was his finest hour. Few Scottish leaders have walked out so confidently – or so slowly – at the head of the tartan army.

Less than two years later, Sole was ready to quit: 'It's not the year the model was made that matters these days. Look at the miles on the clock.' Sole had already told Carling of his intentions to quit after the Calcutta Cup match. 'I was surprised,' explained England's captain. 'I asked him, why wasn't he staying on until 1993 to captain the Lions? But David said that he'd had enough. He joked that he was leaving the way clear for me, but he added in all seriousness that it would be very hard for a so-called pretty-boy England back to captain the Lions. It wasn't a judgement on me, just the image that was perceived among the other nationalities.' England's fly-half Rob Andrew, another 'pretty boy', was also aware of the problem.

ANDREW
I don't think Will's absence from the 1989 Lions tour was a blow to him from the playing point of view. But the tour would have done him lots of good in other areas, such as mixing with players from other countries. The Lions is an amazing experience. The home countries hate each other for two or three years, then they all come together for the Lions. Up to that point, you're

suspicious of players from other countries. And the press like to feed that national fervour. Then suddenly you're rooming, drinking and playing together, and you find out that these blokes are not as bad as they are made out to be. Sharing a common cause breaks down all sorts of barriers – although you still knock lumps out of each other once you return and the championship comes round again. But those friendships remain. Often they're for life. That's why British Lions tours must survive.

Most of us know each other from there or from the old days when we gather at championship dinners. But Will doesn't. He's there on a pedestal, on the top table. That wouldn't matter to players if they had met him on the way up, but they didn't: Will was at Durham University when he was first capped. And before he knew it, Will was captain. So players from other countries haven't got to know him. That side of things has not been helped by the number of big games England have played recently. There's been a lot of tension about, and that doesn't make it easy, either. Still, other international players seem reluctant to approach him. All they know is what they read. Will is shy. Not an extrovert. He won't push himself forward in a group he doesn't know, so he probably seems aloof and arrogant. The only guys who really got to know him before the press got to him are some of the older England lads from the North. We know what a lot of rubbish is written.

Another Grand Slam would definitely make Carling favourite to captain the 1993 British Lions in New Zealand. But Geoff Cooke was not as gushing as Yarranton in England's praise. 'We are still a bit off being the best in the world. Until we can beat New Zealand, Australia and South Africa, we are still only a step down the road. The job is only half-finished. We had one chance to beat New Zealand and we didn't. And we have managed to beat Australia only once in five attempts while I have been manager. The measure is sustaining a run of success over a period of time. I think we have closed the gap. But they are still running ahead of us, and we are running like hell to keep up with them.' If Cooke was concentrating on the immediate present, it was because he had little option. The RFU had still not extended his post beyond April.

Rory Underwood confirmed his intention to retire in the week of the Welsh game, while Jonathan Webb announced that he was reconsidering calling it a day. That Saturday was a big day for goodbyes: the East Stand was also making its last appearance. Carling allowed Dooley to lead the side out to celebrate his 50th cap, although the captain had the ball back within a minute to score England's first try as he followed a kick ahead. Dooley, not to be outdone, scored the third and final try; England won 24–0, and the Twickenham crowd had a second successive Grand Slam to celebrate. England's 118 points was a new championship record, 16 more than Wales had scored in 1976, while Webb's 67 points were 7 more than Hodgkinson's tally the previous year. His career total of 246 also took him past Dusty Hare's 240 points. Records apart, though, it was a subdued day at HQ. Victory was a formality after Carling's try, but England didn't score for 48 minutes in the middle of the match as Wales concentrated on defence, content to keep the score respectable. Carling came off five minutes before the end with a dead leg. Cooke spoke honestly: 'Everyone was a bit disappointed with the quality of performance. But we just couldn't control it for long enough to produce the quick ball we required.'

Cooke was confirmed the following day as England's team manager through to the 1995 World Cup. Although Cooke had the support of the majority of the committee, the dissenting voices were some of the loudest and most influential – one man, one vote has never been the way of the RFU committee. Much of the opposition came from representatives of the north, Cooke's home base. Cooke had succeeded where some of them had failed, and that was resented, along with his high profile. If anyone wavered on the committee or attempted to recite Cooke's remarkable achievements, the Cardiff silence could always bring a hush to the proceedings. Meanwhile, Cooke announced he was stepping back from his 'hands-on' approach. 'The time has come for me to step aside a bit. We will probably be looking for an assistant coach.'

The inevitability of England's Grand Slam had rather taken the gloss off the achievement. 'We were still living the World Cup,' Andrew recalls. 'The championship was on us before we realised it. I really enjoyed it, though. There was less pressure than I can ever remember in the Five Nations.' The England players, especially those who had been with the Lions, were now looking forward to their first summer off since 1986. 'It will be interesting to see how they cope with the enforced lay-off from international rugby,' reflected Cooke.

Carling still had one big game left that season, the Pilkington Cup final against Bath. Harlequins' chances were not boosted when Skinner and fellow-forward Richard Langhorn were sent off the week before the final, and Paul Ackford was persuaded out of retirement to fill the breach. 'It's a one-off game,' said Ackford. 'I'm doing it out of loyalty to the club and to Dick [Best], who was instrumental in my rise to international rugby.' There was still life in the not-so-old dog: Ackford played a blinder. The match went into extra time, and in the very last minute Bath skipper Stuart Barnes dropped the goal that separated the sides to win 15–12.

Carling was magnificent in defeat. Defending, attacking, England's captain was in tip-top form. Tactical kicking had often let him down in the past, but this final art had now been mastered. Here was the complete article. Stephen Jones, of the *Sunday Times*: 'I rate his finest performances as England captain those two games against France, the World Cup quarter-final and the 1992 match. England are no angels but, under his influence, they conducted themselves well. As a player, Will was immense in that Pilkington Cup final against Bath, when he was under a lot of pressure.

'He has always been a guy with talent, but I think he's probably been a bit conservative. A man with his talent should be more extravagant. But he's continued to develop. He's very much the strong man in the middle. Will has always been assured. Now he's a complete player. I rate him highly. Sella has great ability, but he has not contributed as consistently as Carling. As for Charvet: how many games did Charvet's genius turn? The great players do it all the time.'

ANDREW
Will's game has improved each year. He knows what has been required, and he has done it fantastically well. He's always been a quality player, and he quickly became world-class. There have been times when his game has been picked to pieces, and that's been unfair. When he's playing well, his captaincy has been attacked; when his leadership is no longer an issue, it's Will's game that's under the microscope. The only ones who really appreciate his performance are those on the field. Coaches and team managers know it fairly well but, deep down, it's only the players who see everything.

He's been the first name on the team sheet for the past five years, and that's a tremendous achievement. Will's got phenomenal pace and strength. He works hard at his game, both his skills and the physical attributes. He's naturally strong anyway, but he works to improve his body strength and mauling ability. Will's got great determination. Aside from the captaincy, which he holds in great store, Will is very proud of his own playing performance. Once you get to a certain level, people are looking for you – and at you. Will knows that. His pride won't allow his standards to slip.

CARLING

I don't worry about opposition centres that much. I accept their strengths and weaknesses. Most of my build-up is visualised, how I am going to play. I've never been too deeply into other players. That's that. It's me, not him.

Scott Hastings is a tremendous defensive player, very committed, but he doesn't possess the subtlety of a Charvet. Sella is strong and skilful, and has vision, but was not as effective when he lost the edge on his speed. Tim Horan is a good finisher, very strong with pace. And, like Jerry [Guscott], he has the knack of being in the right place at the right time. That's not luck. Horan works well with Jason Little – they're a combination. Jerry and I have to be on our toes when facing them, aware. They have a good understanding. Jerry and I work well together. I can predict fairly well what's he going to do, his angles – I know what he prefers to do. Occasionally, I just have to admire breaks he's made or even his passes – the miss-pass that put Hunter away against Canada, or the break for Rory's try against Scotland in 1993. We don't do a lot of talking during matches. It's mainly calls.

Carling's status was confirmed when he was named *Rugby World* Player of the Year for 1991–92. Now he really did have the rugby world at his feet. He was an outstanding captain of the outstanding rugby side in the northern hemisphere. On his horizon, after a well-deserved summer off, was that hat-trick of Grand Slams and leadership of the 1993 British Lions tour to New Zealand. Both seemed a formality. But Will Carling was to achieve neither.

Chapter 29

Insight to the Future

Sport seemed a very good way of getting your message across. Audiences can easily relate to sporting situations and concepts.

WILL CARLING

Carling's chosen career has allowed him to cash in on his rugby fame, although claims that he will be Rugby Union's first millionaire are wildy exaggerated. Tony O'Reilly, of the British Lions and the Heinz organisation, has 10 times more millions than he scored international tries. And O'Reilly, like Carling, gained his fame from rugby. But while his sporting ability opened doors, his business acumen kept them open. Now that O'Reilly is one of the most successful businessmen in the world, nobody resents his achievements or suggests that he used Rugby Union for his own ends. But Carling suffers both those accusations.

Carling's Army plans were scuppered in 1988 at a few weeks' notice. After an 18-month spell with multi-national Mobil, he left to set up his own company. His time at Mobil had told him that he was not an office or organisation man. He wanted his own business, with the freedom to expand or develop in other areas. His working life is now organised around his sporting career, allowing him to devote the time he believes the England captaincy needs – although that commitment is lost on those who claim he is using the position for his own ends.

'Inspirational Horizons' duly became 'Insights', offering management seminars and talks, and Carling's company is now one of the leaders in its field. His name and England's rugby success have undoubtedly helped, but corporations are not paying thousands of pounds during a recession just to look at a pretty-boy England centre. Carling has done his homework. While working with Mobil, he had attended a convention in Monte Carlo, where the British athletics coach Frank Dick was one of nine speakers. 'All were good,' remembers Carling. 'But Dick, who spoke about coaching principles and winning, was outstanding. Sport seemed a very good way of getting your message across. Audiences can easily relate to sporting situations and concepts.'

Carling's experiences as England rugby captain give more than validity to his lectures. Audiences are also familiar with his experiences, successes and failures. His business has not slumped because England lost in Wales and Ireland in 1993, or because he was dropped from the Lions Test team. Carling finds the bad times are often more useful than the glory days to emphasise his points.

CARLING

My first six months at Mobil were taken up with marketing training. It was brilliant fun, just like university, except that money was in supply and everything was on expenses. My job was to sell oil to the big car dealerships in London. I did pretty well on my targets. How solid the contracts were was not part of my job, and my weakness was after the deals had been signed. Servicing clients didn't appeal to me. I was sharing a house in Baron's Court with friends, and I worked from home with a computer. I think my rugby name helped, although I never used international tickets to seal a deal.

That time with Mobil allowed me to find out certain things. I enjoyed working from home. Office life would not have suited me and, with my rugby commitments, it would not have been fair to the others to see how often I was away. My prospects were good, but the next step would have given me an office in the Victoria headquarters, and I wouldn't have liked that. Still Mobil were good to me. They were a good company to work for and helped me decide what I wanted to do.

216

The British media, not the Rugby World Cup organisers, were responsible for the successful promotion of the 1991 tournament. England's journey to the final did the rest. Carling was much in demand prior to and during the event. England, the Grand Slam champions, were the main hope of the northern hemisphere against the southern giants, Australia and New Zealand. Carling was the captain and figurehead of England's drive for the World Cup. He was to be found on the news pages, the women's pages, the feature pages and, of course, the sports pages, in newspapers and magazines; he was interviewed on TV and radio, on chat shows and news and current affairs programmes; he was filmed and photographed at home, at work, training and playing. Here, Carling is draped in the St. George's flag, the symbolism apparent to all.
(*Allsport/Russell Cheyne*)

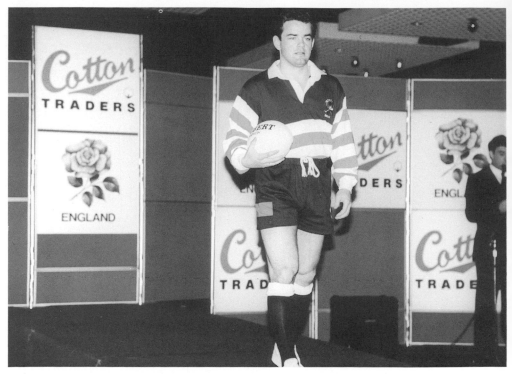

England's reserve World Cup strip, worn by Carling, introductions being made by RFU Marketing Executive Michael Coley. (*Colorsport*)

Publicity shot of the all-action Carling, taken before England's World Cup campaign. (*Allsport/Russell Cheyne*)

Carling, Roger Uttley and Geoff Cooke (standing) relax on the golf course before the World Cup opener against New Zealand. (*Colorsport*)

Uttley, Cooke and Carling, with press liaison officer Dewi Griffiths, at a World Cup press conference surrounded by sponsors' logos. (*Colorsport*)

RIGHT: Carling touches down to seal victory in the World Cup quarter-final against France. Wade Dooley (5) and Brian Moore celebrate England's 19–10 win. (*Colorsport*)

BELOW: England's captain celebrates his quarter-final try and looks forward to a revenge match against the Scots at Murrayfield in the semi-final. (*Colorsport*)

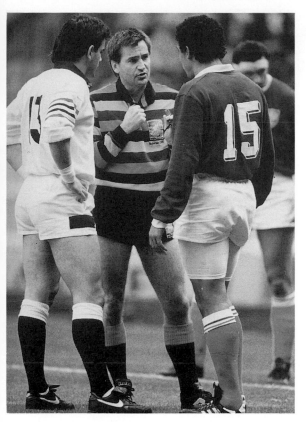

LEFT: New Zealand referee David Bishop lays down the law to French captain Serge Blanco, with Will Carling in attendance, after Nigel Heslop was laid low at the start of the World Cup quarter-final. (*Allsport/Russell Cheyne*)

BELOW: A satisfied Bill Carling and, as ever, a smiling Pam Carling with their younger offspring at the Parc des Princes after the World Cup quarter-final. (*Colorsport*)

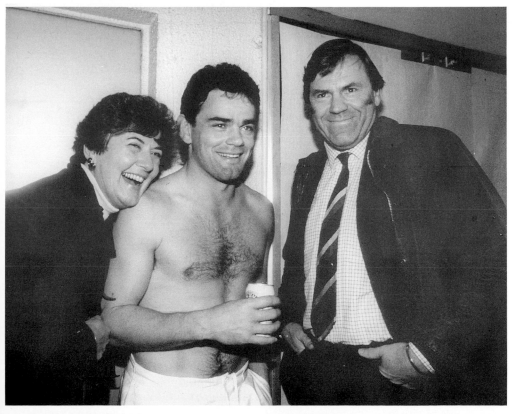

Will Carling meets the press at the Stoop Memorial Ground the day before the World Cup final against Australia. (*Colorsport*)

Carling sets up another attack in the World Cup final, but Australia's dogged defence stood firm to take the trophy. (*Colorsport*)

LEFT: Carling salutes the Twickenham crowd as he comes to terms with the fact that England had failed at the final hurdle to take the 1991 World Cup. (*Allsport/Russell Cheyne*)

BELOW: Carling shakes hands with World Cup official Russ Thomas after receiving his loser's medal from the Queen. (*Colorsport*)

Carling beats Tony Clement to the ball to score after only 61 seconds at Twickenham to set up England's first back-to-back Grand Slam since 1924, when Sedbergh old boy Wavell Wakefield was captain. England's 118 points in the championship surpassed the previous record of 102, set by Wales in 1976. (*Colorsport*)

England celebrate another Grand Slam. When the picture was used in the 1992/93 RFU Handbook, Mickey Skinner's shirt was painted on. (*Colorsport*)

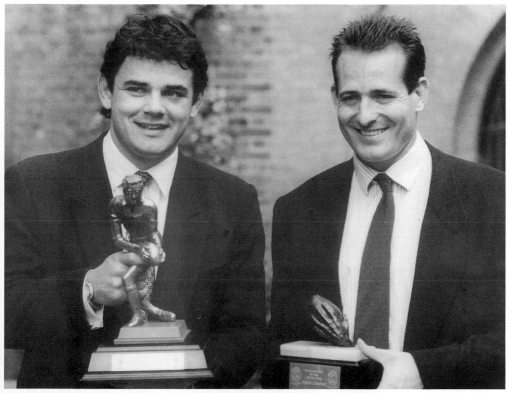

Will Carling, the 1992 *Rugby World* Player of the Year, with his old adversary, David Campese, the International Player of the Year. (*Colorsport*)

RIGHT: Carling with some female admirers at the launch of the *Young England* magazine. (*Colorsport*)

BELOW: Carling agreed to take part in a children's programme, explaining rugby to Mr Blobby. Actually, it was part of 'Noel's House Party' and the set-up was watched by millions. (*The BBC Photograph Library*)

LEFT: Will Carling, OBE, and trendy waistcoat-wearer, at Buckingham Palace after receiving his award.

BELOW: 'Maybe, this Will Carling will pass to me' was Jerry Guscott's remark when Carling's Madame Tussaud's waxwork made an appearance before the game against Canada at Wembley in October 1992. (*Madame Tussaud's*)

Carling and the women in his life. This is his favourite picture of him with his
mum, Pam. Although, if the boys were in trouble, they would go to their
mother first and let her choose the moment to tell Dad, it was Pam who was
disappointed and felt Will had let himself down by not working harder at
Durham University.

Carling and Julia Smith at Chelsea Harbour at the time their engagement was announced just before he left for the 1993 Lions tour to New Zealand. That separation proved costly. 'My phone bill was horrendous,' explained Will, although business took Julia to Australia and she was able to fly over to see him in Christchurch. (*Mail on Sunday/Solo*)

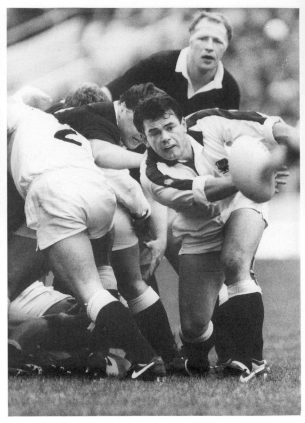

ABOVE: Carling contemplates life during the 1992 Pilkington Cup final. (*Allsport/David Cannon*)

RIGHT: Carling tries his luck at scrum-half in the 1993 Calcutta Cup match. (*Colorsport*)

Carling's seventh try for England, against South Africa at Twickenham in November 1992. (*Colorsport*)

Ireland jubilant, Martin Bayfield stunned, as Carling suffers his biggest Five Nations defeat as captain at Lansdowne Road in March 1993. (*Colorsport*)

Carling breaks through the Otago defence for the Lions. He was forced to withdraw with a thigh strain as the tourists plunged to defeat. (*Colorsport*)

Will Carling, the captain, calling the shots. Already, he is the most successful captain in England's rugby history. Yet Carling wants to go on and now has his sights firmly set on England winning the 1995 World Cup. (*Colorsport*)

I started 'Inspirational Horizons' in an office in Piccadilly before I went on the Argentina tour in 1990. It was a risk and, early on, things were tough. But once I had decided to make the break, other things became clear. As England captain, I was meeting all sorts of sports people, and I was impressed. There was far more emphasis on man-management in sport than there was in organisations like Mobil. After hearing Frank Dick, I had realised that sportsmen were the best way of getting management messages over. Not only did the audience relate to the sporting person, but a famous name added star quality. Eventually, I wanted to expand the presentations into a more interactive service. That was the progression.

I had met Jim Foley through my agent, Jon Holmes. Jim had his own management training company. We set up 'Insights' together in 1991. Our intention was not to make lots of money or assume a very high profile. I was chiefly concerned with where I'd be in five years' time; that was the basic premise. We are in a niche market, and it's a quality product. It's a small specialist concern which I hope will develop a reputation as the No. 1 company in the field.

Sportsmen we use include Gary Lineker, Mike Brearley, Adrian Moorhouse, Sebastian Coe and Tony Jacklin. We put together a day's package for senior managers. Although sport is used to get the message across, it's still very much business-related. I believe that British industry has talented managers, but there is not enough training. Having a good product is not enough: you must have a good team. Back-up is vital. My experiences with the England team have taught me that. The actions of the individual have got to benefit the company. People change jobs more often these days – companies have got to be a lot more fluid. The great weakness is the lack of communication with their people. There's not enough delegation. Few have realised their full potential.

We discuss how you cope with disappointment. When someone in a job is patently not good enough, it's demoralising not only for him, but for others. You have to find him another job, whether it's sideways or downwards. You don't need to disguise it. People know when they are out of their depth. You can't ignore the problem; it won't go away. We tell the story of a company in Japan: when they find someone is not capable in a

217

job, their way out of the problem is to promote him. I don't think that's much of a solution. Mind you, looking at some of the people in top posts in various organisations over here, that policy might have been in operation for some time without anyone knowing about it.

Chapter 30

National Anthem

I really feel that it's time England had its own song. Its own national anthem. Everyone else does in the rugby world: why not England? I want something like Land of Hope and Glory *or* Jerusalem. *Something that is English, not British. That would give the team an incredible lift.*

WILL CARLING

Come autumn 1992, Carling was ready for another big season. The Five Nations championship is rarely the sole international highlight these days. In October, England welcomed Canada, to Wembley instead of Twickenham because of rebuilding. The first tier of the new East Stand was to be ready in time for the visit of South Africa in November, for the first time in nearly a quarter of a century. And, with the domestic season done, the British Lions would set out for New Zealand the following May. Captain Carling looked sure to be much in demand.

England's new rugby strip was launched in September. The Cotton Traders design had a broad red stripe down each sleeve and a blue collar. England's top players had been out in force when the World Cup strip was launched the previous year. Times had changed: this time it was Dewi Morris, Jason Leonard and David Pears. The leading players had decided that something for nothing was a mug's game. The RFU continued to frustrate their efforts to be treated the same as the Australian and New Zealand players, yet they were expected to co-operate by turning up to promote new products and sponsorships. No more. 'Players will wear what they are given,' explained Brian Moore. 'It's something over which they have no control.' But the cream of England's rugby talent had withdrawn their promotional labour. The authorities were left in no doubt as to why.

Carling was happy to go to Twickenham in early September, but that was to launch the Young England Club, a grassroots scheme for kids aged 6 to 16. 'Grassroots' had become a familiar phrase at HQ: it was another weapon to beat down the players' demands. The inference was that any money they took for themselves was denying kids a grounding in the game. And where was the future of the game without those kids? The MCC tried the same tactics on some of their members who called for a special meeting after David Gower's exclusion from the 1993 England cricket tour party to India: 'The £17,500 needed to organise this meeting could go towards coaching youngsters.' The MCC decided not to pursue this line, however, when the rebels, armed with the annual accounts, wondered in turn how many kids could have been coached with the amount that had been spent on entertaining during the previous summer.

Carling might not be prepared to turn up just to fill the coffers of the RFU. Kids are different, though. 'There is a tremendous opportunity to get children involved and interested in rugby. It's vital for the future. Children have so many sports to choose from, and I would like to help ensure that they choose rugby football.' Carling appreciated that rugby and cricket were suffering similar problems. 'Both sports are not played as much in the state schools. We need as many as possible playing rugby. That's why current players, at whatever level, have to play their part.'

The law-makers, too, have a role to play. Unfortunately, the introduction of some new rugby laws for the 1992–93 season were about to turn the game, and England's world, on its head. As with most rugby decisions, those entrusted with the laws are three-times removed in age and contact from the international game. The benefit of consulting current top referees and coaches in the law-making process is so obvious it needs no explanation; even leading players, such as Campese, Farr-Jones, Wayne Shelford, Carling and Sole, would bring an expertise to the process. Yet the law-makers continue to work alone, despite an appalling track record. Even more worrying for Carling and England, the home countries have often been led by the nose over law changes by the southern hemisphere nations – especially Australia – in recent times. Many of these law changes have appeared to take rugby away from its real roots.

CARLING

I just think it's common sense to involve all the top participants in major changes to the game, laws or otherwise. They are the ones with hands on, who can offer interesting observations and thoughts about the effects of the new laws. Often, however, it appears that the full ramifications of changes have not been considered.

I've often wondered why they have to change the laws for all levels of the game. Often new laws are tried out at schoolboy level and, because they work there, the authorities introduce them in all rugby. By and large, though, you don't get cunning players at schoolboy level. The first reaction at the top level when a new law appears is, 'How best can we use it to our own advantage or to disadvantage the opposition?' A bit like tax laws: you either look to avoid them, which is legal, or evade them, which is not.

The international game is the shop window. The authorities have to reflect on how changes will affect that top level, not at grassroots. People judge the game on internationals, and they're what attracts the sponsorship money that keeps the whole game going. I'm aware that safety is an important factor, especially when dealing with schoolboys. But there's nothing to stop rugby having different laws for junior and schoolboy players to make their game safer, more attractive and easier to play.

England's early-season run-out against Leicester gave them more than a hint of what was to come. Winterbottom was missing because of a hernia operation, while Leonard was still fighting his way back to fitness. The Quins prop had not played since the Grand Slam victory, after which the surgeons had removed a disc, then grafted bone from his thigh into his back. At the same time as he was showing off England's new strip, Leonard was filing a claim with the RFU for a 'hardship payment' as he had been unable to work as a carpenter since the injury. Mike Teague and Paul Rendall had already received four-figure hardship amounts under similar circumstances. While the players were grateful for the assistance, it smacked to some of a hand-out. 'No set of players ever gave as much commitment,' insisted Rendall. 'But Twickenham expects every sacrifice and to give nothing in return. So some players duck and dive just to get by. That's the "brown envelope" syndrome, and the RFU's double standards have created it.'

Neil Back, who was to go off with a dislocated shoulder, and Bath's Ben Clarke and Steve Ojomoh formed a new-look England back row against Leicester. Sadly, however, no one was admiring the stars of the future that afternoon at Welford Road. They were watching the game of the future. Stephen Jones wrote in the *Sunday Times*, 'It is apparent that English rugby will suffer even more horrors than the rest of the world when it comes to the new laws. Every cheat and every poor team came out drooling for the new season yesterday. Their time has come. They now have their own charter and can lay down plans for global dominance. It consists of nothing more than a few words added to Laws 21 and 22. Simply, if now you cannot dig your ball out of a ruck or maul, the other lot get it. That's the basic upshot. There is just one ball to attack with. Unless you force a line-out, mistake or score, you lose the ball. And rugby loses one of its staples, the pressure platform.'

Jones produced four expert witnesses in his defence: the coaches of the World Cup semi-finalists were united in their condemnation. Australia's Bob Dwyer: 'It's a very bad law, an awful law. It does not allow superior teams to control the game, and that is ridiculous.' New Zealand's Alex Wyllie: 'An unholy mess. A complete shambles.' Scotland's Ian McGeechan: 'I am afraid it could fundamentally alter the game.' England's Geoff Cooke: 'It seems against the first principle of the game.'

Cooke received some good news, however, when Rory Underwood officially reversed his retirement plans. 'I still loved playing, but other aspects of the game were becoming a chore,' explained the winger. 'Having decided to step down from international rugby, I applied and was subsequently selected for an intensive fast-jet cross-over course at RAF Chivenor which starts in November. About a month ago, after a summer without rugby, I started to reassess the situation and talk things over again with my wife Wendy. I asked myself whether I had to leave this situation behind. I decided that perhaps I didn't. After speaking with my flight commander and station boss and making a couple of phone calls, I wrote formally to request a deferment of my fast-jet course. The RAF have been incredibly supportive throughout my career, and I heard on Tuesday that they had granted the deferment. Their willingness to accommodate my request has been an important factor in my decision.' Every time the RAF gained this sort of publicity, there was a great gnashing of teeth at Army headquarters for allowing Carling to slip away. Some regard it as one of the great blunders of British military history.

Both Doolcy and Underwood had brought out autobiographies at the start of the season, a clear sign they intended their retirements to be final. Now, however, both were back. The Wales and British Lions wing Gerald Davies had caused an upset at Cardiff in the late 1970s when he retired suddenly at the start of a new season. His view was that then was the right time to find out if the enjoyment was still there. Why make the decision at the end of a season, then wonder if you'd done the right thing four months later? As England gathered for the Canada game on 17 October, Carling expressed his relief that, in the event, only Simon Halliday had called it a day. He added: 'We still have to go forward. These players can still develop, and we can refine our mental and training techniques. And, although the same players are still around, there is no guarantee that they will be picked. You don't pick people for sentimental reasons. But there has to be someone better to take their place.' Bath prop Victor Ubogu was given his chance to prove that point when Jeff Probyn was left out against Canada, while Ian Hunter and Tony Underwood were given the chance to fight for Halliday's vacant wing spot.

The good news that Rob Andrew was returning from Toulouse to play club rugby in England was then ruined by the Senior Clubs Association, who told Andrew that he was now regarded as an overseas player and could not play league or Cup rugby for his former club Wasps until February. Geoff Cooke was furious: 'I think it's totally nonsensical and I shall be saying so most strongly. I was staggered that a guy who gets moved as part of his business and then returns to his old club could be affected in this way.' So much for the amateur game. Two weeks later, on appeal, Andrew's ban was upheld. 'It is the reasons I have been given which so confuse me in this matter,' Andrew said. 'I have been informed that the decision was taken on the grounds that I had played for another English club prior to joining Wasps. That club was Nottingham, but I left them in 1985. I find it strange that the committee has to go back seven years to find something on which to prevent me playing. That was pre-registration and pre-leagues.' The Senior Clubs were adamant, however. They could not make an exception for anyone, least of all an England player.

What has happened to an amateur game with such restrictive regulations as these? Rugby players have always gone where their professional careers have taken them, especially in times of recession. Now they were being given an ultimatum: follow your work, and you won't play top-class rugby. The Senior Clubs claim that the regulations are there to stop players being induced to join top clubs. But they have not been effective, often because of self-interest. The outcome was that one of England's most respected players was treated abysmally.

All the England players were looking forward to playing at Wembley for the first time. Dean Richards was photographed sparring with Frank Bruno, Britain's popular heavyweight boxer, who was fighting South African Pierre Coetzer after the game. Most of the England boys fancied that Deano would give Big Frank a tougher fight. Meanwhile Wembley was treated to two Will Carlings: England's captain was about to enter Madame Tussaud's. When the waxwork was unveiled for approval, Jerry Guscott offered the opinion: 'At least the model might pass to me.' When the press went to interview Carling on the match prospects, Terry Cooper, of the Press Association, continued the theme. Instead of laughing, however, Carling clamped up. 'Will took it to heart,' remembers Tony Roche. 'He said, "Everything seems to be at my expense." He saw it as another personal attack.' Roche puts it down to the onerous nature of the England captaincy. 'A month later, we saw him at Lensbury before the Barbarians game with Australia. It was a cold, windy Thursday. As we passed time with him, he tried to trip Coops up. His body language was so different: he had his hands in his pockets, the shoulders were down. He was so relaxed. That day, he had a different hat on. He wasn't England captain.'

Canada gave England a good work-out. The home side were more than a little ring-rusty, though Hunter looked sharp and stole the march on Tony Underwood by scoring twice. Carling, who enjoyed the atmosphere of Wembley, reflected on England's 26–13 victory. 'It was always going to be hard this early in the season against a very committed side. It's a one-off blast for them, and they played well. It's easy for sides to lift themselves for one match. It was the biggest match of the season for them. But for us, it's just the start of a long, hard campaign. Mentally, it was a little hard for us to adjust out there, but all the newcomers did very well.'

That same afternoon, South Africa were recording their first win since returning to the world rugby fold with a 20–15 success in France. They lost the second Test a week later and for a time, it looked as if England might lose their leg of the tour. The National Olympic Sports Congress announced from the Republic, 'We don't feel obliged to protect rugby any longer.' They objected to references to the South African tourists as Springboks, a reminder both of the old white supremacy and of apartheid. Initially, the African National Congress backed the NOSC, then they decided that the tour of England should go ahead. But there was a casualty: the national anthem. The South African rugby authorities had shown all their old tact with the passionate playing and singing of *Die Stem* – 'The Call of South Africa' – before their home clash with New Zealand in August. With the Afrikaaners' anthem blaring out, the ANC must have wondered if anything had really changed. An impromptu rendition by the South African team in a French hotel was also heavily criticised. The RFU decided that the safest way was to have no anthems, British or South African, especially with South African state president F.W. de Klerk due to be in attendance at Twickenham. It is remarkable how affairs of state increasingly revolve around sporting events. The players were not the only ones up in arms over the proposed silence.

CARLING
The anthem has come to mean something very special to the England team before matches. We were angry that we were going to be denied part of our normal build-up through no fault of our own. It's a tense time coming out on to the field. Really, you're ready and desperate for the match to start. I'm not keen on presentations. It was a great honour and privilege to meet the Queen before the World Cup final, but I would have preferred different circumstances. You are so keyed up, but you're expected to make small talk.

Although we reacted to the anthem being dropped, I really feel that it's time England had its own song. Its own national anthem. Everyone else does in the rugby world: why not England? I'm not being unpatriotic or disloyal, but *God Save the Queen* is Britain's national anthem, not just England's. I've actually talked to Prince Edward and the Princess Royal about it, and they've both hinted that it's not a bad idea. I want something like *Land of Hope and Glory* or *Jerusalem*. Something that is English, not British. That would give the team an incredible lift. Look at the impact of *Swing Low, Sweet Chariot*. That's become the current side's anthem. It's a tremendous feeling to hear it being sung wherever England's sporting teams are playing.

England's anthem was indeed restored the day before the match. But South Africa's old ways were still given a salute prior to the kick-off with a public announcement welcoming the Springboks and F.W. de Klerk back to Twickenham. The undisguised implication was that they should never have been away. It was an unnecessary prologue, especially from the chairman of the new UK Sports Commission.

South Africa showed for at least half an hour that they will be a real threat on home soil in the 1995 World Cup. England were in some disarray as the visitors took a 14–8 lead towards the end of the first half, before Andrew turned the game with a neat chip for Guscott to catch and score unopposed shortly after the interval. England subsequently added 22 points without reply in the second half, and Tony Underwood marked his full Test debut with a try, taking the final pass off brother Rory. Hunter had originally been picked ahead of the younger Underwood, but he withdrew after injuring himself in a kick-about at club training. The other newcomer, Ben Clarke, made mistakes but undoubtedly had class, while Bayfield, a slow international starter, was now beginning to fill Ackford's place. Carling collected his seventh England try with a typical chase and jump – and just a hint of a knock forward – in the final minutes.

South Africa's disappointment continued after the match with the news that Naas Botha was to retire. Botha was either loathed or loved, depending on your standpoint. The South African fly-half was one of the greatest kickers in the game, but too often he wasted the enormous talents of Danie Gerber outside him by putting boot to ball. Even on his swansong, this rugby Jekyll and Hyde remained true to the end. One inspired swivel led to his record 18th international drop goal; but several times Gerber was left shouting as Botha took the kicking option once again. Gerber's frustration was understandable. The South African backs had shown themselves on the rest of the tour to be a match for anyone.

Carling was now having problems with the Barbarians. He had been chosen in the centre for the game against Australia a fortnight later, the climax of the world champions' short tour of Wales and Ireland. But it's the way they have in the Barbarians – they will never announce beforehand who the captain is. Carling had a long-standing business appointment in Southampton on the Friday. He offered to move the timings and catch a helicopter back. Carling was discovering what Campese had discovered a year earlier: the Barbarians believe that players will move heaven and earth to play for them. That is now a myth. Barbarians' training requirements have increased because even the best players can no longer turn up and turn it on against well-drilled Test teams. Carling debated dropping out, but still they wouldn't tell him if he was captain or not. He was not bothered, but just wanted to know. The chance of partnering Gerber was also an opportunity Carling did not want to miss. There was a lot of Gerber in Carling's style. Both are strong, fast and hard. Carling eventually said 'yes', and Gerber duly dropped out, to be replaced by Scott Gibbs.

Rugby's growing demands were evident elsewhere in the Barbarians side. Stuart Barnes, back in the international fold, was selected, along with the out-of-favour Skinner and Probyn. Skinner had left Harlequins at the end of the previous season to return to Blackheath, where 'Mick the Munch' had spent his formative years. It was a mistake. And a shame. The spirit was still willing, but the flesh was now weak. Skinner had played a significant part in England's World Cup campaign and Grand Slam, but the Barbarians game showed that he needed the class and competitiveness of the Harlequins to keep him up to the mark. For his part, Barnes's day was also spoilt when, on camera, he was told that his Bath side had been knocked out of the Cup at Waterloo. His face was a picture, until it hurriedly disappeared, stage right.

The Barbarians match brought Carling face to face again with David Campese. Earlier, Campese had claimed that Carling refused to shake hands with him after the World Cup final, adding, 'England have beaten no one. Scotland have lost a lot of players, Wales are rebuilding from the bottom up, France have all sorts of political infighting, and Ireland are still celebrating the World Cup. England should be more realistic. They claim they are a "Run with the Ball"

227

team. That is a joke. I am fed up of reading about Captain Marvel this and wonderful Will that. I saw him in action, and if he gave me a team talk I would fall asleep.'

There is no doubting Campese's class. The Australian had a wonderful World Cup, especially in the semi-final. He has the rare ability to think and react immediately in the heat of battle. Former Wallaby coach Alan Jones called him the 'Don Bradman of rugby'. But his mouth has been known to run away as often as his legs. He had already upset the Irish on this tour with his usual pre-match verbal barrage. Fortunately, Campese's rugby usually has the last word, and that rarely leaves a bitter taste. This time, Carling refused to get involved in a war of words, and the pair shook hands in front of the TV cameras after the Barbarians had lost.

The Australians had done well to win the big matches this autumn. Nick Farr-Jones did not tour, and Michael Lynagh was sidelined during the Test against Ireland. The Barbarians ended up being a much tougher proposition than either Ireland and Wales, losing 30–20. The Irish had been an absolute shambles, while Wales at least fought better than in their World Cup group game the previous season. The Principality rejoiced, however, when club sides Swansea and Llanelli overcame the World Cup champions.

Carling and England had enjoyed a perfect 1992 on the rugby field: six matches, six wins. And the Grand Slam. At Christmas, Carling seemed the only choice as Lions captain. But the previous two Lions tours to New Zealand in 1977 and 1983, had both witnessed captaincy upsets to the obvious candidates: Mervyn Davies and Bill Beaumont, who were also picked to captain the Barbarians against the Australians a few months before departure, both failed to make the tour because of injury. It was a Lions captaincy jinx that would wander across Carling's mind over the next few months.

Chapter 31

Carling Mythology

For Gareth Edwards, rugby was his only route to glory. But for Will, if it hadn't been rugby, then he would have found some other route. Gareth gave it his heart and soul. Will is more mechanical and less passionate.

STEPHEN JONES

Carling's place in rugby legend is assured. A world-class three-quarter, England have regained their place as a rugby force under his leadership. The last great era for England was in the roaring 1920s. Rugby, like soccer, has become a universal game in the past quarter of a century. England, once the kings of the soccer world, are now among the also-rans, unlikely ever to recapture their former glory and status. That the national rugby side have recovered lost ground is down to the players and the personality of Geoff Cooke. Yet Carling has been his representative on the field, and it is doubtful if Cooke or England would have achieved as much without him. Carling is the inspirational figure identified by thousands of supporters and youngsters. He symbolises England's rugby success.

While Carling's fame has grown, so has the mythology surrounding the captain. Carling rejects the majority of it, good and bad. The remainder he objects to; the half-truths and untruths anger him.

229

Carling prefers to maintain a dignified silence for most of the time, and that makes him a silent target as well as a sitting one. As Carling won't fill in the gaps in his life, public and private, others are only too happy to oblige. No one has a higher profile in British rugby, and resentment and jealousy are bound to follow. No one likes a winner, especially in the middle of a recession, and Carling is constantly seen in the right places with right people at the right time. He has dined with the Queen at Buckingham Palace, chatted with Sue Lawley on 'Desert Island Discs', and recently announced his engagement to a girl who has mixed with pop stars such as Eric Clapton. Carling has given rugby's cauliflower-eared, beer-swilling, chauvinistic image a real battering.

Areas of the mythology do suit him: if he has gained a reputation for being a loner and aloof, then people – Carling hopes – will leave him alone. Criticism from outsiders doesn't bother him; uninformed attacks are easily repelled. But stories of dissent and unpopularity within the England squad upset him deeply. Bar talk is cheap and exaggerated: the sportsman has not yet been born who does not moan and belly-ache about his captain, along with everything else, at some point. But Rugby Union has been enjoying a major revolution since the first World Cup, and Will Carling embodies the new world. The old guard hate him because of what has been destroyed, while the new are suspicious of him because he appears to have benefited from the pre-revolutionary promises when they have not. But Carling, because of his particular line of business, is actually playing under the old rules. His critics believe he is playing both sides off against the other. But, as he himself says about Guscott on the field, being in the right place at the right time is not a question of luck. It's judgement.

Rob Andrew dismisses rumours that Carling's status causes problems within the squad.

ANDREW
There may be one or two small bits of resentment. But very minor. Everyone accepts the way the world goes wrong. Some have more deals going than others, but we like to stay as a team. That's one reason we're keen on 'Run with the Ball'. Sponsors are attracted because of Will, Rory and Jerry, but Wade, Jeff and Jason can also benefit. Rugby teams have always had stars.

Will was positive about setting up his own business for the future. He had the balls to make that decision and go for it. If he had been injured or dropped, he would have soon been forgotten, like everyone else. Obviously, if anyone wants to make money, the first priority is to be in a team that is doing well. A lot don't understand that: they say that you're only in the team for the money. That's nonsense. You still need success. Now Will is in a position to make good money, but he will only be successful in his chosen career if he's good at what he does.

There are jealousies in every walk of life. There have always been whingers. But Will's high profile has not been a problem in the England squad. I'm not saying that won't change in the future if the restrictions remain as they are. But, the view in the squad is, 'Good luck to him.'

CARLING

I know people are always going on about Will Carling plc this and plc that. There is no doubt I make use of my name. Who wouldn't? I have set up my own company and I really enjoy it. It's serious. There's a market there. But it's not Will Carling promotions. It's management training. I'd never deny that it makes use of my name, but who doesn't in rugby? Rugby players have always got jobs because of who they are. I'm supposed to be an astute player, and I've never seen the logic of being able to go for and exploit openings on the field, then ignore them in business life because you're wearing a shirt and tie, not the England jersey. That's probably why I get so many hackles up: I'm overtly making use of what I've achieved, but then that's my object in life.

Anything I do, I want to be good at, whether it's business or sport. There's too much that's mediocre. I wouldn't call myself a perfectionist, but I like doing things well. When I finish something, I like to think I've given it my best shot. Otherwise, why bother? If I'm associated with anything, I want it to be successful. It's important to me to be a winner. I'm not materialistic [pause for laughter]. I know what people say, but it's not money that drives me. It's doing well and walking away knowing that it's been successful.

His relationship with Geoff Cooke is another part of the Carling mythology. Cooke is looked upon as Carling's Svengali-type mentor. Cooke brought him into the North side and the England team, and appointed him his long-term captain. Cooke also brought Carling into the England decision-making process. To the outside world, it appears that Cooke saw Carling as a potential captain right from the start, and the past five years have all been part of Cooke's grand plan. Nothing could be further from the truth: Nigel Melville was Cooke's initial choice and, as has become obvious, any captain under Cooke's management would have been required to contribute much more than just speaking at the after-match dinner.

Although history will label it Carling's England, Cooke's England is a more accurate description. The pair have worked well together, and Carling has responded to the challenge as Cooke had hoped. But Cooke is not the father-figure to Carling that many have implied: for one thing, Will has his own important father-figure, Bill; for another, both Carling and Cooke have kept the relationship on a business footing. Cooke believes that it would have been a mistake to get too close to his captain, even if he could. That suits Carling. If he opens his heart to anyone, it will be his father.

All along, Carling has been decried for not standing on his own feet, for not making decisions without seeking advice. The strong inference is that his decisions are not really his own, that he has always been looked after, whether by his father or Geoff Cooke. But Carling seeks advice from a variety of sources because he assumes, correctly, that he doesn't know everything. And when the various suggestions have been digested, Carling makes his own decisions. His critics want it both ways: Carling is a loner, but he is looked after by others. Not very probable and, in the second case, untrue. Carling goes his own way, as Geoff Cooke knows only too well.

COOKE
Much more is made of our relationship than really exists. After that first win over Australia just a few days following his appointment as captain, it was assumed that a magic partnership had just clicked into place. That's not true. Will had very little input in the first year. It was only in the second year that he began to flex his muscles as he grew more confident and stronger. Now he's much more assured, and that's basically natural maturity. I feel he's a bit more tolerant of others failing now. He's certainly more aware of his own strengths and weaknesses.

It's been very hard for him. I know just how much time he

spends thinking about rugby away from matches. Will is a big-time player, and he finds it increasingly difficult motivating himself for other rugby. Everything is focused on his international performance. The Quins have been very understanding of the whole situation.

Much too much is also made of Will's involvement on selection, although he's got more say than any other England captain in the past. We ask Will's opinion, but he doesn't sit in all the time on selection. As captain, he is consulted, but he's not at every meeting. Will is just part of a more significant change, wherein all the senior players are asked for their opinions. Will does have an important role. He gives us valuable feedback from the players. We've had very few arguments, though Will is fairly hard-headed and he sometimes takes a different perspective. He's on the park and doesn't look at the same things.

The biggest mythology concerns Carling the wonder captain, the leader with magic powers. Carling has never subscribed to those suggestions. He is simply very proud of being England captain and has worked professionally hard at the job. That has never been the way with the English establishment, as the *Sunday Times* rugby correspondent will attest.

STEPHEN JONES
Will is certainly the prototype modern rugby captain. I can't imagine anyone now being able to do a nine to five job and lead the side. There are so many demands. Teachers, scientists and bricklayers just won't be able to do the job in future.

Will has worked out what's best for him, although I don't believe that it was inevitable that he had to distance himself from the team. He could make more effort to be one of the boys. Who is the real Will Carling, I'm often asked. Will doesn't want people to know. My theory is that he is not sure himself. I certainly don't know what motivates him, although I can tell you what motivated the rest of the England team. For Ackford, it was the physical challenge, for Dooley, the route to glory, etc, etc. But as for Carling, I haven't got the faintest idea.

Will is the symbol of rugby's new-found status: officer-class, good-looking. He provokes a certain jealousy among the foot soldiers. I think his high individual profile has lost him some of his own team, the Probyns and Rendalls who won him the ball. By setting himself alone, Will has lost support.

I don't agree that he's under extra pressure because he captains a successful side. Take Welsh fly-half Colin Stephens – an average player in an average side. That's real pressure. As for him as captain, you could say that England have lost the tight games. Rob Andrew has better tactical control. But Will, he copes well. He displayed steely moments in the World Cup quarter-final. Off the field, when he's been under pressure, Will has never shown any signs of crumbling.

Has Carling captained the best England team ever? Or is he just a jammy so-and-so! Both Wales and Ireland have been at their lowest ebbs ever, and that's got to be a factor. The Ireland team in New Zealand in summer 1992 was one step up from a joke, while Wales in Australia in 1991 had ceased to exist. And French selection has been always about friends – who's in with who. Only Scotland have consistently provided good opposition. But England were badly beaten in Cardiff in 1989 – they never got out of their own 22. And at Murrayfield in 1990, tactics didn't matter with those mad Scotsmen running around. Rugby is not chess. Anyone who thinks it is should get out.

As for the World Cup, I believe England settled for the final. Even the crowd felt it. I have no doubt about that. The England lads weren't as 100 per cent devastated after losing the World Cup final as they were at Murrayfield in 1990.

Geoff Cooke was looking for his own passport to immortality, and he chose Will to provide it. For Gareth Edwards, rugby was his only route to glory. But for Will, if it hadn't been rugby, then he would have found some other route. Gareth gave it his heart and soul. Will is more mechanical and less passionate. It's rare for great players to make great captains. Australia's Nick Farr-Jones is the best there's ever been. Willie John McBride and John Dawes were great captains, but not great players. Will has come as close as anyone in this country, but he's not quite made it.

Carling's Army background and Sandhurst intentions gave the media plenty of ammunition about a leader in the making. But Carling did not merely swap one army for another. He is amused at the way in which his entire school, university and Army days were all supposedly geared to his future as England rugby captain.

CARLING
My early interest in leadership had nothing to do with rugby. It's true that, at the age of 6, I fell in love with the game and dreamed of playing for my country one day. But journalists and profile writers like to take it a step further. They give the impression that my dream had me running out at the head of my England team. Captaining England never entered my head. Leading the England Schools side was a special honour, but I never saw myself as a special or natural leader. My psychology course at university was designed to prepare me for the Army, not rugby. I can't deny my studies have helped me in coping with the job of captain, but that was just luck. I could have happily played out my international career without the responsibility. I would not have felt unfulfilled. But, as I was given the task, I've tried to bring everything I know and could to that task. I don't like to fail.

Carling's style of leadership is very distinct, very organised. He is not a blood-and-thunder leader, but prefers to work on a player's intelligence rather than his emotions. Preparation and thoroughness are his trade marks. Carling acts, rather than reacts.

CARLING
Captain on the field! People have an exaggerated idea of what that means, of how much influence I can exert. 'Tighten up, spread it, vary the line-out' – I can say it, but it's up to the team to implement it. You have to get the team thinking the same way. It's not cricket. The players haven't got time to assess all the problems themselves. And your decision-makers could have their own serious problems. Also, you not only have to react to the opposition, but to the referee. That's why preparation is so important. There's no time once the match starts. The majority of my captaincy work is done by the time we run out. The hustle and bustle of a Dublin international is no place to be trying to work out a new strategy.

One handicap under which he has worked during his five years as captain is that England have always been expected to win, except perhaps on three occasions – the two Australia and the New Zealand matches in 1991. Otherwise, an English victory was the correct result. On the few occasions when the odds have been upset, the captain has carried more than his fair share of blame. But Carling has never tried to hide from the facts of life. He understands that he is a victim of his own success. Only the best will do now. Anything less is failure.

Rob Andrew led England in Romania in 1989 when Carling was laid low with shin splints.

ANDREW
Unless you have actually done the job, you underestimate how difficult it is. Will has had a lot of guidance. He wasn't a natural; he has grown into the job. Will has worked hard with Geoff in creating the right set-up. The right set-up is fundamental to getting it right on the park. The right tactics, the right environment, the right players together. Rugby is the greatest team sport because you are relying on other people, and other people with different disciplines and skills. The success of the England team is down to collective responsibility.

When I took over for one match, the system was up and running, and I had no problems at all. It was very easy. No worries – especially knowing that Will would be captain again the following season. This is the first time that England have had a team manager and a long-term captain. I know some of the press feel that it's too comfortable, that the best way to get a team to perform is to put them under pressure. Make them feel it's their last match, that the axe is hovering. That is ridiculous. You only have to look at various periods of English rugby to see the folly of that argument. Anyway, nobody takes anything for granted in this set-up. Cooke and Carling still make difficult decisions and change their views as the game develops.

Murrayfield 1990 was certainly Will's biggest lesson. He was still learning and finding his feet. He wasn't imposing his authority, and that led to confusion. 'Should we kick or not?' It was such a shock because we had been blitzing everybody. The 1989 defeat in Wales was different. We were beaten that day by Norster and Jones. Cardiff was wet and windy, and we made a defensive error in a tight game. You can't do that, as we found out to our cost again in Wales in 1993. Murrayfield was a kick up the backside for Will and the team. Although Will was in charge, we learnt collective responsibility in a tight game after Scotland.

That really determined what we would do in the 1991 Grand Slam and World Cup. Had we won in Scotland, it might have taken the edge off our game. Perhaps it was the hardest lesson of all. It certainly helped Will's captaincy.

We had to win in France and Scotland in the World Cup. Even the two games we lost in that period, Argentina '90 and the World Cup final, went to the last minute. We did well in 1991 because we really felt a team. During the Five Nations championship, we are actually not together that much. But in '91, we toured Australia and then we were together for the six weeks of the World Cup. We got on well, and a tremendous spirit was built up. We were fed up at not being successful: we were all on the same wavelength on that one. Those who were new to the squad were pulled along.

CARLING
John Orwin – I don't think his performance in Australia in 1988 influenced me in a positive way. It was not a happy tour. I've tried to learn instead by what people do right, although we all learn from mistakes. I know the principles of leading people, what's right. Cookie is similar. Concentrate on the positive side of leadership, do things right, and praise those who get it right rather than criticise players who have got it wrong.

I have been very lucky with this England team. There are not too many political animals who could have given me a hard time. I'm aware off the field that a certain manoeuvring goes on. I've got no control over that area, and I just have accept that. Maybe I should play the political game more than I do. But I don't like doing it. My loyalty is with the players, and I would never compromise that. Of course, the player might question that if a tough decision goes against him. I don't like dropping players, but it's part of the job. I certainly wouldn't want to stay as captain if I had compromised them for my position. But there's nothing I've done politically to stay as captain that I regret doing. I don't think I play the political game well. It's not in my nature.

My Army plans actually helped me. What had fascinated me was the idea of 30 guys under the control of someone much younger. I would have been 23 when I passed out of Sandhurst. They would have said 'yes' to me because I was an officer, but I wanted that 'yes' because they thought I was a good guy. Not popular, but respected. That's what intrigued me. How am I going to get 30 guys following *me*, the officer who set the standards and who they believed in? I certainly wasn't going to know more about the Army than them. But I wanted them to think, 'I respect him and will follow him because he has our best interests at heart.' That's why I went on that exercise to Germany as an ordinary soldier. I wanted to know what they thought makes a good officer. So I spent three weeks in the backs of trucks. Slowly, you learn what they think makes a good leader. I already knew what the mess side thought a good officer was, through family connections growing up. This was from the other side, and it put quite a different perspective on things. One thing was clear: they weren't looking for someone who wanted to be a good guy, who wanted to be popular. They wanted someone to set the standards, who was fair to all, who was honest with them. If that's how he treated them, they grew to like him anyway. The guys who set out to be popular never worked that out, and that was the major difference. The ranks preferred officers who didn't try to cross the line.

Within a few weeks of deciding not to go to Sandhurst, I was made England captain. And put in charge of a bunch of men who were a lot older and more experienced than me. I've never tried to captain England on military lines. That would not have worked. But I've used what I learnt on exercise to determine how I should behave as captain. What a soldier in the platoon requires from his leader is the same as what an England rugby player expects from the captain. The challenge in both is getting the best out of them.

Rugby is different from the Army. No private is going to tell his leader to get lost. The service is his career, and he is a professional. His length of tenure is cast in stone. There are regulations: break them at his peril. Most of what an officer decides is written down for him somewhere and if it goes wrong, it is more likely a fault of the system. Individuality is suppressed for the team good. Few soldiers have an interest in or opinion on tactics. Nobody wants to swap places with the man giving the orders.

Carling's England squad may have taken on the look of permanence from time to time, but nobody has signed on. They stay or go on their performance. Yet they are sporting amateurs, all professionals in other fields. They are taught to fit into a team pattern, but individual skills and style are learnt elsewhere. Most have strong opinions on the way the game should be played, and some would relish the chance to take over. Like most jobs, it is a lot easier when someone else is doing it. Looking at Will Carling, most see the good times, not the bad; the easy decisions, not the hard ones; the back-slapping, not the back-stabbing. 'Giz a job, I can do that!'

Chapter 32

Mr Blobby

I believe Will Carling has done more for rugby in this country than anyone else. As a role model, he has done very few things wrong. Sadly, he is never going to win with certain members of the committee. They feel that rugby has given him that fame and fortune. The truth is the other way around: Will Carling's England have brought fame and fortune to rugby.

COLIN HERRIDGE

Will Carling had been signed up to help with a new children's programme during his summer off in 1992. The captain's role was to explain to Mr Blobby, a giant pink blancmange with yellow spots, how the game of rugby was played for the benefit of youngsters watching.

England's rugby captain is no stranger to world of television. The sporting celebrity circuit these days includes chat shows such as 'Wogan', 'Pebble Mill' and 'Aspel', as well as the statutory 'Question of Sport'. Carling is a competent performer, although his appearance on ITV's 'This Morning' during the 1991 World Cup is not one of his favourites. 'They just went on about me as a sex symbol and wouldn't let up until I admitted it. It made me cringe and wary of putting myself in that position again.'

Carling felt safer with Mr Blobby. The rehearsals went well. The

241

actor playing Mr Blobby only had his false arms and wellies on as they ran through the programme. 'It's bloody stupid really,' ad-libbed England's captain. 'What are the boys going to do when they see this?' What the England boys did was fall about. For Carling's embarrassment was destined not for the relative safety of children's TV, but Saturday night prime-time. He had been set up for 'Noel Edmonds' House Party'. England's captain was one of Noel's 'Gotcha' targets, and Carling received his Oscar with flying colours.

Carling was joined in the studio for the showing of his ordeal by five England team-mates, John Olver, Steve Bates, Jeff Probyn, Martin Bayfield and Ian Hunter. It was only after five minutes of nonsense, when Mr Blobby concluded the episode by bringing down the makeshift goalposts, that Edmonds revealed himself inside the costume and Carling realised his predicament. Still, those five minutes had shown Carling's mischievous sense of humour. Mr Blobby had been stood on and kicked as Carling's comments on the lunacy of the whole performance had to be repeatedly bleeped. One remark – 'We don't have to worry about the Jocks' – caused a furore up in Scotland and was removed when the clip was repeated on the 'Best of . . .' programme.

Carling saw no harm in such frivolous fun. 'People think that you do everything that comes along. But I turn down 90 per cent of requests. There's not enough time, so I just try to do things with a good image. I'm not a natural on television, but I don't mind it. You are at your most vulnerable on chat shows. They always want an answer to the female interest stuff, which is not my favourite subject, and it's difficult to escape. Those appearances promote Will Carling, but they also improve rugby's profile. I think the England captain has a responsibility to present the game in a good light. I know there are complaints that I have too high a profile and shouldn't be seen on television away from the game, but I don't hold with that. The only valid complaint would be if I was presenting a bad image that reflected adversely on the team and on the game.'

England's captain fulfilled his duties admirably on Monday's 'Wogan' programme after the 1990 Grand Slam defeat at Murray-field. The victorious John Jeffrey and coach Ian McGeechan were also guests. Carling had to smile and congratulate the Scots and pretended it was only a game. 'I realise that I was probably still in shock even then. It was only about Wednesday that I realised we had lost the bloody lot!' Those shows allow Carling to meet celebrities from other walks of life, and comedienne Ruby Wax appeared once to give him a rough time on the 'Aspel' show. 'A lot of people thought that she took over the show at my expense. I certainly didn't feel that. She knew I wasn't comfortable or relaxed in that environment. If I hesitated, she came in with a joke. That gave me time to think. She never once interrupted me. I was grateful.'

Carling is careful to give little away on these public occasions. Even Sue Lawley failed to coax him into revealing much on Radio 4's 'Desert Island Discs'. The impression created was thus of a rather one-dimensional character. 'I suppose it is easier for people at the end of their lives and careers to be honest and open up. I deliberately didn't give much away. And since the programme, I keep thinking I should have picked this record and that one.'

His choice of music – including the theme from *The Mission*, Elton John's *Sacrifice*, Eric Clapton's *Layla*, the Police's *Every Little Thing She does is Magic*, as well as Louis Armstrong's *What a Wonderful World* – was, in the main, modern and rather sentimental. His favourite book was *The Hobbit*, and his luxury was a flotation tank.

CARLING

Sting, Phil Collins, Dire Straits, Bruce Springsteen, Tina Turner, Simple Minds and Elton John. That's my kind of music. Julia says that my likes are incredibly middle-of-the-road and middle-aged, but that's always been me. I've never been particularly radical in my music. I suppose my movie heroes are predictable, too: Robert De Niro, Clint Eastwood. And I loved Al Pacino in *Scarface*. It was dreadful, but he was classic, so over the top, really intense. I had a mate at school who looked a bit like Sylvester Stallone. I like his films. This mate knew every line from *Rambo* – not difficult – and we would mimic scenes from the film.

Carling's fame means that his public appearances are less and less rugby-related. He has opened the Boat Show and won a 25-metre dash against a 165 turbo-charged Lotus Esprit at Battersea Park. That helped raise over £10,000 in bets for the Royal Marsden Cancer Appeal. He also receives invites to the Royal Box at Wimbledon.

Royalty has shown an increasing interest in rugby in recent years. The Princess Royal is Scotland's patron, while the Princess of Wales has been a frequent visitor to the National Stadium in Cardiff. Prince

Edward declared the 1991 World Cup open, and the Queen attended the final at Twickenham. Carling has taken part in sporting seminars and congresses with Prince Philip. His OBE award in the 1992 New Year's Honours List took him to Buckingham Palace, where he has also been to lunch with the Queen. 'I sat down with the Queen and six guests. It's quite scary. I've met Prince Charles as well. I feel very privileged. That's all come from rugby. It's fairly unreal.'

His hob-nobbing is resented at Twickenham, for they see that as their preserve. It is another sign that player-power is getting out of control. 'Will tries to promote English rugby in the best way possible,' is Colin Herridge's view. 'I believe he has done more for rugby in this country than anyone else to promote the spread of the game. Everyone knows who Will Carling is. A comedy show like "Birds of a Feather" wouldn't use his name in the script if he was just a sporting star – Will is a national celebrity. As a role model, he has done very few things wrong. Sadly, he is never going to win with certain members of the committee. Will has made a great success of his life already and will continue to do so. They feel that rugby has given him that fame and fortune. The truth is the other way around: Will Carling's England have brought fame and fortune to rugby. And the officials are happy to bask in that glory.'

Chapter 33

Cardiff Catastrophe – Part III

When Geoff Cooke and Will Carling came to the interview room, it was hardly with the smiles of victors. They revealed the slightly gaunt expression that people used to have when emerging from air-raid shelters after the all-clear. 'We've made it.'

DAVID MILLER

The 1993 championship schedule appeared to suit England. Twickenham matches against France and Scotland, and trips to the weakest rugby nations, Wales and Ireland. France were expected to provide the sternest challenge, although Cooke privately thought Cardiff would be the big hurdle. Carling spent the New Year in Lanzarote with the England squad. The pressure of the Courage Leagues, as well as the international and Divisional programme, left few weekends spare for preparation. Cooke tried to play down talk of a Grand Slam hat-trick, indicating instead that the visit of New Zealand to Twickenham in November 1993 was the focal point of this rugby year for England.

Jeff Probyn returned for the France game, and Teague and Winterbottom were either side of Clarke in the back row, while Hunter regained his wing place at Tony Underwood's expense. Probyn's treatment appears to have been one of the few areas of indecision in Cooke's time in charge. Probyn and Carling, nine years

245

apart in age, made their first England appearances together in Paris in 1988. Probyn's propping technique had been under scrutiny even before then: some, like David Sole, have been blunt and accused him of cheating. But Probyn has survived close examination by the best referees in the world and established a reputation as an immense scrummager. He has done England proud. 'Such an odd shape,' is Wade Dooley's view. 'No shoulders, no backside and all stomach.'

The first blow came in 1989 when he came off against Ireland. The Irish doctor Mick Molloy diagnosed Probyn as suffering from concussion, although Probyn made strenuous efforts that night to persuade Molloy to change his mind so as to avoid three weeks' enforced recuperation. His big mistake in the Berkley Court was in talking properly and lucidly late at night in Dublin – no fit person is normally able to. Gareth Chilcott came in against France, kept his place, and went on the Lions tour to Australia. Probyn was devastated. He even considered quitting rugby, but stayed to play his part.

From time to time thereafter, the axe would waver. He and his close friend Paul Rendall were dropped for younger, less experienced props against Fiji in 1989. Carling's New Model Army wanted new-world props, ball-players as well as ball-getters. Probyn did not think much of that. But he worked hard and improved his fitness. He was still always the last man to bed before internationals, watching anything to help him relax. Probyn felt his days were numbered after England's second Grand Slam, even taking £50 bets with two journalists that he would not be in the line-up against South Africa. But he was not going to bow out without a fight. He sat on the bench against Canada and South Africa (the £100 he received did not infringe his amateur status) – then he returned against France, as Cooke announced, 'We have always said that Jeff is the best tight-head scrummager in the business. We need his ability against France. He causes problems to the opposition. He has been very hurt that he has been left out. But we have been pleased with the work he has put in.'

CARLING
Jeffrey has tremendous pride in his performance. When he's been left out, it's because we've wanted him to develop in other areas. And he has developed. He's played some of his best rugby

in recent years. I'm pretty sure he doesn't appreciate what I do, though. I'm just a flash boy to him.

Probyn, the 'Fat Boy', certainly feels that Carling has come from a privileged background, and has accused Carling's dad of looking after his son better than most. The Wasps prop has aired those views publicly from time to time. When Carling received the OBE, it was Probyn who went into print, wanting to know why. 'It's a bit ridiculous. All the hard work was done by Geoff Cooke. Will is just a playing figurehead. He said he was embarrassed to be singled out. He hasn't done anything for an OBE, but Geoff has. He's the man who has transformed England. Alf Ramsey got a knighthood in 1966 and Bobby Moore got an OBE. Will got his OBE for another successful World Cup for England, but Geoff has received nothing. He hasn't even the guarantee of a job after this season. The players believe his contribution deserves something.' Carling did not argue with that. Where was Cooke's honour? Well, only the RFU knew that one.

Money, too, has reared its ugly head. Probyn is a team man – one for all, all for one. But the commercial world does not work like that. Nor does the rugby one. Forwards have been resentful of backs since the first threequarter came off the field without getting his shorts dirty. Probyn runs his own family business as well as a family, and his sacrifices for England have been greater than most. No wonder he gets upset when the RFU charge him for an extra tea ticket. Only Probyn would send a letter to a national newspaper stating: 'There are some who bathe in the financial success that winning brings, but for the majority it's a matter of struggling through the Sahara of amateurism, balancing a job and a hobby, trying to reach the top in both. Yours sincerely, J. A. Probyn.' So, occasionally, he does get resentful of the 'flash boy' who seems to be making a lot of money and is able to make decisions affecting the composition of the England rugby team. But Probyn's anger is actually directed towards the system.

Still, comments in Carling's *Captain's Diary* did not help: 'As I suspected, there was much debate about props. On the one hand, Paul Rendall and Jeff Probyn are easily the best set-piece props we have. On the other hand, their fitness levels are not all they could be. There are fitter props around and, while these may not be ready for international rugby yet, there's a feeling that Probyn and Rendall could do with the jolt of a little competition for their places.' And earlier: 'What we don't have is mobile props. My own feeling is that, given the quality of the other six forwards, we ought to be able to incorporate two young props into the pack and bring them along for a year or so while they mature. The accent of forward play is moving away from big juggernauts towards a more athletic type.' Hardly likely to endear the skipper to his props. And a little naïve, rugby-wise. The fact he was still there four years later gave Probyn intense satisfaction. Normally, however, Carling holds his hands up when front-row play is mentioned. 'I always ask the feelings of the other forwards. What do I know about a good prop? I've never played against one. It would be ridiculous for me to sit in selection and air my views on props.'

As for playing against a good prop, Probyn would dearly love the chance. It was a tragedy when he missed a second successive Lions tour in 1993, and the Lions certainly missed him. In that respect, Probyn has perhaps been punished for a bad tour report from England's 1988 visit to Australia, where he was entrusted with the Herculean task of looking after Skinner. Still, even if he never plays for his country again, Probyn has become England's most-capped prop of all time. And, in turn, Probyn felt the 1993 championship was the stage when Carling finally grew up. England's captain showed his worth when England were struggling, and Probyn, as ever, was happy to give credit where it was due.

Carling did not have a happy New Year in Lanzarote. Bath centre Phil de Glanville had won his first cap against South Africa when Tony Underwood came off near the end, and he now laid his skipper out for four minutes with a crunching tackle. Carling received treatment on and off the field, and took no further part in the final practice match. Carling was also to come off after 14 minutes after hurting his right ankle playing for Quins against Orrell the following Saturday. Since he was unable to take part in the subsequent squad session, those 14 minutes were all the competitive rugby in seven weeks that Carling took into the first international against France. Peter Winterbottom and Dewi Morris also joined Carling on the injured list that squad session.

All three reported fit, but Carling was forced to go into the game without Dooley. The England lock withdrew the day before, and Leicester's Martin Johnson was awarded his first cap at very short notice. Carling has great respect for Dooley's honest endeavour and continuing enthusiasm. He had slipped him a note under the door before the 1991 Grand Slam decider: 'Wade, with over 40 caps, there's bugger all I can say, but you know how important you are to us tomorrow. You've carried us through three games. Let's kill these buggers off in the fourth. Make sure you get to run with the ball, too. Hurt those idiots in the tackle. This is our biggest game, so let's show everyone how powerful we are. Good luck, mate. Will.'

Carling felt the need to reassert his claims on the captaincy before the championship opener. 'I'll never give up the captaincy. I don't see myself being just a player. I'll never relinquish the captaincy voluntarily. I'd find it very strange to play for the side if I wasn't skipper. I love the job and I'm getting better at it. I want to go on leading England until 1995 – and maybe even beyond that, although I'm very aware of the danger of becoming stale and players not responding to what I say to them. I would still play for England if the captaincy was taken away from me, but it's not what I want.'

New cap Johnson played well, but England did not. Webb's hesitancy under the high ball allowed France an early lead and, ultimately, it was only the woodwork which enabled England to scrape home 16–15. Hunter was on hand to score when Webb's penalty attempt bounced off a post before the interval, and the bar then denied Jean-Baptiste Lafond a dropped goal and France victory ten minutes before the end. Lafond had given an outstanding display of full-back play in wretched conditions, but Cooke refused to make excuses. 'We made more errors than we would expect to do in the whole of a season. It was the most disciplined and well-organised French performance against us for a while. Given that sort of start, they are likely to win their next three games.' Cooke was spot-on there.

David Miller, of *The Times*, recorded the aftermath. 'When Geoff Cooke and Will Carling came to the interview room, it was hardly with the smiles of victors. They revealed the slightly gaunt expression that people used to have when emerging from air-raid shelters after the all-clear. "We've made it." In 1991, France lost at Twickenham by only 2 points when victory would have given them the Grand Slam instead of England. Carling said afterwards that being captain of England had become easier over three years. That would be enough to infuriate the French even further. What had become grindingly evident was England's refusal, no matter how close the call, to become frayed, to lose their presence of mind whatever the pressure.

249

That is part-coaching and organisation, part-captaincy. You can picture Carling still pouring the wine in a restaurant that was on fire. No panic.'

Carling was panicking, though. The captaincy was getting to him again, although this was different from the problems that beset him towards the end of 1990. Then Carling had felt he was under attack from all sides. Now the pressures came from within. England's captain had set such high standards and expectations that they were becoming impossible to live with. Winning and playing well was expected. Anything less was failure, and Carling knew the price of failure. At the start of 1993, Carling had said: 'If we lose a game in the championship this year, I'll get absolutely murdered again. I've been put up there and I'm a target. Gary [Lineker] didn't get that when he was captain of England. The England soccer captain doesn't get slagged off for his team losing. I've always seen the England rugby captain as midway between the cricket and soccer jobs. I'm not as involved as the cricket captain, but much more than football. I'm much more actively involved in selection and tactics than Gary ever was. But, the cricket captain does the job all day. He has much more time to make his decisions, and even longer to live with them.'

The almost daily analysis of his suitability to lead the British Lions was little more than an irritant, however. At the time, Carling thought he wanted the job and was sure he would get it. But already the responsibilities of that position were beginning to prey on his mind. And they increased after another disastrous visit to Cardiff.

Wales had missed the opening championship weekend. Alan Davies and Bob Norster had worked a minor miracle since the World Cup, but Wales were still not in the same class as England. Nevertheless, Jonathan Webb's fumbles against France were bringing some relief to the Principality: BBC Wales were repeating three of his errors in their trailers for the Cardiff match. 'There was no slight intended to Jonathan Webb,' insisted former Wales skipper Gareth Davies, now the station's head of sport. 'It was a marketing ploy and, although we are impartial, we are a Welsh channel. We wanted to show something which would give our boys – [very impartial] – a bit more confidence. If we had used clips of recent Wales-England matches, there wouldn't have been too much that was upbeat about them.'

Gareth Davies knows well enough that the Five Nations championship is about commitment as much as anything else. The purists may complain, but the rugby upset is very much part of championship life and is a big part of the tournament's attraction. Every genuine rugby follower was thrilled at the emotional comebacks of two rugby nations in the doldrums at the expense of Grand Slam England in 1993. And it is doubtful whether the National Stadium, even in the glory years, has ever echoed quite so much to the roars that greeted Wales's latest win over England.

The contest turned again on a few seconds' aberration by Rory Underwood, who has been enticed into several lapses by the Welsh *hwyl* over the years. Flanker Emyr Lewis kicked ahead down the right, and Welsh captain Ieuan Evans set off in pursuit – only in hope because, well, you never know. Underwood's 58-cap experience went out the window. The RAF flier was the only man within 100 metres of the ball who could not see the danger as he covered across. Evans steamed past him, hacked on and scored, and the crowd went wild. England had half the match in which to recover, but the tide had turned. Morris had already been denied a try by French referee Joel Dumé; Bayfield lost the ball over the line; Carling was as guilty as anyone of fumbling chances; Webb hit the post, and England did not take a last-minute penalty shot from 50 metres. It was just not England's day. It was a day of mistakes, below-par performances. Underwood admitted, 'I didn't think there was any urgency.'

Cooke had earlier predicted, 'Simply getting to the other end of the field doesn't necessarily bring you points.' Afterwards, England's team manager said: 'When there's a mistake, it's a collective mistake, and everyone shares Rory's disappointment. It is a major setback. But we simply have to pick ourselves up and go on, even though it hurts. It was a combination of skill and judgement failure.'

CARLING
It dawned on me suddenly this year. Why was I playing? Was I captaining England for the right reasons? Was it just ego? I began to question my motives. Was I interested in me, or the team, or just in being heralded? Did I want to be the greatest captain there ever was? If the answer to that question was 'yes' – then I'd got it all wrong. I always felt I'd been for the team, but now I wasn't sure. Cardiff gave me the answer. It was very sad to lose. But I knew afterwards that I was still doing the job for the right reasons. I don't like being in the dressing-room with my team-mates when we've lost.

* * *

The defeat ended England's hopes of a third Grand Slam. And Carling's progress towards the Lions captaincy was now being studied more closely than ever. Stephen Jones, in the *Sunday Times*: 'What of Carling and the Lions? How did Cardiff change his life? He did make one or two electrifying bursts, but they were delicious single notes of a symphony which remained unheard. Carling is a brilliant player, but for an inside centre who is also captain, he was disturbingly peripheral. He was peripheral because England do not have the capability to launch him to strike for victory, and because he showed again that, in tight games, he can allow the England tactics to meander. England captains of the past would have killed for results half as good as those of Carling's men. Yet, in Carling's era, had England been tactically harder of head and more inclined to chase the close games, they could have been unbeaten in the northern hemisphere since 1988 – a run which would have included victory in the World Cup final and against Wales last weekend. All this is Carling's triumph and failure.'

Chapter 34

Mr Arrogant

Will was catapulted so quickly. First of all, it was the captaincy. Then the World Cup happened, and nobody's life was the same again. Will is now among the six most famous sportsmen in this country alongside Mansell, Faldo, Lineker, Gower and Gooch.

ROB ANDREW

Carling was increasingly aware that his performance off the field was being analysed just as closely as his displays on it. Carling's leadership demands loyalty and respect, not popularity. Five years into the job, his captaincy style is well established. He does not trust the media or the rugby authorities. His players, he feels, expect certain standards, so he keeps himself apart. His contact with players from other countries is limited, except as England captain. Carling works closely with Geoff Cooke and Dick Best and devotes a lot of time to his role as captain. That, coupled with running a successful business and other outside work interests, leaves very little time for being social, for the PR side of the job. England's captain does not hang around bars and clubhouses chatting, because he does not have time. That, though, is only part of the reason: Carling does not want to.

CARLING
I don't enjoy the spotlight that much. Many make the big

253

mistake of thinking that I do. But I hate going to functions and dinners if I'm not working. I don't like people pointing and staring at me. I much prefer being with a few close friends. I am shy and introverted. I find it hard work. That's where the press have never worked it out. I don't crave TV and newspaper coverage. I admit I'm no shrinking violet, but I choose carefully.

I've become the symbol of England's recent rugby success, and that's lovely. But they don't know the truth, which is something very different. I can't ever see myself standing up and saying, 'It's me. Christ, I'm a good guy and a great captain.' I place far too much importance on the rest of the squad who've been there all the way through. It's been a hell of a team, and I think there are four or five people who would have made good captains. Rob Andrew, Simon Halliday and Winters are the most obvious, but there have been several other potential leaders around. I don't think I've done anything startling. It's not a big deal, and it's not fair to attribute England's success to one person. Sure, I've done my bit, but so has everyone else.

The perception of me as arrogant and aloof is strongest in the media. I know Geoff talked to Ian McGeechan and others from the other countries about it before the 1993 Lions tour. That is just not the way the players view me. I certainly got on with everyone when I captained the Barbarians. I remember someone telling me that the reason Nick Farr-Jones was so successful as a captain was that he was always slightly detached from the other players. You room alone, and you do have to be slightly apart from them. They know you have to sit in on selection and you have to set standards. If you are trying to get people to adhere to those standards and you are continually late or out on the beer, it just doesn't work. By definition, the job is a lonely one.

Carling, like most people, is conditioned by his experiences. He comes from a very close-knit, loving family. His mum and dad don't regard him as a rebel. 'He's not bolshy, not a trouble-maker,' says his father. 'Nor is Willie a fool. He can see the dangers and would prefer diplomacy to conflict. But he won't cave in.' Nor is Carling the cold fish: he is openly affectionate with his parents and his brother. But he does keep his emotions under wraps, although he cares passionately about playing for England and captaining his country.

* * *

CARLING

I keep my emotions in check. The Scots are fairly canny like that. My grandmother is Scottish – I was eligible for Scotland. I was sent away to school, and I don't know if that had anything to do with it. At Sedbergh, I was put a year ahead of myself at every sport. That singled me out straight away. If I'd have shown any pride, I would have been crucified by my own year. The team I was playing with didn't want to know me – I was from the year below. So you kept everything to yourself. You concealed the fact that playing well at sport meant a lot to you. I didn't want to appear arrogant and different from the boys in my year.

Carling has been singled out all through his life, and that has played a major part in his make-up. The basic shyness has always been there but, because England's captain has learnt to disguise it well, people assume there is not a problem.

ANDREW

Will was catapulted so quickly. First of all, it was the captaincy. Then the World Cup happened, and nobody's life was the same again. Will is now among the six most famous sportsmen in this country alongside Mansell, Faldo, Lineker, Gower and Gooch. Will's life changed the most because he was captain and because of the career he had chosen. A captain with a high profile has double the pressure.

Will is definitely more suspicious and wary than he was. I think it's part of his nature, but after all he's had to put up with, who can blame him? When I started, there were half a dozen or so die-hard rugby journalists. You might not have agreed with what they wrote, but they travelled around with the team, and you got to know them well. That number seems to have increased 10-fold. Nowadays, few have any sort of relationship with the players, so we are all a bit more suspicious. A lot of the press hasn't been too kind, despite our success. Maybe that's why this team has a reputation for being rather stand-offish. We don't bother with outsiders. It's the inner strength that has helped us. You do get knocked about a bit, and it's not just Will. I've had the knife twisted badly by the media. And it hurts. But I don't think that behaviour is peculiar to the rugby press. The profile of the team has grown and because of our professional attitude, we are seen as fair game these days. Many of the younger players do not appreciate that there has been a change. The sniping and digging for dirt is all that the likes of Will have experienced, and that's bound to shape his thinking. And if rugby continues to grow, it will become the norm.

'The more successful Will has become, the more guarded he is,' believes *Today*'s Tony Roche. 'I remember the press chatted to him at the Stoop before the start of the 1992 championship. He explained that he was still frustrated by the way we considered England had played at Murrayfield and in the World Cup final. He doesn't forget. I believe he's got his scars off the field, not on it.'

CARLING
Arrogance is not my style. Nor is it England's – it's not a tradition in this country. Players such as Blanco and Campese have a lot to say for themselves, but that doesn't make them superior in my book. If I'm facing those sorts of bloke, I don't give a damn about them. I know I can beat them. England players have arrogance, but it's inside, not to be shown. I'm arrogant on the field, but I've got to be if I want to be good. I have to believe in myself, that I'm better than the man opposite. I would like to believe that the best thing about this England side is that they can turn it off. If you meet them off the field, they are not arrogant. They prove that you don't have to live the part all the time. Jerry is arrogant, he has a swagger. That's his style, it's not put on. And we don't attack people off the field. I have never been a great believer in that. We get our satisfaction on the field.

Most of Britain's top sporting stars face a backlash once they have made the top. The drive to succeed rarely allows much time for pleasantries. And that drive which will separate them from the pack can bring resentment from fellow-competitors or team-mates. Few escape: even Britain's Olympic 400m hurdles gold medallist Sally Gunnell felt the change. 'It's a horrible enough thing to have to say,' admitted Gunnell. 'But there are those who wish I had not won. I have had this feeling since of jealousy – an impression that some begrudge me making it because it proves that anybody can if they do the work. I get the feeling that they think I believe I'm better than anyone else. I don't. I believe it is possible for far more people to do what I've done. They just have to really want it. The problem is that nothing prepares you for the change. Nobody gives you lessons in coping, in how to act, who to trust. For a while before Christmas, I was so worried that people would think I was above myself if I said no to anything that I was doing everything.'

There is not enough of Will Carling to go round. Better to be selective rather than to spread himself too thinly. But England's captain is public property, be it in a bar or restaurant – 'I'm sorry to disturb you, but . . . !' Carling is rarely rude, for he was not brought up that way. In the end, however, England's captain has come to avoid public places and resents this loss of freedom. Sometimes, though, there is no escape – especially when you have just lost in Cardiff, the whole of England is ready to tell you where it all went wrong.

Chapter 35

The Best Lost Weekend

Dropping Rob was about the toughest of the lot. I feel that it has taken the edge off our relationship. I am involved in selection, but it's not all my decision. Still, I can't say, 'Sorry, you're dropped. Personally, I wanted you.' You have to toe the party line. That's best for all concerned.

WILL CARLING

Rob Andrew was the main casualty of Cardiff, and that cost Carling his main link with the players. Andrew was the one who relayed the rest of the team's input or feelings of disquiet to the captain. And Carling used Andrew to gauge the side's reaction to his own performance as captain. Stuart Barnes was brought in instead at fly-half. The side to face Scotland was announced five days after the Cardiff defeat, even though England sat out the next round of Five Nations matches. Cooke had brought the selection forward to pre-empt any unsettling suggestions. 'Now the players brought in can prepare themselves mentally for the game, and the two we have left out can reflect on their roles in the squad.' Ian Hunter was also replaced, by Tony Underwood. Hunter had needed an eye operation after a freak accident in Cardiff, but Cooke stressed that the Northampton back had been dropped. Meanwhile, Andrew's demotion put quite a strain on his relationship with Carling.

* * *

ANDREW

Will and I have always been close. I wasn't expecting it, but I obviously misread the situation. I didn't think there would be any changes. I believe that if we'd played for another three weeks, we were still destined to lose. You just had to look at the circumstances of their try. It was Geoff who rang me with the bad news. Then I talked to Will. These things happen. When a guy has picked you for 39 consecutive Tests, you can't argue. That's the way it goes. I know Will is involved in selection but, ultimately, it was Geoff's decision. What disappointed me was that mistakes led to the try, and there were others, too. And I wasn't involved in any of them.

In a way, it seemed more awkward for Will than it was for me. We've discussed it since, and it's a difficult situation. We've been in the same side for a long time, since 1988. And we are close, on and off the field. I've been heavily involved and suddenly, that changed. Will finds that part of captaincy difficult. By and large, England have had a very settled side, and that's probably made the times when players have been left out all the harder – when Deano was left out, when Webb came in for Hodgkinson, Hill for Morris, Morris for Hill, Probyn in and out. There haven't been many more. We've all been through so much.

Defeat in Cardiff was difficult. The press were really gunning for the side, and that had started right back in September before the Canada and South Africa matches. There was a lot of speculation about Stuart [Barnes] and me. I had a good game versus South Africa, and I didn't think I played too badly against France. But I've drawn experience from the past. You just get on with life. I was delighted to go with the British Lions in the summer. I won that head-to-head with Stuart, but the debate looks certain to continue.

CARLING

I'm glad I have some say on selection, but it comes at a price. When players are dropped, they know I've had some input. Still, it helps to know why players are picked and the decision-making process behind it. Cookie is very clever: he knows that he gets an input from the players through me, and that's never happened

260

before. Sometimes we agree to disagree. What happens then? Cookie gets his way, of course. I remember when he wanted to bring in Simon [Hodgkinson] at full-back against Romania, while I wanted to play an attacking full-back, someone outrageous, like the other Simon [Halliday]. I suppose we've had three or four such clashes over the years, but nothing serious.

Deano [Richards] has been such a tower of strength, such a tough man. I have tremendous respect for him. After we lost in Cardiff, where he had been on the bench, he was in the bar, head bent. He just asked, 'You okay?' It might not sound much, but it was. I've always felt disloyal leaving him out. But that's not why it's done. Leaving out Simon [Halliday] for Jerry, who I didn't know at all, was hard, too.

And dropping Rob was about the toughest of the lot. It's about having the strength of mind to be honest. Provided it's done for the right reasons, then I can live with that. It would be terrible if personal reasons entered the argument for not wanting someone to play. I feel that it has taken the edge off our relationship. You don't know what's said behind your back. I'm not dissociating myself from the process: I am involved, but it's not all my decision. Still, I can't say, 'Sorry, you're dropped. Personally, I wanted you.' You have to toe the party line. That's best for all concerned.

Wales's revival came to an abrupt halt a fortnight later at Murrayfield, while Ireland faded against the French at Lansdowne Road. Now the tide was turning against Carling. Gavin Hastings had become a serious rival for the Lions captaincy as Scotland won both their home championship games comfortably. Hastings is a much more extrovert character than Carling, a leader by instinct rather than design, and the Scottish full-back had an obvious advantage because of his part in the Lions success in Australia four years earlier. Carling had warned that he would get murdered if England lost in the championship, but the scale of the scorn now surprised even him. The Calcutta Cup was billed as a duel between Carling and Hastings for the Lions captaincy, though Carling realised the outcome would only be considered decisive if Scotland won. If England kept the Cup, then the arguments would rage on. Carling was beginning to feel that the Lions captaincy did not have his name on it after all. He was not even sure that it had not turned the Scot's way already, irrespective of the Twickenham engagement.

Yet even Carling and Hastings were forced to take something of a back seat in the build-up; Stuart Barnes was the man occupying centre-stage. The Bath fly-half and captain was winning his ninth cap, but it was a new beginning: his first under Carling, his first at fly-half in the championship, and his first start at Twickenham since his debut against Australia nine years earlier. Four times Barnes had come on as a replacement, and his four full games at fly-half had been against Australia, New Zealand (twice) and Fiji. Barnes had twice announced his unavailability for England, but his influence on Bath's rise to dominance at the top of English club rugby had been considerable, and that success had kept him in the public eye and mind, even during his periods of self-imposed exile.

Despite Barnes's long absence from the national side, Carling treated him no differently from any other newcomer. 'I'm very trusting of players,' explains Carling. 'When they come into the squad, it doesn't matter what's gone on in the past. Everyone starts with a clean slate. You have to trust players in order for them to trust you.' The captain also appreciated that, for all Barnes's experience and confidence, much was expected of him. It is not always easy or possible to turn it on in the cauldron of the championship.

Barnes started nervously as Scotland began positively. But the visitors' rhythm was disrupted by an injury to fly-half Craig Chalmers, and Barnes began buzzing. England's backs were given both space and opportunity, and Guscott, Barnes's Bath colleague, benefited most and revelled in such conditions. Barnes it was who instigated one of the finest tries of the Carling era. He had to stretch high for a wayward Morris pass from a line-out deep inside England's half, and safety-first seemed the order of the day. But Barnes stepped inside the charging flanker Ian Smith and was off. The burst caught the Scots off-guard. Barnes approached half-way before throwing out a long pass into Guscott's path. Guscott did not have to check in any way and sped off, timing his pass to perfection to remove the two covering tacklers as Rory Underwood raced away for the try. Guscott had already scored, and Rory's brother Tony soon added a third. That set off the proudest mum in Twickenham: Mrs Anne Underwood was captured by the television cameras celebrating the Underwood double in some style.

Although Scotland rallied in the final quarter, England's 26–12 victory was conclusive, but was almost certain to cost them the championship. For the first time, the Five Nations championship had a trophy. There was no sponsorship, but the days of the title being shared (in 1973, for example, all five countries won two matches) were over. The winner would be decided on points difference, although Carling wonders whether in future it would be more reasonable for the top two teams to play off on a neutral international ground to decide the best team in Europe, with the profits going to an injured players' fund. France's points difference, though, now made them firm favourites for the 1993 championship. 'It is unfortunate,' explained Cooke, 'that we did not show the killer instinct after going 23–6 up. We should have gone to town. But our supply of ball dried up, and we did not get our line-out working.'

Carling had little time to celebrate the success as he flew off to join his Harlequins team-mates in South Africa. But his presence in the Rose Room immediately after the Calcutta Cup match had been one of his first public appearances with Julia Smith. Even there, Carling had to evade the lenses of one or two prying cameras, and there was to be no escape in South Africa. Whether by accident or design, one of Julia's faxes to Will was intercepted by some mischievous member of the Harlequins side. It was made public to the team at a later date, to much merriment.

Harlequins have offered Carling much relief over the past six years. It has been the perfect spot for him, and not only because it is a glamorous club with glamorous traditions and glamorous players. They – especially Colin Herridge – have been more understanding of Carling's situation than most. The club helped him when his Army career was suddenly no longer an option. And they offered him advice during his time of turmoil after the 1990 Murrayfield defeat.

The Quins have also allowed him latitude in his club responsibilities. The club-versus-country conflict has not affected Carling. Herridge is well aware of the pressures and problems affecting the modern England captain, and Carling is not required to play in every club match – even in every league match. Like Gareth Edwards before him, Carling is a big-match player. The club scene, even in today's competitive world, is merely a means to an end for him. The routine, the run-of-the-mill, has little place in his world of the pursuit of excellence. Carling would have been no good as a big fish in a small pond in his club rugby career.

* * *

HERRIDGE

We have tried to lessen his load, not increase it. He hasn't had to put up with hero-worship here, and he's not been at the mercy of the crowd. Elsewhere, players like Jerry Guscott and Mike Teague are heroes one week, villains the next. But Will is on an even keel here. We haven't felt the need to make him captain, and he hasn't felt the need to be captain. The club doesn't see Will playing at Harlequins as the be-all and end-all. We know that there are bigger things in his life, and we are happy that he has made his base here. There's give-and-take on both sides. Will's presence at the club is a two-edged sword.

Will has fitted in nicely to the Quins' total game-plan. We have won games because Will Carling has been on the field, but others also benefit because he is around. The opposition expect our game to revolve around him. It doesn't. But their watching Will means space for others. We have many internationals, so Will hasn't had to bear the burden of success for the club. Our officials also understand the pressures of being in London. The rugby clubs here are not the centres of the community.

CARLING

I like being in the Quins dressing-room when I'm not captain. I believe that I have a role to play in encouraging them, although I haven't done as well in that department as I should have. Really, I've just wanted to play, to escape from the hurly-burly, without any responsibility. But I've realised that's not fair to the younger members in the side. I think Winters has picked up quite a bit from me as captain. I know he would never admit that. But Winters has his own style. He's very direct, gives it everything he's got and expects everyone else to do the same. He works on that principle: I'm going to give you everything. I want the same. And you're going to give it to me.

Although I'm not captain, I can't say that I feel like just another player there. I noticed that when I was first made captain of England, my life at Harlequins changed, too. I felt as if I was in a zoo. My every move was being watched. After club games – who is he talking to, who is he not talking to? I certainly had not taken in those implications when I accepted the job. I

264

thought life at the Stoop would go on as before.

The week before the final championship matches, the *Sunday Times* carried an article which was entitled: 'Why Carling must not captain the Lions'. It was written by Stephen Jones. The unfortunate heading angered Carling, but the content did not. Jones's verdict was more a plea for Gavin Hastings to be given the job, arguing that Carling would benefit from a period away from international leadership.

At the time, however, Cooke and Carling were more worried about the Irish. 'They won in Cardiff, and we didn't,' remembered Cooke. 'Their crowd support will have picked up because of that win. Lansdowne Road can be a very daunting place. And Ireland will be more used to the referee, having had him in their last match.' That last statement was polite Cooke-speak for: 'We don't think very much of Australian referee Sandy McNeill.' The liberal refereeing of the French and the Australians, plus the new laws, was a combination that cost England dear in 1993. For his part, Carling was more worried about the laws. The changes relating to ruck and maul had done what no rugby coach or player could do for the Irish: they had brought them back as a force in world rugby. Ireland's display against Australia in autumn 1992 was probably the most inept by a Five Nations country on their own soil since squad sessions took over. Yet, once they realised that the law-makers had given them a licence to hang off, fringe and generally run amok, the Irish had found a new zest for rugby life.

England, the Grand Slam champions, World Cup-finalists, and the northern hemisphere's most successful side, were consequently hustled, bustled and brow-beaten 17–3 by an Irish side full of passion, pride and personality. Eric Ellwood was the latest choice at fly-half and after several attempts, Ireland proved to have found a pivot of character and poise. Ellwood had shocked Wales, and now he destroyed England. Slowly but surely, the visitors drowned in a sea of Irish green. Barnes, who had waited so long to recover England's No. 10 jersey, would have found few prepared to swap places with him in Dublin.

England's forwards continued to underachieve. Any good possession the backs received was accompanied by even better tacklers, and that is how Carling's championship misery ended when he tried one last, desperate attack. The captain was bulldozed backwards, the ball went loose, and Mick Galwey picked up and scored. Carling had started the campaign looking every inch a winner. Now he was down for the count.

CARLING
We were really struggling. I remember talking to Stu [Barnes]: 'What can we do to get into this game?' I had a terrible sense of frustration. But you have to persevere. It's said that you shouldn't look at the scoreboard or clock. Just concentrate on the basics. And don't panic, don't try to force the pace. That's probably right. But when the Irish are flying around at 100mph, it's almost impossible. I was really annoyed to give away that try near the end. I was trying something, but I should have held on to the ball. It just summed up the whole miserable afternoon.

The decisions of Rory Underwood, Dooley and Webb to abandon their retirements had been shown by the 1993 championship to be a mistake. And the notion that England's experienced pack would adapt quickest to the new laws was flawed. Moore's forwards were too set in their ways. Like the older generation faced with computers, England's unit – Ben Clarke apart – struggled to do the new things instinctively. The demise was bad news for the Lions: the core of that summer's party was to be the England scrum. The selectors had waited for several experienced forwards to live up to their reputations, but only Mike Teague did himself justice. 'We will have to stop and think,' explained Cooke, with his Lions manager's hat on. 'Certainly, tomorrow's selectors' meeting will be longer than it would have been otherwise.' The end of the 1993 dream also marked the end of an era.

Ireland always offers consolation for Carling, for Dublin is his favourite rugby weekend. 'The Irish play their rugby hard, then play hard,' says Carling. 'In Cardiff and Edinburgh, the result is everything. But the Irish celebrate whatever, and that philosophy is catching. The most horrendous night out I ever had was with Paul Dean and Michael Kiernan – I'm not sure what time the festivities ended. I must admit that I prefer waking up in London on an international Sunday for two reasons: it's easier getting home, and it tends to mean we've won. But Sunday morning in Dublin is hard work. We normally fly back after lunch, which gives Wade Dooley plenty of time to organise compulsory Guinness for the whole team. And, however badly you've done, the result of a rugby match doesn't seem quite as life-shattering as it was the afternoon before.'

Carling flew home having revealed to the press that he was not expecting to be named British Lions captain. That was no surprise. Carling had already told Cooke that he did not want the job.

Chapter 36

End of an Era

England's national side is at a point of change. And in a few years, the fans – even the administrators – will realise what a great side this was. And I mean WAS, not is. The World Cup, the 1991–92 Grand Slam is finished. It's over. The future belongs to the likes of Neil Back, Tony Underwood, Victor Ubogu and Ben Clarke.

WILL CARLING

The mass retirement predicted after England's World Cup final in late 1991 will now take place before the 1994 Five Nations championship. The reluctance of so many top players to call it a day reflects the spirit and bond that has been built up since Geoff Cooke took over. Now advancing years and the poor showing in the 1993 championship have brought down the curtain on one of the greatest sides in England's history. This was a side to compare with the two best post-war European sides, Wales and France in the 1970s.

Carling knows that 1993 was a great disappointment. Excuses are not his style, but England's captain believes that outside influences played a major part in the national side's failure to consolidate their position.

CARLING
The difference between 1992 and 1993 is that we took our

chances in 1992. The slightest chance, we took it. That's the key in close matches. The 1992 Grand Slam had almost been too easy. We were still on a high from the World Cup, we had so much support, and the team was going well. It was incredible. Winning seemed to take so little effort. The atmosphere was so relaxed, and so different to 1991. Every game had been hard in 1991. The final game against France was so tense and close, and there was so much relief that we had finally achieved something. We didn't have a close game in 1992. The second Grand Slam was more matter of fact – we'd already done it. No game was on the line. The final match against Wales was won in the opening quarter of an hour. People may have claimed we were beating weak sides, but it was still a great year for us.

The level of expectancy did weigh on us in 1993 after two Grand Slams. Most people were putting good money on a third, but the edge had gone. No one from outside could assess that. To be brutally honest, the Lions had a distracting effect. It was hard for Cookie and Bestie in their dual roles, and certain players took their eyes off the ball. They were looking too far ahead to the Lions. Still, we didn't come up to standard. The new laws affected us more than we thought they would. England were not able to establish a pattern of play early on, as we had done in the previous two championships. We had chances against Wales, but we couldn't put them away. And then we couldn't keep the pressure on with the new laws.

Nowadays, it's a case of getting down there and scoring, because it can be 10 minutes before you might get another chance. The new laws have changed the whole emphasis of the game. I have always believed that rugby is about going forwards by passing backwards. That's the way I was taught to play, and you play that way until you are stopped. The new laws reward good cheats: get to the ball and tie it up. It's disheartening as a back to look up and see so many forwards hanging around on the outside. There's no space. It's man-for-man overlaps these days.

Carling admits that his own form was below par, too. Towards the end of the season, he sat down with Peter Winterbottom and after a few drinks, Carling felt able to ask his Quins captain for an honest assessment of his own performance. 'Did I do anything wrong,

Winters?' asked England's captain. 'Well, Will, you didn't give us anything new this year.' Maybe Carling, too, had been distracted by the imminent Lions tour.

England have now lost eight matches out of Carling's 35 in charge. Australia and Wales have triumphed twice each, with single victories for Scotland, Argentina, New Zealand and Ireland. England remained unbeaten at Twickenham in the five championships since Carling took over, losing just four away matches. Only in three matches has Carling felt that the game was lost: Australia in Sydney in 1991, the World Cup opener against New Zealand, and the Dublin defeat last season.

CARLING

It is very frustrating when you realise that you're going to lose. But you have to be sensible about it. It's part and parcel of any sport. It's also the challenge of the captaincy: I've got to keep digging, we might just get a chance to get back into the game. But if I'm ranting and raving, then I might not see that opportunity.

In those three games, the opposition dominated possession – quality possession. So, as a back, it's hard for me to get into the game, except defensively. I'm not blaming the forwards, but at least they can have a crack. I'm stuck out there, and there's nothing I can do. In the other defeats – Cardiff '89 and '93, Murrayfield '90, Argentina '90 and the World Cup final – I didn't think we were going to lose. Defeat only became a reality when the final whistle went. You accept that you might lose, but you believe you're going to win, that it's only a matter of time before that vital score comes. In all those matches, had we got in front, the opposition were finished.

I remember Brian Moore saying that he can never enjoy playing in an international. Maybe that's the difference between backs and forwards, but I don't understand that. To me, that's what international rugby is all about. Sure, there's the pressure, there's the physical confrontation, but that's the test. Anyway, why does Brian keep doing it, if he doesn't enjoy it? In some kind of way, you've got to enjoy the challenge. To me, it's coping with the pressure, and enjoying coping with the pressure. Of course, the games are very physical; but that, in a sense, is what you enjoy.

271

And this England team still has a lot of fun, no matter what anyone else says. Those near to the squad realise that. Why do the old lags want to carry on? If they didn't have any fun, most of them would have retired long before now. It's not the traditional rugby image of having fun, the game being just an excuse for a drinks session until 3 o'clock in the morning. It's slightly different these days, even at club level. But we still have a hell of a lot of fun because of what we've been through. The intense pressure and shared pressure bring you much closer.

Perhaps satisfaction would be a better word than fun. There's a tremendous amount of that within the England squad. We don't show it to other people, but I can feel it when we're together behind closed doors, in hotels, in the changing-room, in the evenings after internationals. A great sense of pride in our achievement. I think the media see us as coming across in a very packaged way. That's more for self-preservation than anything else. We don't want them to build us up so they can wipe us down. We try to keep it low-key, especially when we are favourites. A low-key profile helps us. But in the end, you have got to make sure that you keep getting it right.

England's national side is at a point of change. And in a few years the fans – even the administrators – will realise what a great side this was. And I mean *was*, not is. The World Cup, the 1991–92 Grand Slam is finished. It's over. The future belongs to the likes of Neil Back, Tony Underwood, Victor Ubogu and Ben Clarke.

I have had so many letters of satisfaction from hundreds who've enjoyed watching this England rugby team. Although we had gushing press reports of many of our victories, the overall impression from the media is that, for some reason, we have not been as great a side as we might have been. That somehow, in some way, we have let ourselves down. I think that is nonsense. Just look at the way our *Swing Low, Sweet Chariot* has become a song sung wherever England sides of different sports are playing.

The Twickenham crowd have played a big part in our success at HQ. Other teams notice the atmosphere now and don't like it. The faithful don't worry when they read in the papers about how we should be playing. They know that we've produced the goods for them over the past five years. My first international at

Twickenham is the last one England have lost at home in the championship – Wales in 1988. The crowd must take some of the credit for that. They have been behind us all the way. I'm just sad we didn't give them a World Cup to go with the two Grand Slams.

The most significant thing for me is the number of outstanding performances that will live on from this side. Most great teams have had a few, but this England XV is nearly in double figures. Everyone has their own views, but I think it would be difficult to argue with this list: Ireland and Australia in 1988, France in 1989, France and Wales in 1990, Wales and France (World Cup) in 1991, France and Ireland in 1992. That's the pick of the bunch. And you can add the last two Lions Tests in 1989 and the second at Wellington in 1993, when England's forwards held the balance of power. I've not included the Triple Crown and Grand Slam matches of 1991 and 1992. And last season we scored some great tries against Canada, South Africa and Scotland. In ten years' time, I feel this bunch of players will get a lot more credit than they do now.

We averaged over 30 points and four tries a game in 1992. That's not bad. And we won all six internationals. Yet the team was repeatedly criticised. I accept such a high level of expectation as being the way it is. But it's funny that we will only get the real credit once the team has broken up. Still, that's the English way, and it's probably good from our point of view because it stops people getting carried away. I remember watching the 1980 Grand Slam side: they were heavily criticised when they beat Wales 9–8. Now Bill Beaumont's side is rated as just about the best there's ever been. However you feel about it, you can't let it get to you.

Chapter 37

Private Affair

I handle the press better than Will. He sometimes doesn't understand that you can't muck them around. Will Carling, the rugby hero, thinks he can be a private person in public. It's not on. You just have to accept it and get on with it.

JULIA SMITH

Carling knew that England's poor 1993 Championship performance, especially in Dublin, had not helped the British Lions. Selectors are left in limbo when proven quality players of a certain age are not producing the goods. Several of England's most experienced forwards, especially Peter Winterbottom, who some thought should be Lions captain, and Wade Dooley, had shown only glimpses of their best. Lions coach Ian McGeechan had to decide whether it was a temporary or permanent loss of form; New Zealand is not the place to take a forward on the downward slide. Ireland's rousing finale to the season in particular had several old Irish legends pleading for the selectors to abandon their earlier thinking and go with the men in green.

McGeechan and Geoff Cooke are not men to be easily diverted. The major influences on their selection were the 1989 Lions success in Australia, and England's subsequent domination of the northern hemisphere. The 1993 Lions party, to be led by Gavin Hastings as

275

expected, contained 16 Englishmen, although one of the big shocks was an Englishman who was missing: tight-head prop Jeff Probyn. He was not one of those who had been below par. Although he had been dropped at the start of the season, he had played consistently throughout the championship and was expected to be given the Lions chance that had been denied him in 1989.

The eight Scots in the party included their entire front five. Even before the Lions departed, however, doubts were expressed as to whether those forwards were up to the All Blacks test. 'We looked at the challenge posed by a tour like this and considered Probyn,' explained Cooke at the time. 'But it was decided that the four props whom we have chosen can deliver what will be required.' It was soon apparent, though, that one of those props, Peter Wright, was not equipped to deliver and should never have been exposed to the ordeal.

Dean Richards, currently out of the England side, was one of the twelve 1989 Lions included. Wales's Robert Jones had been McGeechan's scrum-half on that victorious trip, but was originally left out this time. Instead England's Dewi Morris was chosen as Gary Armstrong's deputy – so was this the first time there would be no Welsh scrum-half on a Lions tour since 1959? McGeechan made his policy clear: 'Those who were with the Lions in 1989 have a head start. They know what the pressures are, and that experience must be used, while the challenge to the England players will be crucial to the development of the squad. I hope to set challenges to some very experienced players who can achieve great mobility and pace. All I am asking of them is seven games of top-class rugby.'

Carling offered his congratulations to Hastings. For the third Lions tour to New Zealand in a row, the man who had looked a dead cert to be captain a year earlier failed to do the job. In Mervyn Davies and Bill Beaumont's cases, injury had been the reason; Carling's failure was less straightforward. Still, there was general agreement that the removal of the responsibility of leadership away from Carling was a good thing. England's captain had to concur, especially after a rare public airing of his private life.

His relationship with Victoria Jackson had been on rocky ground for a while. They had split up briefly the previous summer, but went on holiday together in August. Carling finally ended it after a December break with Victoria in the Far East. He explained that rugby was still the most important thing in his life, and that there was not room for a serious relationship in his current plans. When the break-up was made public midway through the 1993 championship, Carling said: 'There is no one else in my life. We are both very sad it is all over. But I felt the relationship had run as far as it was going. It was an unpleasant day for both of us, but there seemed no kindness in prolonging it just for the sake of it. Neither of us has any intention of discussing our time together in public.'

That lasted for a month. Three days after Carling officially lost the Lions captaincy, he was pictured on the front pages with top pop PR Julia Smith. Julia had first met Carling when he was going out with Nikki Turner. She now described their relationship as 'very special. It is in its early stages, and we both hope it will develop. We have known each other for four years. We met at a supper party. Over the years we kept in touch and, suddenly, two months ago we found ourselves together again and realised that our long-valued friendship means much more to each of us.'

Carling's team-mates were surprised that he had agreed to the photograph together. But he had had little choice. Julia rang him from her Kensington office and told him that there were photographers outside who had told her that they would follow her day and night until they got a picture of her with the England rugby captain. To save Julia any more hassle, Carling reluctantly agreed. The matter was not closed, however. The following day Victoria, slighted that Carling now felt able to accommodate a serious relationship alongside his rugby, went into print. 'Life without Will' was the heading as Victoria, billed as Carling's ex, insisted: 'Any career-minded girl would be fed up with just being known as someone's girlfriend.'

Carling was horrified. Despite his many problems with the rugby press, this was the first time his private life had been available for public consumption. England's captain was getting the full Mills & Boon treatment. The article began: 'Victoria Jackson is fed up with being cast as the spurned lover. True, she shared a passionate two-year relationship with England rugby union captain Will Carling. True, their separation was sad and painful.' Victoria herself was less dramatic. 'I'm tired of people coming up and saying how sorry they are that we've split up. I say, "Please don't be". It's happened. Romances break up the whole time. The thing that makes it so difficult is that it's so public. While I was seeing Will, I was always Will Carling's girlfriend. Now I'm Will Carling's ex-girlfriend, and everyone wants to know who I'm seeing. I wish I could go back to being a private person.'

Victoria described meeting Carling. 'We met in a bar. I didn't know who he was. The private side of Will, the part that made him attractive to me, is still very private. We used to have other girlfriends and boyfriends, separate friends, and Julia was one of Will's. But that didn't stop us having a close relationship, and neither of us was sexually involved with friends of the opposite sex. I'm an all-or-nothing person. The reasons Will and I broke up are very, very private. I really don't know if he was romantically involved with Julia before we split, but I wasn't surprised he was seeing someone else; I never thought our relationship was for life. He phoned me to tell me about Julia, but I was so surprised he posed for the newspapers with her. He was always very, very private. I think it's sad, because that was what we agreed on. That was the golden rule. But obviously people change, and Will is now definitely a past stage in my life.'

Just how serious Carling now was about Julia was revealed four days before the Lions set off for New Zealand: they announced their engagement, with marriage plans for the summer of 1994. 'It was fairly obvious to me that this was very different to other relationships. I realised that Julia was the one. We share the same sense of humour and, for the first time, I feel comfortable with a woman and can talk about things that are important to me. I have some very, very close friends, and Julia gets on well with them. Her being there hasn't made any difference. I am very much a man's man, but Julia is a man's woman. Marriage is not going to change me a lot. I'm not a hell-raiser.'

Such openness was very un-Carling-like. He has never been comfortable talking about his feelings. But Julia's independence and confidence have had a marked effect on him. Her name has been linked in the past with several pop luminaries such as Mick Jagger, Bob Geldof and Eric Clapton. 'It is the way of life in show business. There are lots of rumours. In my job as a pop PR you meet those people, occasionally go to parties, or get invited out to dinner.' Her agency is called 'Hands On PR', and clients include Right Said Fred, INXS, French singer Vanessa Paradis, Jade Jagger, Bill Wyman's Sticky Fingers restaurant, and *Playgirl* magazine. Indeed her friend Nikki Turner went to Australia as personal assistant to INXS, fronted by Kylie Minogue's ex-boyfriend Michael Hutchence, after her break-up with Carling. But Julia's pop connections have not all been business: she moved in with pop guitarist Jeff Beck when she was 19, and that relationship lasted six years. Julia is a strong character. She is also a success in her own right. She has her own world, which is a lot more glamorous and less staid than Carling's.

JULIA

I'm a country lass who quit university after a term of history. I then had a six-year relationship with a man who didn't want me to work. I got into pop PR in 1989, working with the Rolling Stones on their last tour, when the most important thing was organising faxes for Mick [Jagger] and Charlie [Watts] so that they knew what was happening with the England cricket team. I met Will through Nikki, his girlfriend. I had heard of Will Carling: my mum liked watching the rugby internationals on TV, and I'd seen a few. I had also been one of the few girls in an all-male school, and I'd learnt all the rugby chants. I suppose I was expecting someone who was brash and arrogant but, at this dinner party, he was desperately uncomfortable. He didn't say a word. He felt on show. I just couldn't believe how incredibly shy he was.

I used to go with Nikki to watch him play at Twickenham. Then Nikki headed for Australia after they finally split. Will and I have always had a phone relationship, abusing each other and I went out with him a couple of times as an escort. I suppose we always knew there was something there, but it took him four years to ask me out. It was pathetic really. He said he was waiting for me, but I would never have asked him.

When he was first asked about us, Will insisted that we were just friends. That annoyed me. You can't handle the press that way. He gets very protective and doesn't want me bothered. But dealing with the media is my job. I was half Jeff's age when I went to live with him, and he had another girlfriend and family, so I know what the press can be like. I handle the press better than Will. He sometimes doesn't understand that you can't muck them around. Will Carling, the rugby hero, thinks he can be a private person in public. It's not on. You just have to accept it and get on with it. He doesn't like to give too much away in interviews. But the less you give a journalist, the more he's going to have an input.

I know Victoria's comments annoyed Will. They split because of his love of rugby and the need to concentrate on it completely. Suddenly, Will's with someone else and getting married. Often I was piggy-in-the-middle when Will and Nikki were having problems – and Victoria, too. That was difficult for me, because nothing could happen with me while they were together. I had been potty about Jeff, but I knew it wasn't love; Will's the first person I've been in love with. Will doesn't like it when I say all his friends are the same, the rugby stereotype. It's like the blonde he has to have on his arm, the standard prop. My friends are all weirdos, most of whom have never heard of him. That's great.

One of the papers did a piece about me as his new girlfriend. It described how all his attitudes, behaviour and life were part of a standard pattern, and how I had to fit in. It was hilarious, and spot-on. Will thought it was a load of rubbish – a bit near the mark, I think. 'The amateur sportsman is not unduly complicated and does not expect his girlfriend to be. Amateur sportsmen are not as promiscuous as one might expect them to be, first because they are often sweet-natured, and second because they don't want all the hassle. They expect a trap.' It went on: 'The first item of marital furniture will be an orthopaedic chair in front of the television. Her sportsman husband will ask her sweetly to rub his ankles and the back of his neck.'

I remember sending Will a fax before the Welsh game. I rang the number of the hotel and asked for their fax number, then I sent off my message. But I hadn't rung the hotel, just an office in Cardiff, so they got my fax instead. They rang back and said: 'Are you Julia?' I was so embarrassed. I said 'no' and put the phone down!

Carling spent a lot of time with Julia after the championship and before flying out with the Lions. He had injured his shoulder in the defeat by Ireland, and his only subsequent appearance before the tour was the Pilkington Cup final, when Quins went down for the second year running, this time to Leicester. A fortnight earlier, Carling had travelled to Edinburgh for the World Sevens, which England won, and shared the TV expert analysis duties with Gavin Hastings. While the two were together, England's captain offered the Lions leader his full support and help at any time. But it did not work out that way. Hastings' leadership style was not the Carling method. The Scottish captain left the running of the side to the coach, Ian McGeechan. That meant Carling was to be redundant on the input front over the next two months. Hastings had no need for support and help. But Carling did. The British Lions tour was to offer him the toughest challenge of his sporting career.

Chapter 38

One of the Lads Again, Briefly!

*You can never reach perfection. But, apart from a couple of mistakes
late on, it was as near to a perfect game as I have played.*

JERRY GUSCOTT

Carling learnt a few facts of his new life as one of the boys even before
the Lions left for New Zealand. Ian McGeechan gathered the tourists
together for a weekend towards the end of April and, after five
seasons as a single man as England captain, Carling found himself
sharing a room. Scotland's Andy Reed was the forward who was
going to have to educate Carling and, after half a day together, Reed
thought the time was right. 'You carry on, Will. Don't mind me. Use
my bed as an office. That's not a problem.' Carling, used to the
solitude and the space, had spread himself out as usual.

  McGeechan split the Lions into six teams, who would operate as
units for training and games throughout the tour. Carling's bunch
included Welsh centre Scott Gibbs, and they called themselves the
Taxi Drivers. That was a less than subtle reference to Gibbs's recent
arrest for pinching a taxi after Swansea's game against the
Barbarians. The car was driven only a few yards, but Gibbs was none
the less ordered to appear in court a few days before the Lions
departed. Still, he was lucky: in the good old days, that prank might
have cost him his place on tour.

Scotland's Gary Armstrong was one who had been forced to withdraw before the off, and Robert Jones was the beneficiary. Wales skipper Ieuan Evans was meanwhile named *Rugby World* Player of the Year in succession to Carling. It had not been a vintage year, but Evans had been an inspiration to his country in bad times, not least for that kick ahead which destroyed England, and he was destined to display his skills to the full with the Lions.

Once in New Zealand, Carling had not even appeared in a match before the word was out that his Lions Test place was under threat. Stuart Barnes led the Lions as they overcame North Auckland in the opening match, although the victory was overshadowed by an injury to England's Ian Hunter. The Northampton wing-cum-full-back had fought a desperate battle to overcome a succession of injuries during the season to make the tour, but he dislocated a shoulder after 39 minutes and his tour was over. The Lions sent for Richard Wallace, who had been to New Zealand with Ireland the previous summer, as a replacement.

Both centres, Scott Hastings and Jerry Guscott, had impressed in that first game. Carling's Lions debut came against North Harbour. The club was founded as recently as 1985 but, with Wayne Shelford's influence, they had already become a power in the land. Carling and Scott Gibbs were up against the All Black centre pairing of Walter Little and Frank Bunce, but it was the forward battle – and battle it was – that will be remembered in the Lions' bruising 29–13 victory. Dean Richards left the field for a precautionary X-ray to his jaw, Paul Burnell received two black eyes, and Bunce needed 20 stitches in an ear wound, all sustained during a ferocious second-half brawl. Such confrontations are inevitable on a tour of New Zealand; the alternative is not to compete and let the home sides walk all over you. McGeechan's 1989 Lions had shown that they would not be intimidated, and nobody expected their 1993 counterparts to be any different. Geoff Cooke made the right noises afterwards. 'The players have been reminded of the need for discipline, but they are not going to back off. I cannot accept that Dean started it. It was an isolated flare-up in an otherwise cleanly fought game. Of course the players know they cannot back off here, but we do not want to be the ones to start anything. Both teams have to share the blame for what happened.'

Carling had not played well, while Gibbs had. Purely on the respective centres' tour form, England's captain was already lagging behind in fourth place. He was paired with Scott Hastings for the third match against the New Zealand Maoris, when the Lions staged a magnificent comeback after trailing 20–0 at half-time to win 24–20. They were still 17 points adrift with only 19 minutes remaining. But the Lions' inspirations were their captain and the rest of the backs. Match-winning tries came from Evans, Rory Underwood and Gavin Hastings, and Evans, especially, was unstoppable. The fightback was the perfect setting for Carling's pace and power, but something was missing. He limped off rather dejectedly in the final stages, to be replaced by Guscott.

Carling was beginning to find the tour a strain. Despite his offer of help, Gavin Hastings was running things his own way and felt no need to involve England's captain. And, training and playing apart, Carling had little to do and nothing to occupy his mind. That was a new experience. So was feeling homesick – or rather, lovesick. That was down to Julia.

Carling and Cooke's thoughts returned to England when the 1995 World Cup draw was announced. It was the organisers' third or fourth such attempt in five months. In January, England's likely quarter-final opponents had been announced as Wales or Ireland. By April, England were lined up against New Zealand. Then, after a complaint from Australia, it became France or Scotland. England's World Cup was growing tougher by the month. That last draw was then retracted because of a 'printing error'. The latest circular put England against either the holders, Australia, or the hosts, South Africa, in the quarter-finals. Cooke described the situation as 'staggering'.

The Lions' next game, a victory over Canterbury, was dominated completely by a virtuoso performance from Guscott. 'You can never reach perfection,' he said. 'But, apart from a couple of mistakes late on, it was as near to a perfect game as I have played.' The Lions' likely Test line-up was then given a dress rehearsal against Otago, with Carling paired with Guscott in the threequarters. But, despite leading 18–8 at half-time, the Lions' plans crumbled in the face of a succession of injuries and mistakes. Carling was the first to leave the field with a thigh strain. Then Scott Hastings, his replacement, came off, his tour ended with a fractured cheekbone. Finally, Martin Bayfield was stretchered off after being up-ended at a line-out and landing on the top of his spine. The injuries distracted the Lions, and they conceded five tries as Otago won 37–24. The tourists' forwards looked off the pace, and the defensive work was shoddy. A week before the first Test, the Lions looked anything but ready.

Fortunately, Bayfield's injury was not as serious as was first suspected. But the second-row problems mounted up when Wade Dooley had to return home because of the death of his father, Geoff. Martin Johnson, who had made his international debut against France in January after Dooley's late call-off, was again required to fill the breach, flying out with Ireland's Vince Cunningham, the replacement for Scott Hastings, who had undergone a four-and-a-half-hour operation to rewire a broken jaw and rebuild his fractured cheekbone. The New Zealand Rugby Football Union broke the rules and, in a generous gesture, told Dooley that he could return if he wished to do so after the funeral. Meanwhile, Carling's battle to get fit intensified when Scott Gibbs was injured in the midweek victory over Southland. Gibbs was ruled out of the Test with damaged ankle ligaments after an accidental collision with Tony Underwood, and the Lions were left with only one fit specialist centre, Guscott. Stuart Barnes was also sidelined by a severe head cut that needed 12 stitches.

Although the Lions' back play was being hailed as some of the best seen in New Zealand for many years, it was the performances of Bath's Ben Clarke that had the wily old campaigners of All Black rugby purring. Clarke had already appeared on tour at both open-side flanker and No. 8, but was picked on the blind-side flank for the opening Test in Christchurch. Although England had preferred Clarke at No. 8 in the championship, Dean Richards remained the cornerstone of McGeechan's pack. The coach had not transported the Leicester stalwart half-way across the world to play in the midweek side. Clarke responded to the challenge in precisely the way you would expect from someone under the influence of Jack Rowell. He showed himself just as adaptable to the new positions as he had been to the new laws. McGeechan was impressed. Such versatility must have reminded him of his colleague Roger Uttley on the 1974 tour of South Africa.

Declaring himself fit for the Test, Carling found himself paired with Guscott almost by default. Still, he was in a good frame of mind entering the match: Julia, who had been working in Australia, had flown to Christchurch to see him. Elsewhere in the side, the English combinations continued with Andrew and Morris at half-back, and with Winterbottom completing the back row. Reed filled Dooley's place, while England's Leonard, Moore and Teague failed to find places in the scrum.

The Lions lost the first Test, as expected. But the tourists' performance stunned the All Blacks, who kicked a penalty with only two minutes left to win 20–18. New Zealand are traditionally at their most vulnerable in the first Test of a series, but the home side had not expected such a fight after the Lions' recent run of poor form and injuries. The Lions actually cried 'robbed', and they had a point. Australian referee Brian Kinsey had awarded the home side a try early on, when Bunce and Evans had gone up together for a high kick on the Lions line, and had crashed over, each with an arm on the ball. Kinsey claimed that he checked with the touch judge before raising his arm for Bunce's score. Unfortunately, however, from where the touch judge was standing, he could not have seen whether Evans had got under the ball or whether Bunce had managed to touch it down.

New Zealand led 11–9 at the interval, the score signifying an impressive recovery by the Lions from the early setback. The backs, especially, seemed to have the beating of the home unit. Grant Fox then kicked two more penalties, but Hastings matched his accuracy into the wind, and the Lions went ahead 18–17 with nine minutes left. The All Black pressure was intense, without their ever looking likely to breach the Lions defence. But the 1-point margin indicated that Fox, who had earlier passed 1,000 points for the All Blacks, might still have the final word. That the inevitable penalty came was all the more cruel because the Lions were being so careful, Kinsey blowing up after Richards tackled Bunce and, allegedly, killed the ball. Such was the blatant injustice of the official's action that Kinsey would be ill advised ever to drive around the Hinckley area of Leicestershire with an out-of-date tax disc. He might find policeman Richards equally strict in interpreting the letter of the law.

As so often happens in New Zealand, only when they have lost the first Test do the touring team realise that the All Blacks are human after all. Still, the Lions were in for a tough final three weeks. Those weeks would be all the tougher if they dwelt on the travesty of Lancaster Park.

CARLING

I felt on trial from the moment I arrived in New Zealand. 'Carling under pressure' – that gave the media a great story straight away. I'd heard about New Zealand rugby and how much it means to the nation, but I wasn't prepared for the massive interest in the Lions. I felt on trial as a person as well as a player. And I made the mistake of worrying about the personal side, of how I was getting on with the Welsh, Irish and Scottish lads – that was important, but not the most important thing. I didn't spend enough time thinking things through. That was strange, because I had time on my hands. I was desperate to do well in New Zealand, but I didn't prepare properly. I'm normally very thorough. That showed there was something seriously wrong with me.

I don't think I arrived in bad form, but I had had very little rugby in the final two months of the season. In New Zealand, the harder I tried, the worse it got. The injury came at a bad time: I wanted a good game against Otago. I don't know what would have happened if Scott Gibbs had been fit, because he was playing well. I was worried that I might be on the way home after my injury. My leg suddenly had no power in it, and nobody could find out why.

I think we psyched ourselves into thinking that we were under more pressure than we actually were in the first Test. I threw out one pass when I thought I was under pressure; I wasn't. We had thought they were going to play at pace in the backs; they didn't. As soon as the referee awarded that last penalty, I knew it was going over. It was an amazing decision, to say the least. We can't blame the referee, though. There's no point. It was a decision we didn't agree with, but we should have been 4 points ahead by then, not 1. That was the frustration: we should have had points on the board. If you play for the last 10 minutes, and the opposition need only a penalty to win, you leave yourselves wide open. The All Blacks did enough. We allowed them to win the game.

Chapter 39

Captain Again, Briefly!

I was shocked to find out that guys who were internationals were not mentally strong enough. I don't think I've been in a side that hasn't competed before. People let themselves down, and that's always sad. It was about character more than ability.

WILL CARLING

Losing the first Test of a Lions series was not a new experience for Ian McGeechan. The coach also had a dozen players at his beck and call who had fought back to win in Australia four years earlier. Grant Fox for one believed the Lions were still in with a shout. 'Unless we improve by 30 per cent, we will probably lose the next one and the one after that. We can't expect to play like that and get away with it.' The Lions had a fortnight to get it right.

One of the Lions' problems was of the selectors' own making. Jeff Probyn's absence was now proving costly, so Jason Leonard was moved over as an experiment to strengthen the other side of the scrum. Probyn is not one not to say 'I told you so'. What he did say was: 'Obviously, I'm considered too old and too fat. I was not given an explanation for not being picked for the Lions. I had a letter from Geoff Cooke which said that the tour had come a year too late for me. I'm only a player, I don't select the side. I'll know when I'm ready to retire, but it's not yet. When the All Blacks come here in the autumn,

289

I hope to get the chance to show what I could have been doing now.' Leonard, now a prop of the tight-head variety, did not let the Lions down as they overcame Taranaki in their next match by 49–25. The final minutes saw the brief appearance of Andy Nicol, who had just been on Scotland's tour of the South Pacific; the Lions had temporarily called on the scrum-half after worries about Robert Jones.

The tourists' morale was given a further boost with the news that Wade Dooley had decided to take up the New Zealand union's kind invitation to return after his father's funeral. The row that ensued overshadowed even Carling's demotion from the Saturday side to face Auckland. The Four Home Unions, with a characteristic lack of touch, ruled that if Dooley returned, he would not be allowed to play. British officials told Eddie Tonks, the NZ RFU chairman who had made the original offer, that Dooley's return as a player would be in breach of the tour agreement and would create an undesirable precedent.

The Lions were furious. Cooke, again, would not have been popular at Twickenham with his view of the controversy: 'The whole squad is incensed about it. It's an appalling way to treat a person who has done so much for the game. We are talking about the amateur ethos in our game, and if ever there was a case for displaying the amateur ethos, this was it. On the grounds of sheer compassion, he should have been allowed to rejoin the party without conditions. For our people to raise objections is staggering. It started with the secretary, Bob Weighill, who was very negative in his approach to Wade, raising difficulties about insurance that were nonsensical. As for the grounds of precedent, that is even more illogical than it being outside the tour agreement, which is the rules and regulations bit.' Weighill was due to arrive in New Zealand shortly. 'I'm sure you will find some interesting questions to ask him,' Cooke told journalists. 'You'll probably be the only people who'll speak to him.' Gavin Hastings summed up the players' views: 'It totally destroys the ethos that everyone says is great about rugby, and has ruined it as far as I'm concerned.' Other Lions were even more direct.

Carling's tour effectively ended that week as well. Scott Gibbs was given his chance alongside Guscott in the Saturday match before the Test, while Brian Moore, Jason Leonard and Martin Johnson were also given the chance to press their claims. The writing may have been on the wall, but it came as a blow to Carling, who had thought he would get one final opportunity against Auckland.

CARLING

Auckland was a shock. It was the first time in my life that I had been dropped. I had no inkling about it. Nobody had spoken to me or warned me. The team was read out, and my name was not there. I had this terrible sick feeling in my stomach. It wasn't that I thought it was unfair; Scott had been playing really well and deserved his chance. But I wondered what I was doing here. I had drifted along for four weeks, and had just paid the penalty. I was as interested as everyone else was about how I was going to react. Brian Moore had a beer with me after the Auckland game: 'I'm sorry you didn't play. I wanted to say something at the time, but I didn't know how.' Paul Burnell and Andy Reed were also dropped, but 15 journalists wanted to know my reactions to getting the push. One of them even asked how I reacted to the punters saying that I had not been concentrating on my rugby because Julia had visited me.

I was very disappointed to be left out, but that was nothing to what Wade had been put through by the rugby authorities. The England boys especially were most upset. We had all known his dad. It was a chance for this great amateur game to show the world what a great amateur game it is. If rugby had been a professional game, I might have understood – it would have cost a lot of money to have paid an extra man. But this was a player who had won 50 caps for his country, whose father loved rugby and would have wanted him to come out, who had announced that he was quitting rugby after the tour, who had been invited out by the host union. Even now I can't believe the Four Home Unions behaved like that. We instigated a $50 fine for any member of the tour party caught talking to Weighill.

The Lions lost (23–18) for the third Saturday in a row, after leading Auckland 18–11 at half-time. Gibbs, however maintained his high standard, and Carling's Test hopes had gone. England's captain had come on to replace the injured Hastings at the interval and gave an adequate display, but his lack of familiarity with the full-back role was exposed a couple of times, and he damaged his shoulder again. He was none the less cleared of blame when the dirt-trackers lost the subsequent midweek game to Hawke's Bay by 29–17. England's captain registered his first points of the trip with a dropped goal, but Cooke called it 'the worst performance of the tour', and nobody was arguing. The many hundreds of British fans who had flown out to support the Lions were disgusted with the lack of effort and pride. Four days before the crunch Wellington Test, this was not the boost the senior side needed. Skipper for the day Stuart Barnes was the most vocal: 'Not all the players showed 100 per cent commitment here. I simply cannot understand that. I'm bitterly frustrated. I'm not accusing all 15 players, but the boys working and trying hard to get into the second Test side in Wellington on Saturday have been badly let down. Unless certain people react in the right way, this performance will cause internal divisions in the squad. This defeat hurts my pride. I just hope it hurts everyone else's pride as well.' Cooke arranged a clear-the-air team meeting for the following day.

Gavin Hastings's damaged hamstring received intensive treatment during the week. He took little part in the Friday session, and although it was confirmed that he would lead the side in the Test, few expected him to last the course. Stuart Barnes was put on standby. Three Englishmen – Leonard, Moore and Johnson – replaced three Scotsmen – Burnell, Kenny Milne and Reed – in the pack, while the one change in the backs from the first Test was the inclusion of Gibbs at Carling's expense. A record eleven Englishmen were selected, but their captain could not even find a place on the replacements' bench. Carling had been resigned to his fate since missing the Auckland match.

Carling was asked to join John Taylor in the ITV commentary box, and the pair had a grandstand view as the Lions gave their best display in New Zealand for 22 years. Hastings overcame not only his hamstring problem, but an elementary error under a high ball that gifted the All Blacks 7 points after only quarter of an hour. The tourists refused to panic: two Hastings penalties and a left-foot dropped goal by Rob Andrew gave the Lions a half-time lead. Hastings further increased the advantage to 12–7 after the interval as the All Blacks attempted to fight back. Then home captain Sean Fitzpatrick lost the ball while on the drive, and Morris and Guscott countered. The home side were caught flat-footed as Guscott put Rory Underwood away, and Underwood left John Kirwan for dead, went outside full-back John Timu and was over in the corner. There was a quarter of an hour left, but New Zealand were beaten. The visiting fans, so critical in midweek, were now roaring in delight. It was a day even the non-playing Carling will remember. So emphatic was the Lions victory, however, and so dramatic the turnaround, that Carling's last slim hopes of a Test recall had disappeared.

The Lions celebrated, and Carling joined in. It was an historic day for British rugby, and the manner of the Lions' success gave real hopes of a repeat of the 1989 victory in Australia. Rob Andrew, a key member of that side, had given a powerful, calculating display at fly-half, while his scrum-half partner Dewi Morris had the game of his life. The Lions pack were immense, and the All Blacks had no answer to the pace of the touring forwards or backs. The French referee Patrick Robin, too, was a great improvement on Kinsey, and the Lions were delighted that he would take charge of the deciding Test in Auckland.

Carling was finally made Lions captain for the last midweek game against provincial champions Waikato. His charges were humiliated. Carling, scoring his first try on tour, and Barnes battled as best they could, but the Lions second-string forwards again let the side down badly as they lost 38–10. McGeechan must have been especially disappointed in the Scottish forwards. 'I can't explain it,' he said. 'But, mentally, it's very different to the Five Nations, and you have to be very hard to keep performing.' There was some reward for Carling, though. He was selected to replace Barnes on the bench for the final Test.

The Lions could not have started better in Auckland. They led 10–0 after 25 minutes, with Scott Gibbs snapping up an opportunist try. The game, and the series, was theirs for the taking. But the Lions failed and were eventually defeated 30–13. The match was not decided until All Black scrum-half Jon Preston dummied his way over on the blind side with 13 minutes remaining, but all three New Zealand tries were soft. The Lions had lost that 10-point advantage to touchdowns from Bunce and Fitzpatrick in a four-minute spell towards the end of the first half.

The All Blacks were saluted for a magnificent recovery, but the Lions had contributed to their own downfall. The All Blacks captain Sean Fitzpatrick summed it up: 'We were desperate to win; more desperate than the Lions.' The All Blacks coach Laurie Mains in turn criticised the Lions for being too negative – an attitude that probably saved his job. He was right in that the Lions backs had repeatedly exposed New Zealand's lack of pace and flair outside, yet that road to victory had been ignored. It was a naïve performance, and bitterly disappointing after the euphoria of the previous week. The Lions' second-Test victory was the undoubted highlight of the tour, but they could have left with so much more. The Lions won seven and lost six matches, scoring 33 tries and conceding 31.

CARLING
I had a varied series: I played the first Test, commentated on the second, and sat on the bench for the third. The bench was easily the hardest. In the commentary box, I accepted that I would not be involved. But the bench is limbo-land. I hadn't expected to get called up for that job. Now I know what it's like for players such as John Olver, who've sat on the bench countless times. I've got a bit more sympathy now that I've been through it myself.

I don't understand how we could be so focused for the Tests – and so poor in midweek. I know that the Tests are the thing, while nobody really remembers the other results. But I was shocked to find out that guys who were internationals were not mentally strong enough. I don't think I've been in a side that hasn't competed before. People let themselves down, and that's always sad. It was about character more than ability: Waikato were a good side, but Hawke's Bay were not.

Once my Test chance had gone, it was down to personal pride. I had to take that responsibility. The tour was going down the tubes, but I was still keen to play. The results might have been disastrous, but I got a lot from the last two midweek games. My game was back, I was happy with myself, and I had solved a lot in my mind. I was under pressure – I had to show a bit of character. Most people have been dropped at some time. Certainly, the Carling silver-spoon image took a battering. It did me no harm to see life from the down side. It gave me all the incentive I need to play again.

Just being a player in New Zealand took a lot of pressure off me. I could pick and choose my interviews. Colin Herridge said afterwards: 'I don't think you can estimate how much good this has done you.' I think the players have seen a different side to me. I believe most of them think I've always had it easy. Now I've probably dispelled a lot of preconceived ideas. I'm sure the England boys could see that I was a lot more relaxed. I had seven weeks of imitating the Roger Moore puppet on 'Spitting Image'. Winters would say, 'Show us anger, Will – or happiness!' And I was expected to remain stony-faced and raise one eyebrow.

But I did miss having an input. I'm used to being involved. I tried to find a balance of not butting in or treading on anyone's toes. Gavin has his own style, and he played very well, too. That's the most important thing in New Zealand – to be at the top of your game.

Gavin left a lot to Geech [McGeechan]. And, again, Cookie found that hard. He's used to being involved, too. But Geech does things his own way. He thinks long and hard about his rugby. I admire the amount of work he does: most of his spare time is spent either preparing or studying. We didn't see a lot of him outside the sessions. He was rarely about for a drink. It was very much his tour, that's what he wanted. He was the driving force in 1989, and again this year. He was more wound up for the New Zealand tour, though, the 1989 tourists recognised that. He tried to show the same intensity as the All Blacks, to match them in that department. But it's not possible just to switch it on for seven weeks. The All Blacks have been doing their thing for over 100 years – it's part of their nature.

I think Dick [Best] found it tough, too. He had no defined role. Dick and Geoff must have looked at me half-way through the tour and wondered what was going on. They must have thought I'd had enough. But I had my chat with Geoff and told him I was keen to carry on. I have tremendous loyalty to Geoff, and I felt I had let him down. I hope the final two games repaired the damage to some extent.

A tour like that is very intense. There are no easy matches, and you are travelling every third day. We trained on every travel day, except one. I enjoyed the experience, but I'm not sure the Lions will survive, purely from the practical point of view. Players need so much time off nowadays. I think I shared a room with every forward, apart from Winters, Mooro and Jason. I spent a lot of time with the Welsh contingent – Tony Clement has a very dry sense of humour, which I like. We had only two players' courts on the trip, and the fines were fairly unimaginative. I thought I would really cop it when the lads heard Julia had come out, but all they did was make me drink a can of beer. I think there was a social committee, but nobody seemed to know who they were.

A tour like this, if you're not captain, allows you a lot of time to think about yourself. It was the wrong time for me to be doing that. It's no secret: I missed Julia terribly. I've never been in that situation before. The hotel phone bills were horrendous. From a playing point of view, I'm glad I sorted out my problems there and didn't give it away and wait until I got home. I was determined to prove that Will Carling was not finished: far from it.

Chapter 40

Back to the Future

The All Blacks appear in adverts wearing kit. It's up front. They now have the All Blacks Club. The authorities must realise that you promote the game through the players.

WILL CARLING

Carling returned home from New Zealand with his reputation restored, even enhanced. His tour had gone wrong; one Test appearance represented failure. Yet Carling was more positive about his and England's future than he had been for a long time as he prepared for the new season. As in 1989, England's rugby hopes had taken a giant step forward on the Lions tour. 'Well, that helped England sort out her pack problems for 1994,' claimed Ian McGeechan at the end of the trip. And the staggering progress of Ben Clarke, the emergence of Martin Johnson, and the switching of Jason Leonard to tight-head prop, did indeed give England options for the future. Wade Dooley and Peter Winterbottom have now joined Paul Ackford in retirement; Mike Teague, Dean Richards and Jeff Probyn will follow soon. But Carling believes that England already have the core of a pack that will challenge for the 1995 World Cup.

CARLING
It was Wales's coach Alan Davies who first described it as the

297

'England Development Tour'. There was a joke among the dirt-trackers that they would be terribly honoured to play for the England tour team. The performance of the Englishmen was fairly staggering. It looks good for England, although you can take nothing for granted. Certainly, it appears as if we have plenty to work with in the year ahead. We've got New Zealand, the Five Nations championship, and then a tour to South Africa in less than a year. We have got to be focused.

New Zealand's appearance at Twickenham late in 1993 is Carling's immediate challenge, but he already has the next World Cup in his sights. His original intention had always been to bow out after that tournament, but midway through the Lions tour England's captain wondered whether he had the motivation to last even that long. Those doubts have now been swept away, along with many of the reservations held about him by the rest of British rugby. Scotland's Peter Wright, for one, said at the end of the Lions trip: 'For me, the biggest surprise of this tour has been getting to know Will.' Carling was able to remove most of the misconceptions by simply being himself, by not playing the part of captain. He had been determined to give the other players a look at the real Will Carling. If they still did not like what they saw, fair enough. 'Everyone hates you when you are captain of England. They build up an idea of what you are like. It irritates, but there is no point in getting upset. I just try to do my normal thing and hope that, at the end of it all, people think I'm not too bad.'

That should make life easier for Carling over the next two years. So should his improved relationship with the British rugby media. England's captain has taken money off two newspapers for what they have written about him: one had claimed that he swore during his World Cup semi-final team talk; recently, another paid up for having suggested that he was not declaring money to the tax man. That money went to the Trinity Hospice, a cancer hospital in Clapham. Carling is not naïve enough to think that there will not be problems with the media in the months ahead, but he has now destroyed for ever the image of a pretty boy living off the back of his team. When it counted, Carling stood up.

His life is hectic enough without battling against misconceptions. Geoff Cooke has indicated that Carling is still the man whom he wants to take England to the next World Cup. Carling is in for a busy time: England have two Five Nations championships as well as that tour by New Zealand and a tour to South Africa before then. There's also the matter of marriage to Julia, and a fast-growing business that needs his full attention. That is why Carling gave serious thought to his future during the Lions tour. Unless the rugby fire was still there – because that is what will carry him through – he would be better advised to get out now before the pressures and problems of the 1993 championship flared up again.

Julia's absence caused Carling problems in New Zealand, but her presence will be a great benefit over the next couple of years. She is not star-struck over his world, she has her own successful business, and is skilled at handling the press. Carling has found an equal, who will tell him straight. She is also likely to become his best friend. Carling has never denied he is a 'man's man'; his friends, not his partners, have always previously been party to his worries and real thoughts. Not now. Julia is someone he can trust completely with all aspects of his life.

Carling will continue to clash with the rugby authorities. But in August, it was the turn of Dudley Wood to get into hot water. Carling and other members of the England squad signed a public letter disassociating themselves from the RFU secretary's remarks. Wood had attacked runners Linford Christie and Carl Lewis for 'putting nothing back' into athletics. He also described athletics and boxing as 'sports for the underprivileged, unemployed and ethnic communities.' Wood then added that he believed 'cricket is the greatest game ever invented.' Carling's reply was to state that Rugby Union was a sport for everyone.

And accusations of Will Carling plc will not die, either. But Carling saw how the amateur regulations, southern hemisphere-style, work in New Zealand. 'The All Blacks appeared in adverts wearing kit. It's up front. They now have the All Blacks Club. The authorities must realise that you promote the game through the players.' Indeed, Gavin Hastings will be representing the All Black players as their marketing agent when they tour England and Scotland in late 1993.

The Lions tour grossed nearly £2 million in profits, half of which was gate receipts. The British Lions are still big business. Yet the Four Home Unions continue to act like amateurs. Umbro, who have provided the Lions kit for many tours, offered the authorities big money to market the jersey: the Lions badge, like several others, had been redesigned for copyright reasons. But the Four Home Unions were horrified by the idea, especially when Umbro asked to put their name on the jersey. The upshot of the dithering was that, a few weeks before the Lions left for New Zealand, they had no kit. Nike came to the rescue, and that is why the Lions jersey had the Nike name and logo on it. And they did not pay a penny. Even England did not give their jersey away for nothing.

Rugby Union cannot remain amateur while it goes down the commercial road. Despite the phenomenal success of Will Carling's England, the RFU have money problems. Everything has been ploughed into building new Twickenham stands; how much that can be seen as ensuring and providing for the future of the game is debatable. Carling simply wants all international rugby players to be treated the same, whatever the regulations are. It is blatantly obvious that the All Blacks live in a different world from the England players. The England players have been trying to get consistency for over four years; while cant and hypocrisy remain the watchwords for their treatment by those in authority, their struggle will continue.

Carling, though, remains in demand. Since England's captain came under the wing of the agent Jon Holmes, who also looks after Gary Lineker, Mike Atherton and David Gower, Carling has become one of the most sought-after sports stars in the country. Holmes's Big Four have all captained their country, and Carling has got to know Gower, Atherton and, especially, Lineker. That contact has enabled him to see how professional sports work and to realise that others have come under even more intense media scrutiny than him.

Carling the rugby player has too often got lost in the glare of Carling the captain, rugby's biggest superstar. The 1993 British Lions tour gave him and the rest of the world a chance to rediscover his undoubted talents. Carling went back to basics. He had no choice; circumstances dictated that he had to play for pride, for fun, for himself. That has not happened since he took over the England captaincy in 1988. Will Carling soon realised that Rugby Union, the sport he fell in love with at the age of 6, is still a hell of a game, whatever the problems. And it is a love affair that is far from over.

Carling's Career Statistics (to 1 September 1993)

Carling's England career

16.01.88	France 10, England 9 (Parc des Princes)
06.02.88	England 3, Wales 11 (Twickenham)
05.03.88	Scotland 6, England 9 (Murrayfield)
19.03.88	England 35, Ireland 3 (Twickenham)

23.04.88   *Ireland 10, England 21 (Lansdowne Road)

12.06.88   Australia 28, England 8 (Concord Oval, Sydney)
17.06.88   Fiji 12, England 25 (Suva)

05.11.88†   England 28, Australia 19 (Twickenham)

04.02.89†   England 12, Scotland 12 (Twickenham)
18.02.89†   Ireland 3, England 16 (Lansdowne Road)
04.03.89†   England 11, France 0 (Twickenham)
18.03.89†   Wales 12, England 9 (National Stadium)

04.11.89†   England 58, Fiji 23 (Twickenham)

20.01.90†   England 23, Ireland 0 (Twickenham)
03.02.90†   France 7, England 26 (Parc des Princes)
17.02.90†   England 34, Wales 6 (Twickenham)
17.03.90†   Scotland 13, England 7 (Murrayfield)

28.07.90†   Argentina 12, England 25 (Buenos Aires)
04.08.90†   Argentina 15, England 13 (Buenos Aires)

03.11.90†   England 51, Argentina 0 (Twickenham)

19.01.91†   Wales 6, England 25 (National Stadium)
16.02.91†   England 21, Scotland 12 (Twickenham)
02.03.91†   Ireland 7, England 16 (Lansdowne Road)
16.03.91†   England 21, France 19 (Twickenham)

20.07.91†   Fiji 12, England 28 (Suva)
27.07.91†   Australia 40, England 15 (Sydney Football Stadium)

World Cup
03.10.91†   Group A England 12, New Zealand 18 (Twickenham)
08.10.91†   Group A England 36, Italy 6 (Twickenham)
11.10.91†   Group A England 37, USA 9 (Twickenham)
19.10.91†   Quarter-final France 10, England 19 (Parc des Princes)
26.10.91†   Semi-final Scotland 6, England 9 (Murrayfield)
02.11.91†   Final England 6, Australia 12 (Twickenham)

18.01.92†   Scotland 7, England 25 (Murrayfield)
01.02.92†   England 38, Ireland 9 (Twickenham)
15.02.92†   France 13, England 31 (Parc des Princes)
07.03.92†   England 24, Wales 0 (Twickenham)

17.10.92†   England 26, Canada 13 (Wembley)
14.11.92†   England 33, South Africa 16 (Twickenham)

16.01.93†   England 16, France 15 (Twickenham)
06.02.93†   Wales 10, England 9 (National Stadium)
06.03.93†   England 26, Scotland 12 (Twickenham)
20.03.93†   Ireland 17, England 3 (Lansdowne Road)

† Captain
* Millennium Match

Other England matches

08.06.88   NSW B 9, England 25 (Wollongong)
01.05.90†   Italy 15, England XV 33 (Rovigo)
14.07.90†   Banco Nacion 29, England 21 (Buenos Aires)
21.07.90†   Buenos Aires 26, England 23 (Buenos Aires)
29.09.90†   England XV 18, Barbarians 16 (Twickenham)
07.07.91†   NSW 21, England 19 (Waratah Rugby Park, Sydney)
14.07.91†   Queensland 20, England 14 (Ballymore, Brisbane)
07.09.91†   England 53, USSR 0 (Twickenham)

England tries

v France, Twickenham, 1989
v Ireland, Twickenham, 1990
v France, Parc des Princes 1990
v Wales, Twickenham, 1990
v France, Parc des Princes, 1991
v Wales, Twickenham, 1992
v South Africa, Twickenham, 1992

England matches missed

05.06.88   Australia 22, England 16 (Ballymore, Brisbane)
             (Sitting university exams)
13.05.89   Romania 3, England 58 (August Stadium, Bucharest)
             (Injured, shin splints)

Carling's England record

Career	P	W	L	D	For	Agst	%
England	42	30	11	1	899	472	72.51
England captain	35	26	8	1	789	392	75.71

Five Nations championships

Year	P	W	L	D	For	Agst	Pts	Pos
1988	4	2	2	0	56	30	4	3rd
1989†	4	2	1	1	48	27	5	2nd
1990†	4	3	1	0	90	26	6	2nd
1991†	4	4	0	0	83	44	8	1st
1992†	4	4	0	0	118	29	8	1st
1993†	4	2	2	0	54	54	4	2nd=
Total	24	17	6	1	449	210	35	72.31%

Opponents	P	W	L	D	For	Agst	%
France	7	6	1	0	133	74	85.71
Wales	6	3	3	0	104	46	50.00
Scotland	7	5	1	1	109	68	78.57
Ireland	7	6	1	0	152	49	85.71
Australia	4	1	3	0	57	99	25.00
Fiji	3	3	0	0	111	47	100.00
Argentina	3	2	1	0	89	27	66.66
New Zealand	1	0	1	0	12	18	0.00
Italy	1	1	0	0	36	6	100.00
USA	1	1	0	0	37	9	100.00
Canada	1	1	0	0	26	13	100.00
South Africa	1	1	0	0	33	16	100.00

Venue	P	W	L	D	For	Agst	%
Twickenham	20	16	3	1	525	203	82.50
Paris	4	3	1	0	85	40	75.00
Edinburgh	4	3	1	0	50	32	75.00
Dublin	4	3	1	0	56	37	75.00
Cardiff	3	1	2	0	43	28	33.33
Sydney	2	0	2	0	23	68	0.00
Suva	2	2	0	0	53	24	100.00
Buenos Aires	2	1	1	0	38	27	50.00
Wembley	1	1	0	0	26	13	100.00

Other representative matches

19.10.88	North 15, Australia 9 (Otley)
22.04.90	Four Home Unions 43, Rest of Europe 18 (Twickenham)
28.11.92†	Barbarians 20, Australia 30 (Twickenham)
26.05.93	North Harbour 13, British Lions 29 (Auckland)
29.05.93	NZ Maoris 20, British Lions 24 (Wellington)
05.06.93	Otago 37, British Lions 24 (Dunedin)
12.06.93	New Zealand 20, British Lions 18 (Christchurch)
19.06.93	Auckland 23, British Lions 18 (Eden Park)
	(Replacement for Gavin Hastings)
22.06.93	Hawke's Bay 29, British Lions 17 (Napier)
29.06.93†	Waikato 38, British Lions 10 (Hamilton)

Carling's rugby career

1981/82	First season in Sedbergh 1st XV
1982/83	Yorkshire Schools
	England Schools
1983/84	Captain of England Schools
	Captain of Yorkshire Schools tour to Zimbabwe
1985/86	Durham University
1986/87	Debut for North in Divisional Championship
	Debut for Barbarians at Leicester
	Joins Harlequins
	Rest XV in England Trial
	Debut for England B
	UAU final – Durham 15, Bristol 6
	Debut for Army in Inter-Services Tournament
1987/88	England debut in Paris
	John Player Cup final – Harlequins 28, Bristol 22
	England tour to Australia
1988/89	Appointed England captain
	Misses British Lions tour because of shin injury
1989/90	Moves from North to London Division
	Loses Grand Slam decider at Murrayfield
	Plays with Barbarians in Hong Kong Sevens
	Carling in Quins side that wins Middlesex Sevens

1989/90	One of *Rothmans Rugby Union Yearbook* Five Players
(cont.)	of the Year
	England tour to Argentina
1990/91	RFU twice investigate Carling's amateur status
	Carling left out by London after missing training
	England's first Grand Slam since 1980
	Pilkington Cup final – Harlequins 25, Northampton 13 (AET)
	England tour to Australia
1991/92	World Cup final – England 6, Australia 12
	Passes Bill Beaumont's record of 21 times as England captain in USA World Cup game
	Passes Paul Dodge's record of 32 caps as England centre in Scotland game in Five Nations championship
	England achieve a second successive Grand Slam
	Pilkington Cup final – Harlequins 12, Bath 15 (AET)
	Carling named *Rugby World* Player of the Year
1992/93	England beat Canada at Wembley
	South Africa back at Twickenham after 23 years
	Pilkington Cup final – Harlequins 16, Leicester 23
	British Lions tour to New Zealand
	Carling dropped for the first time in career

Index

307

Index

Oti, Chris 34, 36, 52, 56, 64, 65, 78, 149, 172
Otley 24
Oxford Union debating society 144–5

Parallel Media 160
Paris 62, 64, 158
Pearce, Gary 169
Peard, Les 142, 199, 200
Pearey, Michael 126, 159
Peters, Lt John 139
Pilkington Cup 9, 86, 88, 166; *1992* 213; *1993* 280
Player Vision 124, 159
poaching players 162
Portugal 35
press conferences 131, 203, 207; after Cardiff *1991* 124–8, 133–4, 136–8, 159
Prisma company 87, 108, 134, 158, 159
Probyn, Jeff 62, 79, 112, 162, 173, 184, 195, 210, 223, 245–8, 276, 289–90
Pryce, Jonathan 125

radio broadcasting 165, 166
Reason, John 56
Redman, Nigel 67, 149
Reed, Andy 283
Rees, Gary 66, 79, 80
referees 199–200, 265
Rendall, Paul 144, 162, 173, 222, 246, 247–8
Reynolds, Mike 161
Richards, Dean 37, 144, 162, 165, 197, 224, 261, 276, 286; in play 26, 63, 141, 196, 284; disciplined 36; dropped 172, 195
Richmond 169, 204; Petersham Hotel 202–04
Ricoh UK 156
Ringer, Paul 90, 113
Robinson, Andy 26, 36, 85
Robinson, David 27, 55, 67
Roche, Tony 25, 29, 68, 119, 135, 172, 224, 256; *quoted* 136–7
Rodber, Tim 195, 196, 197
Rodriguez, Laurent 63
Romania 82, 100, 236
Rose, Marcus 148
Rothmans Rugby Union Yearbook 6
Rowell, Jack 133, 210
Royal Air Force 66, 72, 139, 222–3
Royal family 113, 166, 183, 185, 225, 226, 230, 244–5
Rugby Football Union (RFU) 2–4, 32, 33, 36, 66, 67, 100, 101, 205–06, 209; amateur regulations 105, 106–09, 124–8, 130, 157–62, 220, 246, 247, 299–300; disciplinary panel 112–13, 114, 133–4; hardship payments 221–2; marketing 124, 125, 140, 153–5; relations with Carling 106, 144, 244; relations with Cooke

106, 126–7, 196, 212, 247; WC organisation 153–7, 160–62, 164–9
Rugby League 67, 107, 132, 196; Au 150
Rugby Limited 158
'Rugby Special' programme 10
Rugby Union Writers' Club 134
Rugby World 9, 44, 100, 214, 284
Rugby World Cup 155–7, 177
'Run with the Ball' campaign 160–61, 169, 230
Russ, Tony 162
Rutherford, Don 69, 100, 205
Ryan, John 93

Salmon, Jamie 58
Sandhurst 18, 71, 72–3
Saracens 101
Save & Prosper 140
Schools *see* England Schools
Scotland: nationalism 182; Grand Slam 85; *1986* 58; *1988* 32, 34, 64–5; *1989* 35–6; *1990* 93–8, 99, 100, 105, 106, 121, 127, 139–40, 234, 236, 237, 242; *1991* 139–40, WC 154, 169, 180, 237; *1992* 196; *1993* 261–3
Scott, John 132
Scottish Rugby Union 36, 94
Sedbergh School 39–40, 41–7, 52, 118, 121–2, 255
Sella, Philippe 63, 176, 213, 214
Senior Clubs Association 223–4
Simms, Kevin 45, 53, 56, 58, 62, 63
Skinner, Mickey 1, 62, 63, 144, 172, 173, 174, 184–5, 199, 213, 227, 248
Smith, Anna 115
Smith, Graham 114–15
Smith, Ian 262
Smith, Julia 12, 191, 193, 230, 263, 277–9, 285, 286, 291, 295–6, 299; *quoted* 279–80
Smith, Steve 100
Sole, David 9, 95, 96, 98, 99, 121, 182, 210, 246
songs and anthems 65, 66, 95, 161, 166, 194, 225–6, 272
South Africa 209, 225, 226–7, 263
Spencer, John 44
sponsorship 86–7, 107–09, 140, 144–5, 153–61, 230
Sports Council 209–10
Squire, Jeff 78–9
Stanger, Tony 95, 98
Stephens, Colin 234
Stirling, Brian 86
strip 219–20, 299; jerseys 153–4, 219–20, 299
Sun 187
Sunday Telegraph 56
Sunday Times 23, 56, 89, 90, 100, 114, 197, 222, 252, 265
Swing Low, Sweet Chariot (song) 65, 66, 161, 166, 194, 226, 272

311